PIMLICO

556

TUNES OF GLORY

Richard Aldous lectures in history and music at
University College Dublin.

TUNES OF GLORY

The Life of Malcolm Sargent

———

RICHARD ALDOUS

PIMLICO

To the memory of my father

Published by Pimlico 2002

2 4 6 8 10 9 7 5 3 1

Copyright © Richard Aldous 2001

Richard Aldous has asserted his right under the Copyright, Designs
and Patents Act 1988 to be identified as the author of this work

First published in Great Britain by Hutchinson in 2001
Pimlico edition 2002

Pimlico
Random House, 20 Vauxhall Bridge Road,
London SW1V 2SA

Random House Australia (Pty) Limited
20 Alfred Street, Milsons Point, Sydney,
New South Wales 2061, Australia

Random House New Zealand Limited
18 Poland Road, Glenfield,
Auckland 10, New Zealand

Random House (Pty) Limited
Endulini, 5a Jubilee Road, Parktown 2193, South Africa

The Random House Group Limited Reg. No. 954009
www.randomhouse.co.uk

A CIP catalogue record for this book is available from the British Library

ISBN 0-7126-6540-4

Papers used by Random House are natural,
recyclable products made from wood grown in sustainable forests;
the manufacturing processes conform to the environmental
regulations of the country of origin

Typeset in Bembo by MATS, Southend-on-Sea, Essex

Printed and bound in Great Britain by
Clays Ltd, St. Ives PLC

Contents

Illustrations

Unless otherwise attributed, all photographs are from the Sir Malcolm Sargent archive.

Malcolm aged four with his parents
Stamford choirboy
Private Sargent
Organist at a Melton wedding (*courtesy Richard Snodin*)
Sir Henry Wood (*Hulton Getty*)
Leicester Symphony Orchestra, 1925
Royal Albert Hall, late 1920s
Diaghilev with Cocteau, 1924 (*Hulton Getty*)
Samuel Courtauld (*Hulton Getty*)
Hiawatha
Eileen
Pamela
Peter
Lord Horder
The Rivals: Sargent and Adrian Boult (*Hulton Getty*)
Sir Thomas Beecham (*Hulton Getty*)
Auction of Toscanini photograph

Acknowledgements

I would like to thank University College Dublin for a period of leave in which to write a first draft of this book. I am grateful to colleagues for making the arts faculty such an engaging place to work. Special thanks go to Ronan Fanning, James McGuire and Maurice Bric (a Barbirolli fan). Hutchinson's Tony Whittome, assisted by Sophie Wills and Poppy Hampson at Pimlico, has been a most sympathetic and helpful editor. Georgina Capel at Capel & Land has brilliantly combined enthusiasm with hard-headed advice; I am grateful to Andrew Roberts for introducing us. Publication of this book affords me the opportunity to acknowledge some long-term debts. Michael Rothwell was an early mentor. Sally Warwick-Haller was the first to encourage me to consider history as a profession. David Reynolds and Peter Clarke remain role models.

Among the pleasures of research was interviewing Sargent's contemporaries. His immediate circle was encouraging from the outset. Peter Sargent, the conductor's son, was frank in discussion about his father. Sylvia Darley gave me access to Sargent's papers, wrote letters of introduction to his friends, and shared her recollections of working for 'the Maestro'. I am grateful to all those I interviewed, many of whom have since died, for their time and memories. I hope that I have been fair in my representation of their views. I am also indebted to the archivists and librarians who helped my research. Many are cited in the end notes, but special thanks go to Neil Somerville at the BBC and Ruth Edge at EMI.

Simon Ball, Harry White, Mark Lytle and Gillian Brennan read a full draft text. Judith Brett read the Australian chapter. They all devoted much time and energy to improving matters of style, judgement and taste. I salute their collegiality in taking time away from their own work to enhance mine. Simon Ball, in particular, read the book as part of a dialogue that goes back to our time at Christ's College, Cambridge. Errors that remain are mine and I must rely on eagle-eyed readers to alert me to them.

No one has been more involved in this biography than my wife, Kathryn. She read and commented on every draft, provided solutions to apparently intractable problems and offered unceasing support. Quite literally, the book would not have been the same without her.

My greatest regret about this book is that my father will not read it. He inspired my love of music and history, and, along with my mother, encouraged my every endeavour. I had him in mind as I wrote. *Tunes of Glory* is dedicated to his memory: I hope he would have enjoyed it.

Richard Aldous
Dublin, 2001

Preface to the Pimlico Edition

Shortly after publication of the Hutchinson edition of *Tunes of Glory*, I received a letter from Jean Fonda Fournier, son of the cellist, Pierre Fournier. He enclosed a private letter written to him by his father in the days immediately after Malcolm Sargent's death. The letter is an extraordinary testament to the esteem in which Sargent was held at the highest musical levels. 'I am deeply distressed about Sir Malcolm's passing away,' he wrote. 'You have witnessed, dearest Jean Pierre, our appearances in London, Berlin, Edinburgh during which this Guardian Angel surrounded my playing with an ever flowing pulse, provoking freedom and total control. Do you remember the 1958 Proms? The *Don Quixote* [Richard Strauss]. Certainly through the years, as wonderful as the one I did with [Georg] Szell or even Herbert von K[arajan]. I shall surely miss him, having been one of the few who understood his wonderful human side, together with Jascha [Heifetz] who totally agreed with me.'

That judgement supplements the assessment of Yehudi Menuhin recorded later in this book. 'Malcolm was a much deeper man than his rather light-hearted, superficial aspect would convey, and was much, much more of a musician than you would presume from his bearing,' observed Menuhin. 'From my experience with Russian or

German conductors, they usually carry a certain portentous weight, but Malcolm with his carnation never conveyed that over-seriousness. He was natural and elegant yet always master of his scores and no mean musician: a person of stature. I always enjoyed working with him.'

I happily defer to the critical judgement of Heifetz, Menuhin and Fournier – three of the finest instrumental soloists of the twentieth century – on Sargent's musical ability. The rest of what follows is history: the story of one man's struggle to get to the top, the contribution he made to British cultural life when he got there, and how he helped to define the image of his country abroad, not least at a moment of maximum danger.

Dublin, 2002

Prologue

Backstage at the Royal Albert Hall, Colin Davis was getting ready for his big night. Well-wishers called in to say good luck. Officials hovered, speaking in hushed voices, making sure that everything was in order. In the auditorium, television lights blazed down on the BBC Symphony Orchestra. Almost within touching distance stood row after row of predominantly young people. Most were covered in brightly coloured streamers. Many were waving Union flags, bouncing balloons or blowing sirens. This was the Last Night of the Proms, an occasion embedded in the British national psyche and watched worldwide by a television audience of millions.

As the atmosphere built, it might have appeared to the casual observer in 1968 that this was just another Last Night. Yet it was a poignant moment, the first such end-of-season celebration to have taken place since the death of Sir Malcolm Sargent, Chief Conductor of the Proms from 1948. Promenaders had expressed themselves 'doubtful' about whether a diffident Colin Davis had the glamour to carry it off.[1] Sargent, immaculate in evening dress, with trademark carnation in his lapel, had presided with a control and panache that whipped the audience each year into a state of exuberance bordering on hysteria. When Davis now emerged from the bull-run into the hall, there were sniggers and gasps of astonishment. He had abandoned his tailcoat for a white dinner jacket, which to many had the unfortunate effect of making him look like a wine steward on a P&O liner. 'Gin and tonic, please, waiter,' quipped a member of the orchestra as the conductor swept past.

'That jacket' was not the only change introduced at the Proms in 1968. Davis and William Glock, Controller of Music at the BBC, freed from Sargent's objections had moved away from the traditional populist programmes and chosen to emphasise the European avant-garde. The First Night of the Proms, transferred from a Saturday to a Friday night, had abandoned the light touch associated with Sargent's opening to a season. When Promenaders asked if a bronze bust of the conductor might be placed alongside that of Sir Henry Wood, founder of the Proms, which watched over the concerts, Glock refused point blank.[2]

Changes at the Proms were part of a battle for Sargent's historical reputation that took place in the critical eighteen months after his death in 1967 when supporters worked valiantly to keep his memory alive. At the funeral in Stamford, thousands lined the streets to pay their respects.[3] Weeks later, 3,000 people crowded into Westminster Abbey for a memorial service at which the entire nave was set aside for Proms season ticket holders. Fifteen hundred more heard the service relayed in St Margaret's church, Westminster.[4]

The first anniversary of Sargent's death prompted an extra-ordinary event. A group of Promenaders undertook a pilgrimage of more than a hundred miles between London and Stamford to lay a wreath on Sargent's grave. The walk began with a service of dedication at St James's church, Piccadilly. Mstislav Rostropovich played all six Bach cello suites in support. Cardinal Heenan, Archbishop of Westminster and Sargent's friend, preached a sermon. It was one of only a handful of occasions since the Reformation at which a Catholic cardinal had spoken in an Anglican church.[5] The walk was undertaken to raise money for a charity, the Malcolm Sargent Cancer Fund for Children, established in the conductor's memory.

Sargent remained even after his death the most famous English conductor, throughout the world instantly recognisable in photographs by his ubiquitous buttonhole. But just as the flag-waving and singing of patriotic hymns of the Last Night seemed incongruous to many in post-Imperial Britain, so revisionists argued that Sargent represented the style and values of a defunct age. He symbolised to them the way of the amateur in a world that had now decisively turned professional: white jackets and the 'white heat of technology' not white carnations epitomised their vision of the future.[6] Sir Malcolm Sargent was as irrelevant in their brave new world of Technicolor as the leading man of a 1930s black and white film.

Sargent in his final years had been increasingly troubled about how he would be seen by posterity. In 1965 he finally agreed to write an autobiography, having previously refused all offers, however lucrative. The publisher Hamish Hamilton enlisted a music critic, Charles Reid, to ghost-write the book.[7] In the weeks before he died, Sargent annotated 40,000 words of the first draft. Immediately after his death, the project descended into acrimony.[8] Reid, who was known for brusqueness, arrived at Sargent's apartment from the funeral to demand the conductor's papers and diaries. Not only was the request refused but it also precipitated a complete withdrawal of cooperation by Sargent's executors. Reid, however, possessed enough material from the ghosted memoir to create a fair and well-written contemporary biography.[9]

Published on the first anniversary of Sargent's death, Reid's book ignited a debate from which the conductor's reputation has never recovered. Neville Cardus had written in the conductor's obituary that 'critics would have raved' over interpretations of Beethoven and Schubert had Sargent been a foreign maestro.[10] Those same critics now took the opportunity to assert their view that Sargent was a musician of limited vision. 'In spite of the fierce admiration that he inspired in the huge choirs and the massed brass bands he loved to conduct, and in spite of the adoration lavished on him by princesses and Promenaders, he was not generally admired by his fellow musicians, who were not alone in doubting his ability to get to the heart of the greatest music,' concluded the *Observer*.[11]

Review after review echoed the opinion that Sargent was superficial, unadventurous and stuck in an Edwardian mind-set. No one doubted his ability to 'put on a show' to please the masses, but any suggestion that he might be considered among the ranks of the great conductors was plainly ridiculous. He was at best a 'Choir-master Extraordinary'.[12] Attacks did not confine themselves to Sargent as a musician. 'Why did this *bon capitaine*, spruce, busy, successful, devoted genuinely to music as a great affirmative tonic and blessing, confident of social and probably divine approbation, "beloved of millions" – why does he trail a faint question-mark behind him, shadowy figures shaking their heads and smirking?' asked the *Spectator*.[13]

The myth of Sargent as 'Flash Harry', the not entirely affectionate nickname that dogged him throughout his life, had been consolidated. That assessment has changed little in the decades that have followed his death. Fashions in the choral music at which Sargent excelled have moved towards historically-aware performances with small forces, the antithesis of – and partly a reaction against – his interpretations. While his music-making has increasingly been seen as outmoded, so details have emerged of an apparently less palatable side to his nature. Those who knew him have often presented an unflattering portrait in their published diaries and memoirs. 'He is not a friend and in spite of his undoubted wit and vitality, his intelligence and drive, I do not like him,' Cecil Beaton wrote in his diaries, serialised in the *Sunday Telegraph* in 1976. 'He is appallingly conceited and says things to honour himself that curl one's toes.'[14] William Walton's wife, Susana, serialised a memoir in *The Times* in 1987 that was excoriating of Sargent as both man and conductor.[15] In 1998 Sir Edward Heath recalled in his autobiography a supervision at Oxford with Professor Sir Hugh Allen at which he was told that to succeed as a conductor 'you must be prepared to be just as big a shit as Malcolm Sargent'.[16]

Shortly after the thirtieth anniversary of Sargent's death, Michael Kennedy reviewed the conductor's life and career for the *BBC Music Magazine*. His brutal assessment summed up three decades of criticism. 'Sargent was bargain basement,' wrote Kennedy. 'He has perhaps been over-vilified, but one cannot make out a convincing case for drastic rehabilitation. He was a star musical propagandist, not a great conductor.'[17]

Few would disagree that Sargent was a star propagandist; it is difficult to think of many great conductors of whom the same might not be said. The claim that Sargent was bargain basement, however, shows a failure to understand the conductor's life in its proper historical perspective. The dust is beginning to settle on the rows and personal animosities that swirled around a man who evoked such strong reactions in those who knew him. A generation later, it is time to take another look at this cultural icon.

Authorial detachment when writing this book was made easier by the fact that I was born after Malcolm Sargent had already conducted his last concert. Rooted in the historical record, this account has benefited from the wide range of archival material now available to researchers, including major collections at the BBC, the Victoria and Albert Museum, EMI, the Public Record Office and many others. I have been privileged to use a number of private collections, including, most importantly, exclusive and unfettered access to Sargent's own papers held by his secretary, Sylvia Darley. Many letters and diaries were destroyed in bombing during the Second World War but the record is complete from 1942 onwards. I have also profited from talking to many of Sargent's contemporaries, including Peter Sargent, the conductor's only son.

This life of Sargent tells how a boy without privilege came to dominate English musical life, enjoying both fame and social cachet. Alongside the narrative, a number of important themes emerge. First, Sargent's career reinforces that today's amateur is often yesterday's professional. Although critics later portrayed him as a gentleman-amateur, Sargent's ascent came as an accomplished professional who established new standards of excellence. Second, his career coincided with the emergence worldwide of the Maestro as arbiter of taste and high priest of the canon of great repertoire. Third, Sargent's utilisation of the rise of the conductor was possible because by training and taste he was able to present himself as the embodiment of English musical tradition. Fourth, England in the twentieth century, despite its class structure, was a fluid society possessed of an open elite to which boys of humble origins might legitimately aspire. In music, the Church of England was central to the process of identifying and developing talent from all backgrounds. Fifth and last, more than any of his English rivals, Sargent understood the mid-century transition to mass culture and society. His adept self-deployment in broadcasting and the mechanical reproduction of music made Sargent an international celebrity.

Sargent made a unique contribution to an English conducting tradition that continues to thrive. Sir Simon Rattle, who in 2002 takes up the post of Chief Conductor and Artistic Director of the Berlin Philharmonic Orchestra, the most prestigious conducting job in the world, embodies that tradition today. His inheritance is direct: Maurice Miles, a rare Sargent pupil, was, according to Rattle, among his most important influences.[18] Rattle is the first English conductor since Sargent to achieve celebrity status. Like Sargent, his showmanship on the podium and exploitation of mass communications have enabled him to step beyond the elite world of classical music.

To comprehend Malcolm Sargent is an exercise in understanding Europe's musical future not just an English past.

1

One Day He'll Be a Knight

Many of the world's greatest conductors and lovers have been Italian: Malcolm Sargent was no exception. So runs generations of gossip in the Lincolnshire town of Stamford where Sargent grew up. Stamfordians remain divided even today about the conductor's origins. Rumours go back to the nineteenth century, when it was whispered that he was the product of his mother's affair with an Italian peripatetic music teacher at Stamford High School. One town resident was told by his own grandmother, who lived around the corner from Mrs Sargent, that Malcolm was illegitimate.[1] Another, Marjorie Gesior, who was born in 1909 and knew the family, is sceptical. 'It was just nasty gossip,' she says. 'I never thought he was anything but his father's son. In fact, as I remember Harry Sargent, Malcolm was definitely his. They were so alike.'[2] Only DNA tests could have conclusively settled the question. What matters most is Malcolm Sargent's own reaction to the rumours that swirled around his family. When he looked in the mirror, an olive complexion and dark features suggested Mediterranean blood; yet he could also see Harry's unruly, brush-like hair. The truth is that young Malcolm Sargent probably did not know what to think. That insecurity helped spark a lifelong craving for recognition.[3]

Harold Malcolm Watts Sargent was born on 29 April 1895. Despite the fact that he so often spoke of his childhood in Stamford, Sargent was actually born in Ashford, Kent, at 4 Bath Villas.[4] His first two names were chosen at random but the third was a tribute to the friend, Amy Watts, who assisted during a difficult labour. Back in Stamford, tongues already wagged that shame had dictated the choice of Ashford for the boy's delivery, although it was quite normal at the end of the nineteenth century for a woman to return to her own birthplace to have a baby. That it took nine weeks for the baby's birth to be registered only fuelled the rumours.[5]

Sargent's mother, Agnes Marion Hall, was born in 1864 and moved to Peterborough as a child when her father, Benjamin, was looking for gardening work. When old enough, she was sent to work on the domestic staff at Stamford High School for Girls. Agnes was striking rather than beautiful: tall, big-boned, with nutmeg-brown hair and green eyes. Her father's decision to place her in service at the school was in part an attempt to instil respectability into a rebellious nature. Instead she quickly gained a reputation as a flirt with both colleagues and local young men: she was engaged to be married four times. When Agnes finally walked down the aisle at the late age of thirty, she found waiting a bizarre sight.[6]

Henry Edward Sargent was unconventional in both looks and tastes. He was a small, stout man, several inches shorter than his wife and two years younger. Everyone knew him as Harry, which explains why his son quickly became 'Malcolm' to avoid any confusion with diminutives. Sargent senior would rush eccentrically through the town's streets at breakneck speed with chest puffed out and trilby hat barely able to contain his shock of curly hair. 'If you met him anywhere he always had a joke for you, especially if you were a child,' reminisces Margaret Hare. 'He was a very convivial man with a good circle of friends.'[7]

Harry worked as a clerk for a coal merchant on Red Lion Square, taking orders in the front office. From there he could see his great love: the church of St John Baptist, at which he was organist. The members of St John's choir adored him.[8] Harry had the fanatical passion of the autodidact, having taught himself not just to read music but also to play the violin and organ. Tellingly, when registering his son's birth, he wrote 'organist' under profession and beforehand had told everyone that 'if it's a boy I shall make him a musician'. His dearest hope was that his son should become a cathedral organist. Agnes thought music was unlikely to make her son prosperous, thinking instead that he might become a banker.

Whilst they might have disagreed about professions, both parents were intensely aspirational for their son. Neither thought to constrain Malcolm by the conventions of their own class. Each was determined that he should 'get on'. 'They did not have much money but they must have been ambitious for him because they made such sacrifices,' suggests Marjorie Gesior. 'I know they had to go without.'[9] An insight into their progressiveness came when a daughter, Dorothy, was born in 1896. She did not assume second place but enjoyed the same benefits of parental drive as her brother.

Ashford was Sargent's birthplace but the Stamford landscape shaped him. Visitors had gone into raptures over Stamford for centuries. Cecilia Fiennes, the seventeenth-century traveller, thought it 'as fine a built town all of stone as may be seen'. Sir Walter Scott doffed his hat at the view up to St Mary's church and pronounced it the finest sight on the road between London and Edinburgh. Pevsner later described Stamford as 'the English country market town *par excellence*'. When late evening sunshine fell on the golden ironstone and sheep-grey limestone, playing on the river and spires, framed by the water meadows and Burghley woods behind, it is not difficult to see why many thought Stamford the most beautiful town in England. It had been one of the five controlling boroughs of Danelaw between the ninth and eleventh centuries, and, positioned on the Great North Road, was a prosperous trading centre throughout the early Middle Ages. When the focal point of the wool trade moved to East Anglia during the fifteenth century the town fell into decline. The revival of its fortune came with the rise in prominence of the Cecils, a local family.[10]

The Cecil line has been the root of perhaps the most powerful family in British political life during the past 500 years. William Cecil, 1st Baron Burghley, was Chief Minister to Queen Elizabeth I, who called him her 'spirit', and gained a reputation for *realpolitik* in the vicious world of the Tudor courts.[11] His sons were the 1st Earl of Exeter and the 1st Earl of Salisbury, each of whom established important political dynasties. In 1895, the year of Sargent's birth, there was a Cecil in 10 Downing Street.[12] Burghley House dominated Stamford socially and economically. Lord Exeter remained intimately involved with the affairs of the 8000 residents of Stamford. He owned 27,000 acres, dispensed justice from the bench, appointed priests at sixteen parishes, and provided for the poor at the workhouse. Burghley House owned even the town's water supply. Like most towns of its time and type, Stamford had a stifling social order and small-mindedness that might have been the enemy of ambition had it not been for the attentions of this local aristocratic family. 'You were always aware of the Marquess,' observes Marjorie Gesior. 'He regarded the town as part of his duty. He certainly helped people get on.'[13] Lord Exeter's *noblesse oblige* included providing scholarships for local boys to Stamford Grammar School and St John's College, Cambridge. That the Exeters were willing to further the careers of those with ability but not money would be crucial for Sargent.

In the summer of 1895, Agnes Sargent returned to Stamford with her new son. Her journey did not end in the discreet grandeur of Georgian Stamford but at a grim terraced cottage, 24 Wharf Road, on the outskirts of town, near overcrowded delivery yards. The house was in the shadow of Stamford's twin gas towers where the pungent smell of coal gas always lingered in the air. Gesior remembers that 'Wharf Road was not a nice place to live although it was not the worst: there were slums around Bath Row that were even worse.'[14] Neighbouring roads were named not for heroes of victorious overseas battles but with drearily practical directions. Gas Lane and Gas Street were both within yards of Sargent's front door.

The house itself was small. There was a parlour with an ornamental cast-iron fireplace, kept for Sundays and 'best'. The focus of family life was the kitchen-cum-living room. Dominated by a range, it was a long, narrow room with plenty of books and a piano. Upstairs there were three tiny bedrooms, which ensured that Malcolm and Dorothy had their own rooms. Outside was a backyard with a lavatory. This was the lot of the Stamford respectable working class. 'Most of us then were working class,' reflects Gesior, 'but you could be down at the bottom or up near the top: the Sargents were upper working class.'[15]

Not for the last time in his life, Malcolm Sargent found himself ideally placed to take advantage of social change. The beginning of the twentieth century was a time of flux in English society. In 1900 the average family enjoyed a standard of living better even than during the mid-Victorian boom. In 1906 a radical Liberal government was elected that championed the underprivileged and introduced a programme of major reform, culminating in the 1911 National Insurance Act which addressed the dual threats of sickness and unemployment. Those who had been marginalised now found their lives explained, if not quite celebrated, in popular novels by the likes of H. G. Wells. Works including *Kipps* and *The History of Mr Polly* illustrated the trials which the ambitious had to endure and offered a vision of the shape of things to come.[16]

Malcolm Sargent was reared on ambition. His parents were determined that he should make something of himself. Whatever the final destination, both supposed that education was the key to his future success. Harry, who would pound away on the family's battered upright piano, inspired in his infant son a love of music. When Malcolm started playing, the old piano was replaced by a new instrument bought on the 'never-never' and paid for in monthly instalments.

Harry thrilled to all kinds of music. 'My father was a musical man,' recalled Sargent. 'As soon as I could read music, which was before I could read words, I sang in the choir, and soon I sang alto because it was more difficult.'[17] At the piano, father and son, with Dorothy squeezed between, would range from works by the great composers to tunes from music hall and light opera.[18] They scoured music and second-hand shops to find new piano transcriptions by their favourite composer, Sir Arthur Sullivan. The combination of technical facility and sheer brio displayed by Sullivan in his comic operas appealed to Harry Sargent's own sense that enthusiasm for music was a serious business. He wanted his son to enjoy music but also to excel. This meant lessons.

If searching for the name of a piano teacher in a story, it would be difficult to find one better than Mrs Tinkler. 'I still revere and love [her] dearly,' said Sargent more than sixty years later.[19] Frances Tinkler was Stamford's leading piano, singing and theory teacher, who prepared candidates for examination by the Associated Board of the Royal Schools of Music. Lessons took place in the garden room at her handsome double-fronted house in Broad Street, where she combined rigorous training with a kindly if firm manner.[20] She taught not only Malcolm Sargent but later the composer Michael Tippett, who found her 'wonderfully encouraging'. He remembered her as 'bourgeois in the best sense of the word, with a mature, warm personality – the sort of person to whom a schoolboy could take his troubles (as I often did) and be listened to understandingly and helpfully'.[21] Her teaching centred on Bach's *48 Preludes and Fugues* and instruction in counterpoint.

Malcolm Sargent went to Mrs Tinkler when aged six and for the next ten years flourished under her care. He had near-perfect pitch and always came top in theory. But precocity did not make him popular. Even as a young child his self-confidence came close to arrogance. When 'Tinkie' asked questions in class, Malcolm's hand was always first in the air. He sat at the piano with a straight back and laughed at fellow pupils who could not identify notes played at random. Other mothers might compliment Mrs Sargent on her little boy, who looked like a soldier on parade, but his contemporaries often ridiculed him. On more than one occasion, Mrs Tinkler admonished the class for not paying more respect to her favourite pupil. 'You may laugh at Mal now,' she told them, 'but one day he'll be a knight and the rest of you will still be in Stamford.'[22] Such remarks, whilst flattering, were unlikely to help a boy already regarded as teacher's pet. Back at 24 Wharf Road, his neighbours despaired of the constant piano practice and christened him 'the Banger'. Even his mother's patience wore thin. 'I used to drive her mad,' said Sargent. 'I would do my homework and everything else sitting at the piano strumming, which shows I suppose that I was musical.'[23]

When Malcolm's legs were long enough to reach the pedals, his father sat him at the organ in St John Baptist. This fifteenth-century small Perpendicular church was not the most prestigious in Stamford but it was the only one to have a three-manual organ, built in the 1870s. The springs were rusting, woodworm was rife and the instrument complained wheezily if worked too hard. The boy operated the swellbox by kicking out a stick and jumping on it before the shutters swung up and propelled him several feet in the air. It was not an easy instrument to master, but having done so he was to feel confident in the luxury of any cathedral organ loft. Whilst his father played at Matins, Malcolm beside him learnt organ technique and was inducted into the Anglican choral tradition. Stanford, Wesley and Parry were a counterbalance to the Gilbert and Sullivan played on the piano at home. Harry Sargent had given his son a wonderful musical legacy: a love of both sacred and popular music married to a respect for technical excellence. It was the training on which Malcolm Sargent would base his professional life.

Sargent's musical training, successfully planned by his father, was a joy to him. His formal education at the town's schools also began promisingly, at the infants' department of a school on Wharf Road administered by St George's church where he was taught to read and write by an elderly spinster who used the Bible and hymns as learning texts. Sargent's parents made a 'voluntary' contribution of one penny a week that increased to sixpence when he moved to Bluecoat just before his sixth birthday. Bluecoat was a preparatory school for Stamford Grammar, and in 1907 Sargent was awarded one of six 'free' places to the senior school, which included William Cecil among its old boys. Sargent was unhappy there, although that made him far from unique. His misfortune was to attend a school noted before and after for academic achievement but which at the time placed little value on scholarship. 'It is customary for each generation of old boys from any school to think that the generations succeeding them are softer and have comforts undreamed of in earlier, sterner days,' laconically observed a former headmaster. 'This is probably true of all those who were at School between 1907 and 1912, and they have stronger grounds for their opinion than have some others.'[24]

A new headmaster, E. W. Lovegrove, arrived in the same year as Sargent to oversee the education of sixty-four boys. He believed that books were all very well but it was discipline and physical exercise that turned boys into men. It became more important to win a place in a school sports team than to do well in exams. Between 1907 and 1912 just two boys won scholarships to Cambridge compared to twelve between 1896 and 1906. On Sargent's first Saturday at school, he went through an initiation rite: 'kissing the old man'. This involved prefects lifting up each new boy in turn to kiss the worn stone head of St Paul over the west door of the Old School before being dropped to the ground accompanied by the loud jeers of the whole school. For Sargent, who was 'Stam Scum' – a poor dayboy from the town who did not pay fees – the prefects ensured that the ordeal was more robust than usual.

Discipline and routine characterised the school day. The humanities were marginalised and music was not even on the curriculum. Exercise was central to a boy's everyday life, with rugby replacing football as the school sport. Sargent dislocated his shoulder in a scrum and for years afterwards was able to click his left arm in and out of its socket. At the end of each day, the boys would set out on a four-mile cross-country run and return to cold baths. Later in life, Sargent would make much of his athleticism, but the physical harshness of life at Stamford Grammar did not appeal. His only comfort was that at least it was worse for those who boarded: unheated dormitories, hot water only on Saturdays, and ten-mile runs. The boarders might have roughed him up, but being 'Stam Scum' had its perks.[25]

Boys who boarded rarely ventured into town and this left Sargent free to enjoy life as Stamford's emerging musical protégé. He was actively involved in the local operatic society, where he began toying with conducting. In the winter of 1909, on a rehearsal night when the fog-bound conductor could not get to Stamford, Sargent was given a baton and told to get on with it. The work was Gilbert and Sullivan's *The Yeoman of the Guard*. Sargent knew the opera intimately, having spent hours playing through the score with his father, and directed with all the self-assurance of a cocky adolescent. He was given a big cheer at the end of the rehearsal while Mrs Tinkler looked on with pride. 'That night in Stamford,' he later said, 'I found myself using a natural stick technique. I have been using the same technique ever since.'[26]

Malcolm Sargent left school in 1910, aged fifteen, when he might have expected to be sent out to make his own way in the world. Instead, his kindly and ambitious father told him: 'You'll have to start earning your living by eighteen or drop music altogether and earn it some other way. At eighteen you'll be under your own steam.'[27] The boy converted the parlour into a study and for a year took lessons in organ and harmony with P. J. Murrell at All Saints' church. Murrell was the senior organist in Stamford, with connections to Peter-borough Cathedral. His emphasis was on technical proficiency, with much time spent on transposition, counterpoint and orchestration. Each morning, Sargent worked at home, grinding through exercises. Later in the day, there was organ and piano practice. His aim was to become an Associate of the Royal College of Organists, the first step on the road to becoming professional.

For more than a century, the organ loft had provided the structure for music-making in England. Throughout the nineteenth century, cathedral organists including John Clarke, William Crotch, Samuel Sebastian Wesley and Frederick Ouseley had dominated perform-ance and teaching. Organists were supreme at Oxford and Cambridge universities and the new conservatories of music in London and regional cities. When Ouseley became Professor of Music at Oxford in 1855, he established a system of degree examina-tions that drew explicitly on the keyboard skills of the organist. The best players directed prestigious societies such as the Royal Choral, the Bach Choir and the Three Choirs Festival Chorus, while church organists conducted local choral societies. Success in the organ loft could also bring prominence in society. To be appointed organist at the royal peculiars, such as the Chapel Royal, Westminster Abbey and St George's Chapel, Windsor, ensured not just a life of 'grace and favour' but also friendly acquaintance with royalty. The Church could educate a boy in its choir schools, offer employment in the great cathedrals and propel the most gifted or tenacious into the realm of the 'great and the good'. The nineteenth-century Church provides one of the most potent examples of an enabling organisa-tion giving boys of natural ability from all backgrounds an opportunity to show their mettle. Turn-of-the-century England offered greater social mobility than any other country in Europe, with an elite to which those clever or skilful enough to force their way in might reasonably aspire. For young Malcolm Sargent, living next door to the gasworks, the organ loft promised a means to achieving respectability and a tantalising sight of eminence.

In January 1912, aged sixteen, Sargent travelled to London to present himself for examination at the neo-Gothic monstrosity in Kensington Gore that housed the Royal College of Organists. Near-by stood the Royal Albert Hall and the Royal College of Music. The

Associate examination, overseen by Walter Alcock of the Chapel
Royal, was long and demanding.[28] First, Sargent sat at the organ,
hidden from the examiners by a green curtain, and followed barked
instructions. He transposed hymn tunes, accompanied in the
Anglican style two men and a boy singing a canticle, and performed
the *Fantasie* and *Finale* from Rheinberger's Sonata in B Minor. There
followed ear tests, counterpoint exercises and a short essay on the
nineteenth-century orchestra. Of the 220 candidates who faced this
rigorous assessment of practical and academic ability, only fifty
passed. Sargent, coming second, was awarded the Sawyer Prize and
£5. His performance marked him out as an organist of exceptional
promise and was enough to secure him an apprenticeship with Dr
Haydn Keeton, the Master of Music at Peterborough Cathedral.
Stamford society rallied. 'Young Malcolm Sargent having distinguished himself in an Examination of the Royal College of
Organists, and knowing of his desire to have a course of lessons from
Dr Keeton, which was an expensive matter, I mentioned a proposal
to Canon Williams of raising a fund of £24 which would give him,
Malcolm Sargent, a season ticket to Peterborough during three
years,' recorded Tom Sandall, the local bank manager, in his diary. 'I
easily collected this myself from 33 subscribers, including the
Marquess of Exeter.'[29]

One word embodied music at Peterborough Cathedral in 1912:
Keeton. 'I could not visualise God very well,' said Sargent later, 'but
he is as near as I could get to it.'[30] Dr Haydn Keeton had been
organist and Master of Choristers for more than forty years. He could
trace his musical genealogy back to Thomas Attwood, organist of St
Paul's Cathedral and Mozart's only English pupil. With thick side-
whiskers, frock-coat and high collars, Keeton was the image of a
Victorian gentleman. Already in his seventies, he was the last
exponent of a system established by the cathedral's sixteenth-century
organist, Richard Storey. Boys were articled by their parents to the
Master of Choristers, who took responsibility for their complete
education. For almost four centuries Peterborough had turned the
most promising pupils into cathedral organists while making highly
competent parish organists of the rest. Only a handful of cathedrals
in England retained the system, and after the First World War it
disappeared altogether.[31]

Absolute discipline defined the Keeton method. 'It was a tyrannical reign,' explains Dr Stanley Vann, who was among Keeton's successors as organist at Peterborough Cathedral. 'He was very hard on his articled pupils. If he was unhappy with the playing of a pupil at Evensong, he would get on the seat and shove him off. He was very strict – a disciplinarian. He seemed harsh to his pupils at the time but they appreciated it later on. They all came out with an impeccable technique.'[32] Keeton smacked boys round the head for wrong notes; counterpoint exercises that displeased him went straight in the bin. He placed pennies on the back of a pupil's hands while he played scales and castigated him for 'impurity' when the coins fell off.[33] His tastes were conservative. 'Music stopped at Mendelssohn – he absolutely thought anything after Mendelssohn was very modern indeed,' recalled Sargent. 'Anything after that period was modern and he did not like it.'[34] In Paris and Vienna in 1912, Schoenberg and Stravinsky were turning the world of classical music upside down; for Malcolm Sargent in Cambridgeshire with Dr Keeton, it might as well have been 1812.

Keeton was a hard taskmaster but at least Sargent did not face him alone. He had been articled with two other boys: Thomas Armstrong and Philip Taylor, who later became organist of Magdalen College, Oxford. Armstrong went on to dominate music education in England much as Sargent did performance.[35] His son Robert, later Cabinet Secretary, remembers that his father considered Sargent 'a lifetime friend', although there was also rivalry.

Thomas Armstrong was the musical golden child of Peterborough and its orbit. His father, Amos Armstrong, had also studied with Keeton and was parish organist at nearby Woodston. As the conductor of many local choirs, including the Stamford Operatic Society, he had inadvertently given Sargent a first opportunity to conduct on that foggy night in 1909. The nine-year-old Thomas Armstrong had won a place in the choir of the Chapel Royal at St James's Palace and sang at the funeral of King Edward VII in 1910. Sargent had often watched him enviously at Peterborough railway station disembarking from the London train in his splendid Tudor-style uniform. He was three years younger than Sargent but appeared so much more sophisticated. He looked sleek in well-tailored suits that enhanced his air of effortless ease. Sargent, on the other hand, had inherited his father's confused dress sense and hair that stuck up like a chimney sweep's brush. Where Armstrong was charming, Sargent was brittle. 'My two young brothers were in the choir and told me the boys loved Armstrong and hated Sargent,' wrote a contemporary. For a boy so desperate to succeed, it was galling for Sargent to be confronted by a younger, more gifted and worldly-wise rival.[36]

Each morning Sargent, Armstrong and Taylor assembled at nine o'clock to start a demanding day. 'It was like a college of music in one man who schooled his students in everything and it was incredibly hard work,' says Stanley Vann.[37] Articled pupils went through the whole gamut of musical work: organ playing, choir training, theory, counterpoint and harmony. They were involved in sung Matins and Evensong every day but Wednesday. Organ and piano lessons took place while the choristers were at school. On the train home there were counterpoint and harmony exercises to complete for the following day. If this were not demanding enough, Sargent enrolled as an external student of Durham University. Working at home in the evenings for a Bachelor of Music degree, he passed his finals in October 1914. Proud members of the choir at St John's church bought and presented him with his violet silk B.Mus. hood.

The cathedral had been a liberating experience for Sargent. He reflected later with Thomas Armstrong that it was the happiest time of his life: 'We had no money and our future was quite uncertain: but it was music, music all the way.'[38] When he returned in the 1960s to conduct a concert, he asked to see the new organ console. 'He played for a few minutes and when he came down he was visibly moved,' recalls Stanley Vann, then Master of Music. 'He said, "Just leave me for a moment to go round the cathedral. I've got such memories." He could hardly speak for emotion.'[39]

Peterborough launched Sargent on the career that his father had chosen for him. He could now earn his living as a musician. In 1914, Keeton recommended him for the post of organist at St Mary's church, Melton Mowbray. More than 150 applied but, as Keeton's man, he was offered the position despite being the youngest applicant. Yet his pleasure was not unqualified, since Thomas Armstrong was appointed sub-organist to Keeton at the cathedral and, after service on the Western Front, took up an organ scholarship at Keble College, Oxford. While Armstrong moved inexorably towards the heart of the Establishment, Sargent looked set for a provincial life in the pretty market towns of middle England.

2

Malcolm in the Middle

Fox-hunting set the market towns of Leicestershire apart from others in England. Melton Mowbray, close to three of the finest hunts – the Quorn, the Belvoir and the Cottesmore – was a playground for the rich and well bred. 'To go fox-hunting in Leicestershire was a deadly serious business, an activity considered superior to almost any other by the Edwardian upper classes and their graded subordinates,' explains the biographer James Fox. 'As a social ritual it was more protected and specialised than any other, with its rules and conventions and its stratified world of cliques and sets.'[1] To many of those who fought in France in the First World War – most famously Siegfried Sassoon, in *Memoirs of a Fox-Hunting Man* (1928) – the hunt represented the essential pre-war England. Blood was shed in unprecedented amounts in that war; the body count was often made in tens of thousands per hour or hundreds per yard won. Yet to all outward appearances, life in Leicestershire carried on between 1914 and 1918 seemingly oblivious to the conflict. The pages of the *Melton Mowbray Times & Vale of Belvoir Gazette* were always more concerned with news from the hunt than the Front.

Life for the townspeople of Melton revolved around servicing the hunt. Serious huntsmen and women often needed to maintain a dozen horses each at hunting-boxes such as Wicklow, Sysonby, Staveley, Hamilton and Warwick lodges. Hunting-boots were made and polished, hunting-ale brewed and hunting-cake baked. The famous Melton Mowbray pork pies were made to fit snugly in the pockets of hunting jackets. Saddlers, breeches-makers, suppliers of fodder, oats and straw, horse dealers and grooms all flourished.[2] 'But the lot who came to hunt were not Meltonians in any way, shape or form,' remembers Edith Hammond, who grew up in Melton during the First World War. 'I didn't always like people who followed the hunt. They owed more money to people in trade than poor people did.'[3]

When Malcolm Sargent arrived in Melton Mowbray, sporting 'a lot of hair which stood up on his head like a brush', he was there as part of the town, not the visiting smart set.[4] The imposing, cathedral-like medieval church of St Mary the Virgin dominated Melton architecturally. It was built of Ketton limestone, with windows at roof level in the nave, and was presided over by the rector, Richard Blakeney, an imposing and severe man who was never seen out of church without a frock-coat and silk hat. 'Canon Blakeney kept himself above you, removed, and was always very much the rector,' says Edith Hammond.[5] Blakeney, who had enjoyed the living at St Mary's for more than thirty years, was known for the ferocity of his sermons. 'He was one of those preachers who would bang his fists down on the pulpit and preach properly,' recalls Eva Dickings, a child at the time. 'It was fire and brimstone. My dad would not go to church unless Canon Blakeney was preaching.'[6]

The rector's wife, Alice, was also a dominant personality in the town who personified Jane Austen's Mrs Elton in *Emma*: a parson's spouse of independent means who considered herself a woman of taste, drove her husband to distraction and had a predilection for 'adopting' protégés. From the moment Sargent arrived in Melton, she made him her pet and smoothed his way in the community. He became the leading light of her musical evenings, playing the piano and directing the assembled musicians – with Alice to the fore – in chamber music and arrangements of folk-songs. Since childhood, he had always been the star turn, encouraged to perform for family and visitors. At the Blakeneys', Sargent now honed that skill, adding to it an ability to flatter influential older women that would serve him well.

The rector, despite his wife's pestering, had little interest in the music at St Mary's. He was happy to leave its planning to his new organist. The church had a 'low' tradition, and Matins and Evensong dominated the services. Sermons often lasted for more than an hour. 'St Mary's would have been quite austere,' says the present rector. 'It is easy to see how Malcolm Sargent would have added a certain colour.'[7] Sargent took advantage of the freedom Blakeney offered to begin restructuring the choir along Dr Keeton's lines. He insisted that members attend practices regularly and weeded out those whose enthusiasm outstripped ability. The remainder and new recruits were cajoled and rehearsed to higher standards of performance. 'I can't remember any good music at St Mary's until he came but he gave it a real push so the choir was absolutely lovely,' says Eva Dickings.[8] They sung the staples of Anglican worship – Parry, Stanford and Wesley – and the 'Hallelujah Chorus' on special occasions. Keeton had shown him that discipline and authority were the best ways to achieve results. Sargent often taught his choir note by note to sing a new setting and developed a caustic wit to get his way. 'I knew some of the boys who were in the choir then and they used to tell me how strict he was,' writes Greta Gastall.[9]

Work with the choir was praiseworthy, but it was Sargent's organ playing that drew crowds to Melton. He was now a player of great prowess who used the recessional at the end of services as an opportunity to display his talents. In 1890 the church had partially installed a new organ that featured a full thirty-two-foot open wood stop with the capacity to produce an overwhelmingly powerful sound. Many parishioners stayed in their pews and often were joined by those who had not attended the service while Sargent thundered his way through classics of the organ repertoire.

Life as a well-received parish organist brought some satisfaction but not financial rewards. Sargent's modest stipend forced him into simple lodgings, including with Harold Furness, the local GP. Like many struggling organists, he taught to supplement his income. He took up the post of music master at the recently opened King Edward VII Grammar in Melton and later added a similar job at his old school, Stamford Grammar. The official history of King Edward's records that Sargent was disliked by other members of staff, who found him offhand, but that his good looks made him popular with schoolgirls.[10] He gave two lessons a week for five guineas a term, composed a new school song and conducted the choir. 'He was such a handsome man, very energetic and smart but he was very severe in his job,' remembers Eva Dickings. 'If you were five minutes late for class or were ill, he would get very cross. I liked him but thought I had to mind how I talked to him.'[11]

Sargent had advised his friend and rival, Thomas Armstrong, that an organ scholarship at Oxford would be a waste of time and told him to go to London. Yet he was not in a position to take his own advice; and nothing emphasised his distance from the cosmopolitan world of London music more than conducting the boys and girls of the local grammar school. The situation was simple enough: Sargent was bored. Respected parish organist, star turn at the vicarage and local schoolmaster: this was not enough to satisfy Sargent's ambition.

There was another, more troubling doubt. When he stood in front of the Melton Mowbray Choral Society on 4 April 1918 to direct Elgar's patriotic work, *The Banner of St George*, he must have wondered, as did others, why he was not out slaying dragons himself. War had been raging in Europe for over three years. Why was this energetic and vital young man at home entertaining 'Mrs Elton' while so many of his contemporaries were dying on the battlefields of the Western Front? All around him men were going off to fight in France. The roll of honour at Stamford Grammar shows that fifty-five old boys and teachers died in the war – the equivalent to wiping out an entire school year. The story was similar at King Edward VII Grammar, and, from Peterborough, Thomas Armstrong went to Flanders with the Royal Artillery. Each week men left the Melton Mowbray Choral Society or brass band for armed service and often did not come back.

The Western Front was the defining experience of Sargent's generation, if not for the man himself. At its worst, the war could mean days such as the first of the Battle of the Somme, 1 July 1916, when 60,000 British soldiers were wounded and 21,000 men killed, most within the first hour.[12] Even before the introduction of conscription the pressure on young men to sign up was immense. Whether or not to fight became a question of moral and physical courage. Women were asked, 'When the War is over and someone asks your husband or your son what he did in the War, is he to hang his head because you would not let him go?' Could fathers of the future, posters demanded, bear the shame when children asked, 'Daddy, what did *you* do in the War?' Those who would not fight often found themselves branded traitors and presented with white feathers for cowardice.[13]

Sargent's military record shows that he had enlisted into the Durham Light Infantry on a short-service engagement in 1916. He signed up on 19 January only to fail the medical the next day. Devastated, he was released to the reserve as 'unfit for service'. The Duke of Wellington may have won the Battle of Waterloo on the playing fields of Eton, but Sargent's war had been ruled out on those of Stamford Grammar. The rugby injury to his shoulder had left him susceptible to dislocation and unfit for active duty. When he was eventually conscripted into the 27th Battalion Durham Light Infantry on 9 May 1918, it was in a low medical category. Manpower shortages meant that anyone who wanted to be in the army was allowed to join the war effort. When his call-up papers came in 1918, Sargent left immediately, glad finally to be involved in the war and, it was rumoured, to escape the wrath of a local policeman whose daughter he had seduced.[14]

The Durham Light Infantry offered a passport to the worst experiences of the Great War. The regiment fought in most of the important battles, including the Somme, Ypres, Loos, Arras and Messines. Around 13,000 Durham soldiers died on these battlefields, with thousands more wounded, gassed or taken prisoner. By 1918, the Durham Light Infantry had raised forty-three battalions, with postings as disparate as France, Italy, Egypt, Salonika and India.[15]

99935 Private Sargent was sent to Herne Bay in Kent for basic training. Coming from the relative comfort of Melton Mowbray, life in the army was a terrible shock. He found himself sleeping in a bell tent with fifteen other men and using facilities that fell a long way short of basic. Food was scarce and manners coarse. Men worked at least twelve hours a day, seven days a week. It was an unsettling environment for a man whose mind had been on counterpoint and organ practice since childhood. Sargent's contemporary in the army, Steuart Wilson, later Head of Music at the BBC, found the military camps in Kent 'stuffy and depressing and full of ill-assorted smells'. His mind was preoccupied not by thoughts of war but 'food, clothes and drains'.[16]

Sargent was not happy as a soldier. He worked hard to please his sergeant major with immaculate appearances on parade, and marched with the straightest of backs. This did not endear him to fellow conscripts who gave him the nickname that would stick for the next fifty years. 'From day one he must have turned out meticulously in his uniform,' says his son, Peter. 'His first name was Harold and so they called him Flash Harry. He had the name for most of his life and never really minded. I think it did have a lot to do with his appearance and the name just stuck.'[17] Sargent's only real friend in the army was Private Wilfred Aris, a teetotal Baptist preacher. For the next eight months the two men became inseparable, and when recruits were needed to form a signals unit, both volunteered. They were transferred to a prep school in Broadstairs where Sargent's musical training helped him master the intricacies of Morse code, and flag and heliograph mirror signals.

The closest that Sargent came to death during the war was a serious bout of Spanish influenza. The 1918 pandemic killed at least forty million people, and perhaps twice as many, in just a year.[18] Healthy young adults were its prime target and soldiers in trenches or the close confines of army barracks were particularly at risk. When Sargent displayed the usual symptoms – runny nose, fever and muscle pain followed by breathing difficulties and the onset of pneumonia – he was immediately quarantined in a single room with twenty other patients. Steuart Wilson expressed scepticism about the level of medical care provided in the army, telling his sister that 'Nobody would induce me to trust myself to any Red Cross show [unless] one is well enough to enjoy rodgering the young ladies who smooth one's pillow.'[19]

Sargent was terrified that confined living with so many ill men would kill him, and was lucky to recover, helped by Aris, who smuggled in a supply of oranges and lemons. By the time he returned to duty in November 1918, an armistice had been signed. Organists were in a low category, but university graduates planning to read for a post-graduate degree were 'category one' and given early release. Sargent, who already had an offer to read for a doctorate at Durham University as an external candidate, was out of the army within two months. He had not had 'a good war' but could rightly claim to have 'done his bit' for King and Country. He had answered England's call and survived: for men of his generation, this was an achievement in itself.

Sargent was returned to the reserve on 27 January 1919.[20] Musical Melton, having suffered during his eight months in the army, was keen to re-establish him as prime mover. At St Mary's church, Sargent dazzled parishioners with increasingly flamboyant organ voluntaries; he was even rewarded one Sunday with the offertory takings in recognition of his talents. In 1919, he founded the Melton Mowbray Operatic Society, enlisting the Duke and Duchess of Rutland as patrons. 'The speed with which the society got into working order was little short of amazing,' wrote the critic of the *Melton Times* after an inaugural performance of Gilbert and Sullivan's *Patience* in March 1920. 'That they accomplished this [perfection] was due in no small measure to the skill and resourcefulness of Dr Sargent whose musical abilities are so well known and recognised that they need no recapitulation here.'[21] The following year, Sargent conducted and directed another Gilbert and Sullivan operetta, *Iolanthe*, to even greater local acclaim. 'This [undoubted triumph] was, of course, primarily due to Dr Sargent, who was responsible for the dancing, acting, grouping, and everything concerned in the production for in each detail there was evidence of a master mind at the helm,' enthused the *Melton Times*.[22]

Performances by the operatic society quickly established a place on Leicestershire's social calendar and were popular with those who came to hunt. It was among the greatest strokes of luck in Sargent's career that he happened to be in Melton Mowbray when it became the most fashionable country retreat in England. The Prince of Wales began to hunt with the Leicestershire packs and was based at Craven Lodge, a 'hunting club' for those who did not want the trouble of maintaining their own hunting-box.[23] The Prince enjoyed his first visit so much that he had an apartment built overlooking Craven Lodge stabling. Wherever the Prince went, society followed. During the winter months, his royal brothers and intimates including the earls of Dudley, Kimberley, Rosebery, Derby, Sefton and West-moreland streamed to Melton. Each day they attracted hundreds of royal-watchers, who turned up to see the hunt ride out and camped in country lanes to catch a glimpse of the Prince. He would ride to St Mary's for Matins while admirers lined the route. Melton was home to the 'fast set' and that which came with it: money, titles, grand houses, gossip, intrigue and sex. 'Melton was a quiet little town but it attracted a sexy crowd,' remembers Edith Hammond. 'And a very racy lot they were too.'[24]

There was in post-war England no 'surer or quicker way to social ascendancy [than] by cutting a good figure at Market Harborough or Melton Mowbray'.[25] Sargent quickly learnt to ape the manners, style and dress of Leicestershire society, given an entrée by providing its entertainment. The Prince of Wales and the Duke of York, accompanied by marquesses, earls and rajas, came to annual performances by the Melton Gilbert and Sullivan Society. 'This illustrious mark of favour is but another instance of Melton royal hunting visitors' interest in their local organisations, and was an occasion that, from the Society's point of view, will live in history, no matter how many years it may run, which from its continued excellence of productions and all-round popularity, bid to be not a few,' observed the *Grantham Journal*, perhaps a little enviously.[26] Sargent was presented afterwards to those royal visitors, who already knew him from services at St Mary's.

Invitations to Sargent from Craven Lodge became more frequent, where he proved adept at singing for his supper. At the piano, he would play classical sonatas and follow them with songs by Gilbert and Sullivan. His bright and energetic character, coupled with an ability to perform, made him a 'local turn' at the dinners, dances and parties that took place night after night at the lodge. With Mayfair's smartest set at play, Sargent was a hugely popular court entertainer. Many of the contacts, such as Lady Irene Curzon, daughter of the foreign secretary, Lord Curzon, later became important sponsors who promoted Sargent's name in London.[27]

Amusing the upper classes gave Malcolm Sargent increased social status but still no financial rewards. Teaching at Stamford Grammar and King Edward's continued.[28] One day a week, he went to his parents' new house in All Saints Place, Stamford, to give private lessons in piano and singing at half a guinea a time. Sargent rounded off his own education by working for his doctorate. He was required to compose a work lasting forty minutes with eight-part choral writing, a fugue in at least five parts and an overture for full orchestra. By 1920 he had completed a setting of Shelley's *Ode to a Skylark*.

'Pure Tchaikovsky and all the better for that,' he later said.[29] It was not a very original work but it satisfied the academic criteria of the doctoral examination. Alice Blakeney paid for his silk gown, which he wore with a flourish at Sunday services. Malcolm was now Dr Sargent, the name by which he would become known throughout the world.

Aged twenty-five, Sargent could look at his life with a certain pleasure. He paid his way in the world exclusively by performing and teaching music. The pastoral beauty of rural Leicestershire provided an elegant physical and social landscape. St Mary's was charming and its parishioners appreciative of his efforts. He had influential patrons in grand houses where he was petted. His academic credentials had been confirmed by his doctorate. Sargent might have settled for the next fifty years into this successful, almost idyllic, provincial life. Yet ambition remained, and with the door of opportunity ajar, he barged his way through. The man who stood on the other side was Sir Henry Wood, the father of English conducting.

Henry Wood was nothing if not a character. He dressed foppishly in droopy bow ties and sported a flamboyant moustache and beard. It was this unconventional look that caused Queen Victoria (ironically or otherwise) to ask after a command performance: 'Are you quite English, Mr Wood?' His risqué look was mirrored in his personal life. Married twice, he spent the last ten years of his life living with his mistress, who changed her name by deed poll to 'Lady Jessie Wood' since the real Lady Wood would not divorce him. Whatever his personal difficulties, his impact on conducting and orchestral life in England was immense. He modelled himself on the great German maestro Arthur Nikisch, and was perhaps the first Englishman to embrace wholeheartedly the art of conducting. He founded the Promenade concerts at the Queen's Hall in London in 1895 – the year of Sargent's birth – and used them to introduce radical compositions by composers such as Debussy, Stravinsky and Richard Strauss. When he performed Schoenberg's *Five Orchestral Pieces* in 1912, he famously exhorted: 'Stick with it gentlemen! This is nothing to what you'll have to play in twenty-five years' time.' He consistently encouraged young talent and even at the height of his fame continued to rehearse the student orchestra at the Royal Academy of Music.[30]

'It is all very well to say conductors are born not made,' complained Elgar in 1905, 'but have we ever seriously attempted to make them?'[31] Henry Wood agreed, and made it a personal crusade to seek out potentials. He was mentor to Adrian Boult, and encouraged John Barbirolli to make the transition from cello section of the Queen's Hall Orchestra to podium. His discovery of Malcolm Sargent was just as influential. Yet if Sargent had not been something of a 'chancer', he might have had no opportunity at all.

On Thursday 3 February 1921, Wood took the Queen's Hall Orchestra to Leicester to perform a concert in aid of the blind. Since Leicester was not part of the orchestra's regular circuit, the visit became a cultural highlight of the year. The 3,000 seats of De Montfort Hall were sold out weeks in advance. Given that Leicestershire's musical public were so organised in their preparation for the concert, they might have it found mildly surprising that Malcolm Sargent had not been quite so punctilious in his own arrangements. This would have mattered less if he had not been asked to write an overture for the concert. The planning committee had invited him a year earlier to compose a work for Sir Henry's visit, hoping that a local composer would generate added interest. Their calculation was well placed: many of those who had booked tickets also chartered a special train serving Stamford and Melton. Sargent had engineered an opportunity for himself by not releasing the score until late January. Wood was livid and wrote to the committee: 'Whoever this fellow is he will have to conduct it himself.'[32]

The overture, *Impressions on a Windy Day*, was based rather unpromisingly on a day's golf at Cromer with Dr Furness. He composed it 'quickly and easily', sending the score off to the copyists with less than a week to spare. 'It is a surprisingly good work,' says the composer Malcolm Arnold, who performed it often under Sargent as a trumpeter in the London Philharmonic during the Second World War. 'It is a marvellous little piece and always went down very well with audiences.'[33] Henry Wood, who was well known for preparing concerts on very little rehearsal, gave Sargent just half an hour in front of the orchestra. Leon Goossens recalled that the orchestra, having expected the 'organist of Melton Mowbray' to be a balding, whiskery old doctor of music, was amazed when Sargent jumped up on the rostrum. He talked too much in rehearsal but brought a dynamic energy to his composition. When he emerged on to the stage that evening in a borrowed tailcoat, he was greeted with all the enthusiasm of a local boy made good. He sped the orchestra through its paces and for his efforts was given an ovation. Time and time again he was called back to the podium. Wood, kindly and encouraging, insisted that Sargent perform the end of the work as an encore.

Backstage after the concert, local friends claimed Sargent. His proud parents watched as Wood congratulated their son and made a life-changing offer: would he like *Impressions on a Windy Day* to be performed in London? For a young composer to have a new work performed by Sir Henry Wood was a tremendous boost. But Wood was not interested in Sargent the composer. What he had seen was a promising conductor: 'You shall conduct it.'[34] Sargent never forgot that Wood had discovered him. 'I shall always be very grateful to you for having given me my first opportunity of conducting in London, for your great encouragement and for the continued inspiration your work has been to me to endeavour to follow in your footsteps,' Sargent wrote just months before Wood's death in 1944.[35]

On 11 October 1921, Malcolm Sargent stepped on to the stage of the Queen's Hall to make his London debut. *Impressions on a Windy Day* was included in a programme with Tchaikovsky's Sixth Symphony. The young man that night did not look like 'Flash Harry'. The tail-coat was not his own and his thick hair was characteristically bushy. What Sargent already had was stage presence that combined dynamism and poise. If there was no surer or quicker way to social ascendancy in 1920s England than cutting a good figure in Melton Mowbray, Sargent now transferred the swagger and energetic self-confidence learnt there to the London concert stage. 'A vivid memory remains of an extremely thin and wiry young man with flying arms, crashing with a breathless orchestra though *Impressions on a Windy Day*,' remembered Bernard Shore, who played that night.[36]

For most of his life, Sargent had wanted to be part of London's musical world. Stamford, Peterborough and Melton Mowbray had served him well, but here at the Queen's Hall, Dr Malcolm Sargent had announced himself. *Impressions on a Windy Day* had been a useful calling card – 'as breezy as a day with the hounds at Melton Mowbray', wrote one critic[37] – but the manner of its performance was more important. The younger Sargent had aspired to be a 'second Elgar'. Now he knew he must be a second Wood. Introducing Sargent to another protégé, Adrian Boult, and the composer Herbert Howells, Wood himself had declared: 'Here's a young man who may not be one of our next composers but is certainly one of our next conductors.'[38]

3

Une Spécialité Anglaise

By 1921, Dr Malcolm Sargent was a man with a future. He returned to Melton Mowbray after his triumph in London with a promise from Henry Wood that a life in music was assured. Sargent was greeted as a hero. 'Everybody was so proud because our organist was having his name shouted from the rooftops,' remembers Edith Hammond.[1] Sargent had always been confident of his talent but now added the self-assurance of a successful man. His manner and clothes were subtly changed. The brush-hair was slicked back with brilliantine. His dress, paid for by discreet patrons, became more formal and expensive. 'He was such a smart man, so dashing and energetic,' says Eva Dickings. 'I used to feel very proud when I was talking to him, especially if somebody saw me.'[2]

Nowhere was Sargent's increased confidence more evident than in dealing with women. 'He was a bit of a lad, according to my mother,' remembers Maisie King.[3] Sargent was popular with women of all ages and pedigrees in the town. He slept with many of the wealthy, middle-aged women who bought him expensive presents, and often kept things in the family by seducing their daughters. His sexual conquests were legion, with young women in the local musical societies particularly susceptible to his charm. There were no long-term relationships, only a succession of flings born of a determination to enjoy as wide a range of sexual experience as possible within the confines of a busy life. It was no surprise when he finally got caught out.

Sargent still lodged with Harold Furness, Melton's doctor. Furness, his regular golfing partner, had helped inspire *Impressions on a Windy Day* and co-founded the operatic society. As a friend, he may have been shocked to discover that Sargent was sleeping with one of his domestic staff. 'She was a servant girl, just an ordinary maid,' recalls Eva Dickings.[4] Eileen Horne was a striking woman. Three years younger than Sargent, she had a squarish jaw, high forehead and dark brown hair cut into a fashionable bob. She lacked any interest in music but recognised in him a man on the make. What attracted Sargent were her willowy looks, general availability and willingness to put propriety to one side.

When she announced that she was pregnant, it came as an unwelcome and chilling shock. Sargent did not love her and she had no compensations of wealth or status. Whether or not Sargent would have wanted an abortion, Eileen, having secured her man, did not. 'He got her into trouble and so they had to get married very quickly,' recalls Edith Hammond.[5] In September 1922, at the parish church of Beyton, near Bury St Edmunds, Eileen Horne became Mrs Malcolm Sargent.[6] The birth of a baby girl, Pamela Stephanie, was difficult and almost resulted in the death of both mother and child. Greta Gastall remembers walking past the Sargents' new house 'on tiptoe' because 'when their first child was born Mrs Sargent was very ill. To deaden the noise of the traffic (mostly horses in those days) the road outside their house was covered with tan, the material used in riding schools and on Rotten Row in Hyde Park.'[7] When Eileen recovered, the family moved to a bigger house in nearby Oakham, although her husband's philandering continued.

Sargent's shotgun marriage only served to reinforce his determination to succeed as a musician. His problem, like that of most young conductors, was finding an orchestra on which to practise. Not for the first time, Leicestershire provided the solution. Karl Russell, the owner of Leicester's City Piano and Organ Saloons, was something of a musical impresario. He regularly promoted concerts at the De Montfort Hall and was looking for ways to make them more popular with the public. Russell saw that the young man who had conducted the Queen's Hall Orchestra would attract such local support and promptly engaged Sargent to conduct a series of four concerts in 1921. 'These concerts,' his advertisement in the *Leicester Mercury* proclaimed, 'will give Dr Sargent every opportunity to display his undoubted Genius and Amazing Versatility as Composer, Conductor, Pianist and Organist.'[8]

Sargent's programmes in Leicester ranged from a Gilbert and Sullivan night to his first performance of Elgar's *The Dream of Gerontius*. Sargent even performed as soloist in Tchaikovsky's First Piano Concerto with the Hallé Orchestra under Hamilton Harty ('I had the devil of a job to stop him from conducting the orchestra as well as playing the piano,' Harty later said). Such was the success of these first four concerts that Russell formed the Leicester Symphony Orchestra, a semi-professional ensemble of eighty players, with Sargent as Music Director. Mary Thornley, who played in the orchestra, remembered that Sargent conducted rehearsals with 'a quick mind and "a very pretty wit" to quote Gilbert and Sullivan'.[9] He worked his way through the summits of symphonic repertoire such as Schubert's 'Great' C Major and – apparently a first for Leicester – Beethoven's Choral Symphony. He also began a long commitment to contemporary English composition, conducting a 'Modern English Composers' series that included Holst's *The Planets*.

The Leicester Symphony also gave Sargent the opportunity to meet and impress those already making their way successfully in London. Henry Wood, who continued to take an interest, 'presided' in the balcony at Sargent's 'Modern English Composers' concert. One year after his Queen's Hall debut, Sargent was invited back by Wood to the Proms to conduct another of his own compositions, *Night Time With Pan*, and later directed the same work at the Royal Albert Hall. Leading soloists also played in Leicester, including Cortot, Backhaus, Schnabel, Solomon, Suggia and Moiseiwitsch, who also gave him piano lessons. All returned to London telling of Sargent's prowess as a conductor.

That Sargent continued to work as a composer and pianist vexed Wood. He knew that Sargent would not prosper as such but saw the makings of an excellent conductor. Wood encouraged another protégé, Adrian Boult, to befriend Sargent and help him make the 'right' choice. Boult, six years older than Sargent, was already established as a staff conductor at the Royal College of Music. He had conducted the first performance of *The Planets* in 1918. Sargent and Boult quickly developed a friendship. Boult had been in the Queen's Hall when Sargent conducted *Impressions on a Windy Day*. He later recalled that 'the work and the performance impressed me tremendously. I got to know Sargent at once. We saw a lot of each other.' Boult involved Sargent in the general lecture circuit and visited Leicester to conduct the Symphony Orchestra with Sargent as soloist. Sargent's son, Peter, recalls that 'my father always said this was the most important moment of his life. Henry Wood was there and asked him afterwards: "It's time to make up your mind Sargent. Which is it to be, conductor or soloist?" My father thought about it and said "conductor". He never looked back.'[10]

Wood and Boult persuaded Sir Hugh Allen, Principal of the Royal College of Music, to watch Sargent conducting the Leicester Symphony Orchestra. Taking to Sargent immediately, Allen invited him to give a conducting class once a week at the College. The following year, 1924, he appointed Sargent to the full-time staff. It was a moment of epiphany. Sargent, in his thirtieth year, finally moved to London. 'Here is a young man from Melton Mowbray,' Hugh Allen told the Royal College of Music choir on the first day of the 1924–5 academic year. 'You'll be hearing more of him. He's going to be an outstanding choral conductor.'

Sargent's talent had propelled him into the world of conducting but his timing could hardly have been better. The 1920s saw a consolidation of the prestige and influence of the conducting profession, which increasingly came to set a worldwide musical agenda. Music performance had always needed someone to give a lead. Between the sixteenth and nineteenth centuries that direction more often than not was given by a composer either from the keyboard or by stamping his foot, banging a stick on the floor, or, latterly, wielding a baton. During the nineteenth century, conducting developed from time-beating into the art of interpretation, and its most prominent exponents were leading composers, particularly Mendelssohn and Wagner. By the twentieth century, conductors found themselves taken seriously in their own right as interpreters of classical repertoire. If a symbolic moment exists when

authority passed from composers to conductors it must surely be
when Arturo Toscanini routed Gustav Mahler in New York. They
were appointed 'joint musical directors' of the Metropolitan Opera
in 1908, but Mahler had no answer to Toscanini's physical energy
and ceaseless political manoeuvrings. He left the Metropolitan Opera
after two unhappy seasons for a brief, humiliating residency as
principal conductor of the New York Philharmonic. That Mahler
was perhaps the most important composer of his generation counted
for little in New York; a man whose name became a by-word for the
twentieth-century conductor had bundled him out.

Malcolm Sargent revered Toscanini as 'the greatest of all
maestros'.[11] The Italian exuded qualities difficult to define but easy
to recognise: charisma and authority. He was a small, dark man with
eyes that conveyed both ferocity and otherworldly spirituality. His
movements were incisive and controlled in a way that suggested
intellectual rigour but with a physicality implying great passion. His
angular features photographed well and studio shots often left much
of his face in shadow, accentuating his dangerous nature. Orchestras
tolerated his legendary ranting because they recognised it as flattery.
Alfred Wallenstein, principal cellist in the New York Philharmonic
during the 1920s and 1930s, witnessed Toscanini rehearsing Wagner
in Milan and was astonished by his cheerfulness. 'Everybody was
playing out of tune, and you didn't say anything. If that had been
New York you would have been on top of them – as a matter of fact
you would walk out,' he told the maestro afterwards. 'Because in
New York I know they can do it,' replied Toscanini, 'but here I
know they cannot.'[12]

Toscanini was Sargent's hero, but Sir Hugh Allen had a more
direct influence in the 1920s. Allen was dominant in English musical
society and was as full in character as girth. His loud, bullish manner
meant he often gave offence, and according to Michael Tippett, he
'had a reputation for being difficult with everyone, like most
choirmasters'.[13] Yet Allen was more than that: in 1918, he had
spectacularly won not just the directorship of the Royal College but
the chair in Music at Oxford University. During the period between
the two world wars, he personified the 'golden triangle' of Oxford,
Cambridge (where he had been an undergraduate) and the Royal
College of Music. Sir Hugh Allen *was* the musical Establishment.

Sargent, with his provincial background, had been outside the Oxbridge–London elite. His appointment to the staff of the Royal College not only gave him financial stability, it also enrolled him into the 'club' of English musical life.[14]

Sargent left his family behind in Oakham for lodgings in London, off Brompton Road, visiting only at weekends. Royal charter had founded the Royal College of Music in 1883 under the presidency of the Prince of Wales (later Edward VII). It undertook practical training of composers, instrumentalists, singers and conductors. Sargent's duties included instructing the conducting class, rehearsing the second orchestra and taking choir practice when Allen was away. From the moment he arrived, Sargent cultivated a certain image. He would walk most of the short distance to work and then jump into a taxi in Exhibition Road – two minutes away – just so that he could arrive in style. When the more humdrum Boult, who always took public transport, upbraided him for the extravagance of a taxi, Sargent merely replied, 'All the more room for you, Adrian, on the bus.'[15] He dazzled students with tales of the parties he had attended and created around himself an aura of perpetual motion. When students complained about rehearsals at half past nine in the morning, he told them to make more of their lives: he had 'got to bed at four, had two hours' sleep, then got on my horse and rode in the Park for an hour before breakfast'.[16] To credulous young minds, their flamboyant tutor was a man living life in the fast lane.

Sargent's style of teaching was modelled inevitably on that of Dr Keeton. He demanded the highest standards from all his pupils, often lamenting that if only they could have had the training he received at Peterborough they might be slightly better than useless. More than anything, he drilled into them that sloppiness and anything less than total professionalism were unacceptable. 'The curse of English conducting is amateurishness,' became his mantra. 'That's where so much English conducting begins – and ends.'[17] Instruction was given in the practicalities of music-making: knowing the score, keeping hand movements clear and direct, how to accompany, and mentally picturing direction from the podium. Matters of interpretation were rarely discussed, because he believed a performance had to come from within and could not be taught. Tippett was among his students in 1924. He had first met Sargent as a pupil at Stamford Grammar after the war. Tippett remembered Sargent at the College as 'fluent in every conceivable way' but 'right from the start he expressed the view that we were all hopeless and the most useful thing we should learn would be how to conduct amateurs'.[18]

Sargent never warmed to Tippett or his music, but relations were better with two colleagues at the Royal College, Ralph Vaughan Williams and Gustav Holst. Vaughan Williams's tutors and family had despaired of him writing music when 'he was so hopelessly bad at it', but since he was a Wedgwood heir he had the luxury of choosing his own career.[19] He engaged in formal study until his late thirties, which culminated in a year spent in Paris in 1908 with Ravel, under whose influence he wrote his most enduring work, the *Fantasia on a theme of Thomas Tallis*. An opera, *Hugh the Drover*, written in 1914, received its premiere ten years later under Sargent with the British National Opera Company.

Hugh the Drover was a 'problem' piece performed by a 'problem' opera company. Vaughan Williams had wanted to write 'a musical' about English country life, 'real as far as possible – not a sham', but ended up with pastiche.[20] He had been fascinated by folk-song since the turn of the century and was overflowing with tunes for the opera. What he lacked was a dramatic context or even a decent story. He provided his librettist, Harold Child, with a series of musical situations stitched together by a weak narrative. As a result, *Hugh the Drover* was little more than 'an anthology of good tunes'.[21] The British National Opera Company crushed whatever charm it may have had. The company introduced many fine musicians to English audiences and undertook innovative tours of provincial cities that included performances of Wagner's *Der Ring des Nibelungen* sung in English. What BNOC lacked was not imagination but money. It had been formed in 1922 after the Beecham Opera Company went bust and limped along until 1928 before being forced into liquidation.

In 1924, the company presented a season at His Majesty's Theatre in London that included *Hugh the Drover*. Chronic underfunding ensured that *Hugh* was appallingly under-rehearsed. Sargent had little more than a dress rehearsal with soloists, chorus and orchestra. Had it not been for chance, the first performance, on 14 July, would have been a shambles. BNOC had just returned from a lengthy tour and the company were exhausted. Sargent was painfully aware that singers had not learnt their parts, but he knew others who had. The Royal College of Music had given public 'rehearsals' of *Hugh* just days earlier, and Sargent drafted in those same performers to bolster the unprepared British National Opera Company. The premiere was not a triumph, but neither was it a disaster. Afterwards, Vaughan Williams proclaimed that Sargent had 'saved it from disaster every few bars and pulled the chestnuts out of the fire in a miraculous way'.[22]

Hugh the Drover was not a dramatic success, but the music itself, when detached from its plot, was sufficiently charming to encourage His Master's Voice to record it. This first visit to the recording studio marked for Sargent the beginning of a long relationship with The Gramophone Company (which became EMI in 1931). The record industry, still in its infancy, used primitive techniques for capturing sound. For a conductor in 1924 to agree to make a record was a guarantee that dignity would have to be set aside in the name of art. *Hugh the Drover* was recorded at studios in Hayes during September and October. Orchestra, chorus and soloists were crammed into a room that was too small and in which wind players and singers had difficulty breathing. Protruding from the wall were two enormous brass horns. Sound vibrations travelled down the horns and caused a sapphire cutter to gouge out a groove in a disc of wax. The acoustic process was only able to reproduce a limited frequency range. In order to direct events for the best possible sound, Sargent mounted a shelf and was harnessed to the wall to ensure he did not fall off. He conducted the opera from memory but had more to do than simply give cues. It was his responsibility to secure the right acoustic levels, which, in practice, meant pushing a singer's head into or away from the recording horn with his left hand and conducting with his right. To get in place, singers had to slither on their hands and knees along the floor popping up in front of the highly sensitive recorder only when cued to sing.[23]

Sargent's work on *Hugh the Drover* and, in 1925, the premiere of *At the Boar's Head* by Gustav Holst, ensured his growing reputation as an interpreter of new music. This led to invitations to conduct the Royal Choral Society and the Royal Philharmonic Society, personal fiefdoms of Sir Hugh Allen. Allen was a vigorous supporter of new music so long as he did not have to conduct it himself. In 1925, he organised a Royal Philharmonic Society concert of contemporary

English music at which Sargent conducted works by Vaughan Williams, Herbert Howells and Lord Berners. Just as Howells's piano concerto drew to its conclusion, a man in the circle leapt to his feet and shouted: 'Thank God that's over!' The audience, at first shocked – surely this kind of discourtesy only happened in Paris – quickly rallied behind the young composer and gave him a standing ovation. The protester was dragged out by attendants and pursued up the stairs by Howells's now extremely vocal supporters.

Sargent was beginning to get a taste for controversy. In 1924 he had been invited by Robert Mayer to take over from Adrian Boult as permanent conductor/compère of his concerts for children that took place on Saturday mornings at Westminster Central Hall. Mayer was a copper millionaire obsessed by music who in 1923 had established a series of concerts aimed directly at children.[24] Sargent was appointed for his youth and easy ability with audiences. Among his innovations when he took over was the introduction of words and phrases to illustrate themes to a young audience. Beethoven's Fifth Symphony opened with 'fee, fi, fo, fum' and Mendelssohn's *Fingal's Cave* with 'how lovely the sea is'.

The music press was enraged that the great composers should be so denigrated. 'The best place for him is at the door taking tickets,' observed the *Musical Times* of Sargent.[25] The *Music Bulletin* worried that jingles encouraged 'nothing save the categorical sense, which is better developed by mathematics. Children's concerts on the present lines will only help to raise a nation of shopkeepers, bankers and civil servants.'[26] These fulminations sparked a national debate in which Sargent was portrayed by the daily press as a moderniser. *The Times* praised his 'wonderful help in leading from the known to the unknown, which might set many a young mind on the road to both philosophy and music'.[27] The *Morning Post* wondered how many of the critics hostile to Sargent could communicate about the subject with his clarity and enthusiasm.

Most children attending the concerts seemed entranced by the 'explanatory remarks' with which Sargent introduced programmes. 'Explanatory remarks, however, is too formal an expression to be applied to the conversational way in which he outlines for us each composer's life, tells us the conditions under which his music was written, and helps us to understand it by explaining the construction and picking out the chief tunes,' reported two enthusiastic pupils at Haberdashers' Aske's School for Girls in 1925. 'These concerts are developing our taste in music and helping us to appreciate good music of every style, from Boccherini's dainty Minuet to Wagner's crashing *Lohengrin* overture.'[28]

Sargent continued as permanent conductor of the concerts until they were interrupted by war in 1939.[29] They were invariably sold out as eager middle-class parents latched on to such an improving and time-filling scheme. Mayer and Sargent worried about those who had no access to music and started an offshoot at the People's Palace on the Mile End Road in the East End of London. The price of a ticket was virtually nothing and encouraged full houses of children that included the very poorest. Concerns were expressed that youngsters with no sense of concert etiquette would ruin the event, recalled Mayer, but 'you could have heard a pin drop'.[30] The People's Palace concerts were the beginning of a lifelong determination by Sargent to advance music in poorer communities.

The Robert Mayer children's concerts brought Sargent public attention, but it was conducting Gilbert and Sullivan in London that made him famous. Irreverent, mocking and witty, these light operas had sliced through Victorian society. Admirals, high court judges, peers of the realm, and policemen: any in authority might find themselves pitched into the 'topsy-turvy' world of Gilbert and Sullivan. Their skill was to produce an amusing social commentary within a meticulously executed musical structure. *HMS Pinafore*, *The Gondoliers* and *The Mikado* are but a few sensational hits among many that brought the two men wealth and fame. Lytton Strachey debunked most Victorian heroes yet conceded that Gilbert and Sullivan's operas were among the enduring legacies of the century. The two men reached the apogee of their creative output in the 1880s, by which stage they had already been absorbed into English conventional tastes.

By the 1920s, the radicalism of Gilbert and Sullivan's operas had been dulled by tradition and familiarity. The fact that 'Safety First' Stanley Baldwin, the bluff, no-nonsense leader of the Tory party, was a loyal patron only emphasised how comfortable the Savoy operas had become. Rupert D'Oyly Carte had since 1913 been running the D'Oyly Carte Opera Company, founded by his father, Richard, but was deeply affected in the 1920s by new trends in theatre and choreography. In 1926 he decided to give the operas a more contemporary look and in doing so whipped up a storm of public outrage. D'Oyly Carte knew that the operas had gone stale not because the works themselves were ageing poorly but because the productions were tired. The company had the appearance of a nineteenth-century relic. The original staging remained in place. Costumes were rotting. Scenery looked rickety and patched-up. Many of the principal singers had sung for the composer in the 1890s; thirty years later, they sounded like it.

Carte wanted to bring vitality and glamour back. To launch the 1926 season with *The Mikado*, the most popular of all Savoy operas, he engaged a leading English artist, Charles Ricketts, to re-dress the production. Ricketts had lived in Japan and was an authority on its national dress and culture. He had long been a critic of how Japan was portrayed on the stage. '*Madam Butterfly* and *The Mikado* have created a dreary pink dressing gown style quite unlike anything Japanese,' he told Carte. 'The public would be startled by the novelty of an entirely different presentment [*sic*].' New costumes were based on colourful eighteenth-century Japanese dress. Ricketts observed this tradition very closely while allowing himself a few liberties such as the Lord High Executioner's hat, which resembled a big black chopping block. Ricketts's subtlety was so great that he even managed to avoid giving offence to the Japanese by dressing the Mikado himself not as the Emperor but as his Shogun – the Emperor's principal representative. This dramatic new costuming combined, he said, 'beauty, humour, and an element of surprise'.[31]

The new production of *The Mikado* was lavish, but Rupert D'Oyly Carte believed that he needed more than simply a new look. Musical standards in the company were mixed. Carte went to Winchester to see Sargent conduct *HMS Pinafore*. Afterwards, Sargent recalled, 'Mr Rupert D'Oyly Carte sent for me and said that he wanted to put on a big season at the Prince's Theatre, and would I take charge of the music. I could really hardly believe my ears, because it was to me the most fascinating project, and he said I want you to take complete charge of the music, and to do it as you feel it should be done.'[32]

Just as Ricketts attempted to bring authenticity to the costumes, so

Sargent consulted Sullivan's scores and performance notes locked away in the vault of the Savoy Hotel. He restored the band parts, which had previously been rewritten for the purposes of touring with a smaller orchestra, in line with Sullivan's originals.[33] The chorus was purged and younger recruits brought in. 'We in the chorus adored him and sang as never before; we were said to be the greatest [*Iolanthe*] Peers' Chorus ever,' remembered Webster Booth. 'Things may have been different then, the world was less democratised and there were not many famous conductors to whom a quite unknown member of the chorus would have dared to speak but he always had time for each of us, and there was always quick sympathy and wise advice.'[34]

Sargent's musical innovation had its opponents. 'The principals definitely did not like the "the drill Sargent" quite so much,' Booth observed from the chorus line. 'For years they had sung when and how they conceived to be correct; but Sargent, fresh from an intensive study of Sullivan's scores, realised that some very strange notes had crept in through the years!'[35]

Everything that Sargent wanted to change at D'Oyly Carte Opera was symbolised by its star performers. 'When I first became a member of the D'Oyly Carte Opera Company in September 1919 for the season at the Princes Theatre, there was no question who were the stars of the operas,' remembered Derek Oldham. 'Henry Lytton was king and Bertha Lewis was queen.'[36] Lytton had joined the company in the 1880s and sung leading roles for Sullivan himself. He had stage presence and a certain artful incompetence that got to the heart of the major-generals, admirals and other Establishment characters he satirised. Yet he could not read music, and so half-sang, half-spoke his way through roles in a rough approximation of what Sullivan had written. Bertha Lewis was a better musician than Lytton but even more arrogant. 'When Bertha came on, we joked, the opera's commenced,' recalled Oldham.[37] 'There's no room, there's no room,' she would hiss at other singers, barging her way centre stage.

When Sargent took on these outsized egos, 'then the big battles began'.[38] Lytton attempted unsuccessfully to have Sargent dismissed and was furious when he persisted in correcting him on stage. 'It amused us enormously to see the tremendous Henry Lytton, Bertha,

Darrell and "Sheff" [Darrell Fancourt, Leo Sheffield] having music lessons again,' said Booth. 'It certainly did not amuse them – there were frayed tempers, tears and something near to violence sometimes – but the results were worth it and they knew it even when they were fighting their hardest.'[39]

The most controversial aspect of Sargent's interpretation was speed. Sargent used the composer's tempo markings, which were significantly faster than 1920s convention. Critics and singers alike were not pleased. The critics praised the precision Sargent drew from the orchestra but frequently complained that he was 'apt to force the pace'.[40] Singers often tried to ignore Sargent altogether. 'Dr Sargent constitutionally likes things fast, while singers, either for the sake of their traditional expression or because this "particularly rapid, intelligible patter" is hard to sing, like them a little slower' observed *The Times*. 'If they reached an agreed compromise they might neither of them be satisfied but we the audience would probably feel more comfortable.'[41]

The first night of *The Mikado* in September 1926 was a highlight of the London theatrical year. Speculation about Ricketts's new costuming had generated huge publicity in the press: rumours even suggested that Nanki-Poo, the wandering player, would have a saxophone. Tickets for the opening night had sold out months in advance and were exchanged on the black market for exorbitant prices. Such was the interest generated that the BBC transmitted two half-hour live broadcasts from the opera, as much to hear audience reactions as the music. 'Probably the number of people who heard the first half-hour was the largest audience that has ever heard anything at one time in the history of the world,' said the *Evening Standard*.[42] Eight million radio listeners heard an excited audience react to the splendour of the production. There was even political controversy. When Henry Lytton as Ko-Ko sang of 'the apologetic statesman of a compromising kind', he mimed Stanley Baldwin, who was in the theatre, striking a match against his bottom and lighting his trademark pipe. Lytton was booed and struggled to complete the song.

The re-costuming of *The Mikado* was a triumph hailed by the press. 'Is there anything in all the annals of the light lyric stage, in this or any other country,' enquired the *Daily Telegraph*, 'that could be compared with the unending triumphs of Gilbert and Sullivan?'[43]

Sargent not Ricketts faced the ire of conservatives at the first night. The critic of *The Times*, who had sat through the performance with the vocal score, was furious that Sargent appeared to have re-orchestrated the opera with 'additional accompaniments'. It took a letter from Carte to the newspaper to demonstrate Sargent's textual fidelity. 'Dr Malcolm Sargent has most carefully studied the original full score and, in addition to piano rehearsals with the principals and chorus, has had six hours of orchestral rehearsals with the full score before him,' he wrote. 'His main object this season is to bring out the full beauty and humour of Sullivan's orchestral colouring. It would seem that he was so successful in this respect last night and that the details of the orchestration sounded so fresh that some critics thought them actually new.'[44]

The 1926 *Mikado* saw the beginning of a revitalised D'Oyly Carte Opera Company symbolised by the return to a refurbished Savoy Theatre in October 1929.[45] It was at D'Oyly Carte that Sargent began to cultivate a showman's image. In this he followed Gilbert's own advice that 'You must stir and stump it, and blow your own trumpet, or trust me, you haven't a chance.'[46] Sargent was ground-breaking in his professionalism but masked hard work with an impression of effortless ease. An immaculately groomed Dr Sargent, who gleamed like a matinee idol, had dispatched the last vestiges of the brush-haired Malcolm. He nonchalantly arrived minutes before curtain-up to ask, 'Which is it tonight?' Afterwards he would dine at the bohemian Savoy Grill. Sargent took as his model another cathedral-trained organist: the actor Ivor Novello, who epitomised star quality.[47] Talent was not enough; charm, personality and good looks were essential to the equation.[48]

Sargent revelled in the fame that came at D'Oyly Carte, but it did not dull his ambition to succeed Sir Henry Wood as England's leading conductor. Gilbert and Sullivan operas were far removed from the cultural revolution that was sweeping Europe. Unease surrounding *The Mikado* in 1926 only scratched the surface of Establishment concerns that the world was changing too fast. Politics were being pushed to frightening extremes by the rise of communism and fascism. Fanaticism had always seemed a peculiarly un-English phenomenon, but even the General Strike of 1926 seemed to hint at trouble to come.

Extremism was also a question of taste. European culture by the
1920s had been in the throes of an intellectual and artistic revolution
that combined gritty social realism, a fascination with the psyche and
an absolute rejection of tradition. To those of conservative taste, it
was shocking and absurd. The novels of Celine, Broch, Joyce and
Roth, the paintings of Chagall, Miro, de Chirico and Grosz, poems
by Eliot and Montale, buildings by Le Corbusier, van der Rohe and
Nervi, designs by Moholy-Nagy and the cinema of Cocteau,
Chaplin and Eisenstein: all seemed to declare schism with
convention, proclaiming with Marinetti, the founder of Futurism:
'We will teach you to love the living, oh dear slaves and sheep of
snobbism!'[49]

This sense of moving into a vastly superior modern world was
paralleled by a scientific revolution. A tradition of classical physics
stretching from Isaac Newton and Galileo was broken by Albert
Einstein with quantum and relativity theories from which there was
no turning back.[50] It was Gertrude Stein in 1938 who compared
Einstein to Picasso, claiming that both had changed society's understanding of the temporal world. 'The earth is not the same as in the
nineteenth century,' she explained.[51]

Music too was in the throes of revolution. In Vienna, the most
conservative city in Europe and spiritual home to music of the
eighteenth and nineteenth century, radical composers led by Arnold
Schoenberg had reluctantly concluded that tonality was exhausted. 'I
feel air from another planet,' sings a soprano in the last movement of
Schoenberg's *Second String Quartet (with voice)* written in 1908. If
music was to survive as a radical art, Schoenberg argued, it must have
a new atmosphere – and a new language. By 1909, in *Three Piano
Pieces*, he was already breathing the foreign air of atonality and in the
next decade codified a new musical language.[52] Yet it was in Paris not
Vienna that music shifted from one episteme to another. The
premiere of Stravinsky's ballet *The Rite of Spring*, on 29 May 1913,
famously ended in chaos. Modernists and traditionalists hit and
screamed at each other. 'By the time the curtain went up [on the
second scene] we were pretty scared,' remembered a dancer. 'The
uproar in the audience made it hard to hear even the music.'[53]
Fighting inside the auditorium was matched by a war of words in
newspapers and journals. 'Never has the cult of the wrong note been

applied with such industry, zeal and ferocity,' wrote one critic.[54] *The Rite of Spring* was nothing less than 'laborious and puerile barbarism', concluded *Le Figaro*.[55] The work became an immediate Modernist icon. It was, said Jean Cocteau with typical epigrammatic flair, 'the Georgics of prehistory'.[56]

The man who stood at the centre of this revolution was the impresario Serge Diaghilev. His Ballets Russes, founded in 1909, would dominate European music and dance until 1929. Diaghilev was autocratic and ruthless but had an extraordinary ability in spotting outstanding talent. Just to list some of the composers he sponsored – Stravinsky, Debussy, Ravel, Milhaud, Satie, de Falla, Poulenc, Auric, Prokofiev, Strauss and Respighi – illustrates his phenomenal influence on modern music. The choreographers he employed, such as Fokine, Nijinsky, Petipa, Massine, Nijinska and Balanchine, tell a similar story in dance. If Stravinsky, Nijinsky and their like were the children of the Modernist revolution, Diaghilev was their godfather. The riotous first performance of *The Rite of Spring* had shown how Diaghilev could ignite public passions but, if anything, the work of the Ballets Russes by the 1920s was even more radical. Experimental works such as Stravinsky's *Les Noces* and Milhaud's *Le Train Bleu* increasingly baffled audiences in Paris and London.

Malcolm Sargent had established himself as a champion of contemporary English repertoire by conducting the music of composers such as Ralph Vaughan Williams, Herbert Howells and Gustav Holst, but that hardly put him in the avant-garde. Yet Sargent was to have a dramatic chance meeting with Diaghilev in the summer of 1927. He was teaching at the Royal College of Music when an urgent message came: the Russian wanted to see him immediately. Sargent hurried along to His Majesty's Theatre, where he was ushered on to the main stage. Ninette de Valois, founder of the Royal Ballet, thought Diaghilev 'the most extraordinarily frightening man'.[57] When Sargent met him for the first time the impresario was pacing backwards and forwards in extreme agitation. Dressed characteristically in black overcoat and hat despite the summer heat, he caught sight of Sargent and exclaimed, 'You are my saviour!' Eugene Goossens, conductor of the Ballets Russes, had been taken ill. Would Sargent take over that night? If he did not, 'there will be no ballet'.

Sargent had never conducted Stravinsky's *Firebird* or Poulenc's *Les Biches*, but this was Diaghilev asking. Sargent accepted breezily and jumped into a taxi to Goossens's sickbed. Just two years older than Sargent, Eugene Goossens was the leading English conductor of the avant-garde. Sargent spent the afternoon with him going through the scores. Conducting contemporary music was a highly demanding exercise. 'It was necessary to invent, for this kind of new rhythm, a new conducting technique,' said Ernest Ansermet, conductor of the Ballets Russes in 1915.[58] Sargent had already developed his own method based on clarity of line and gesture, which suited perfectly music by Stravinsky and Poulenc. Goossens's sister, Sidonie, remembers how impressed her brother was at 'the lightning speed' of Sargent's quick-study of the complex rhythms of *Les Biches*.[59]

Others were less confident. Sargent recalled that when he arrived, 'Everyone rushed at me, arguing and protesting in ten different languages, each trying to impress on me the importance of the tempo in his or her particular portion of the ballet. The music was hard enough but this representation of Babel did not make things easier.'[60] At the end of the performance, Sargent was brought on to the stage to receive applause from the whole company and orchestra. When the curtain came down for the final time, Diaghilev embraced him and bestowed a blessing. To perform so well, under such pressure, he purred: 'C'est une spécialité anglaise'.[61]

For the next week, while Goossens recovered, Sargent fulfilled a demanding schedule. After each performance, he worked into the early hours to prepare the ballet for the following day. He would rehearse with dancers at the piano in the morning, visit Goossens for advice on the score in the afternoon and then step into the pit for the performance. Diaghilev was so impressed that he invited Sargent to conduct the following season. In total, Sargent would direct fourteen ballets in eighteen months. He was in the pit for the opening night of the London season in 1928 at which he shared the podium with Igor Stravinsky, high priest of modern music. Sargent directed Respighi's *Cimarosiana* and Stravinsky conducted the London premiere of his own *Apollon Musagète*.

The 1928 season was to be Diaghilev's last in London. His sudden death the following year closed the most dynamic chapter in twentieth-century music. Sharing the podium with Stravinsky, Diaghilev's most famous protégé, had put Malcolm Sargent at the epicentre of the European avant-garde.

4

Make the Buggers Sing
Like the Blazes

In the summer of 1928, London commuters were presented with a bizarre and wonderful sight. Each night for two weeks in June, a thousand predominantly middle-aged men and women were to be seen boarding buses and the tubes, driving cars and motorbikes, wandering the streets of London, all of them dressed as Native American braves and squaws. They were members of the Royal Choral Society and the collective stars of *Hiawatha*, the smash hit of the year. Their first entry into the arena of the Royal Albert Hall was guaranteed frenzied applause. When the overture finished, house- and floodlights blazed on and they ran screaming from every door and staircase, and threw themselves to the ground, prostrate before totem poles. Each night they whooped, shouted, ran, jumped and sang to acclaim. Behind them a colourful backcloth presented a scene from the Hudson Valley in which a spectacular waterfall cascaded over rocks and bushes. To add authenticity to kitsch, a Native American chief acted the part of the Medicine Man and wore a long feathered head-dress.

The conductor was Malcolm Sargent, who revelled in this opportunity for showmanship. Each night he would emerge up the bull-run into the hall and was picked out by a brilliant light that followed him to the podium. Pristine, with a white carnation now habitually in his lapel, Sargent's calculated panache added to the sense of occasion. As master of ceremonies he stood under a spotlight for the entire evening. For this show Sargent was visibly in charge. He never fell out of love with *Hiawatha* and dismissed as ridiculous those 'inclined to turn up their noses and think it a little cheap'.[1]

Samuel Coleridge-Taylor's *Hiawatha* was the sensation of the inter-war years. Born in 1875 of a father from Sierra Leone and an English mother, Coleridge-Taylor had modelled himself on Dvořák in trying to absorb non-European influences into his music. His most popular work was a series of cantatas based on Longfellow's *Hiawatha* using 'primitive' rhythm and melodies. This dignified and romanticised presentation of Native American life fed into the late Victorian fascination with the exotic that made it an instant success.[2] Converting the *Hiawatha* cantatas into a staged spectacular was the brainchild of innovative producer Thomas Fairbairn. He had approached Coleridge-Taylor in 1912 to ask whether *Hiawatha* could be changed from the past to the present tense to make it more immediately dramatic. The impoverished composer agreed, but tragically died of pneumonia aged only thirty-seven before the project was staged.

The first production of *Hiawatha* took place in the Royal Albert Hall in 1924, but it was not until 1928, when the show was revived with Sargent as conductor, that it became a massive hit. Each summer for twelve years, *Hiawatha* took over the Albert Hall and played to packed, excited houses. Public and press never seemed to grow weary of the show. The Royal Choral Society won unprecedented popularity. 'For years in succession, the Royal Choral Society has put on its war paint and invaded the arena of the Albert Hall in very un-oratorio-like fashion uttering queer cries that would have mightily astonished members of twenty years ago,' observed *The Times* in 1935. '*Hiawatha* has, in fact, become a regular fixture of the summer season and last night's performance proved that it has not become stale to the singers nor lost its attraction for the audience. [...] And for that achievement great praise is due to Dr Malcolm Sargent.'[3] *Hiawatha* helped make Sargent a household name and established his reputation as an outstanding choral conductor.

The choir over which Sargent presided each summer was England's grandest. The French composer Charles Gounod had founded the Royal Choral Society in 1871, under the personal patronage of Queen Victoria, as the choir of the newly built Royal Albert Hall. It quickly established itself at the centre of London's musical life, with a strong membership list and rich benefactors. By the 1920s, however, the Royal Choral Society was in crisis. It had no permanent conductor, membership was declining and audiences were losing interest. A performance of Handel's *Messiah* could still guarantee a capacity audience, but otherwise the society performed to half-empty houses. The advent of the BBC and the gramophone had enabled many in London to get their musical entertainment at home. The Great War had taken its toll on membership. Annual losses were running at more than £2,000 and financial obligations were met only by the generosity of rich friends.

Sir Hugh Allen had given his protégé a first opportunity with the Royal Choral Society in 1924, introducing him to the members of the choir by telling them: 'You are going to be in the hands of this *boy*.'[4] Four years later, Allen was instrumental in getting his 'boy' appointed Principal Conductor in succession to Sir Frederick Bridge. Sargent had shown that he could offer youth, glamour and vitality. His task now was to attract a younger membership and boost the audience to lift the society out of the doldrums. Sargent made a number of immediate changes. He established continuity through attending regular Monday evening rehearsals, and instilled a Keetonian discipline. This made him respected if not popular. He could deliver sharp ripostes to errant singers and taunted this metropolitan choir with accusations that it was not as good as those in Rutland. Sargent insisted that prospective new members be properly auditioned, and encouraged older singers to take social rather than active membership. He was already displaying a characteristic essential to any great conductor: what Isaiah Berlin described as the 'the indispensable element of *terribilita*'.[5]

This modernisation of the society was not simply musical. Careful consideration was given to the choir's image. By tradition, women at concerts had worn white dresses, with those on the right adding red sashes while those on the left wore blue. The effect had been pleasingly patriotic before the war but in the twenties seemed quaint. Sargent argued that the sashes should go but was told by the committee that they must be worn. At the next concert the sashes were nowhere to be seen. Immediately afterwards Sargent was upbraided in his dressing room by the chairman, Lord Shaftesbury. 'It is in the constitution that they must be worn,' Shaftesbury told him. 'Yes it is,' Sargent replied, 'but it doesn't say they have to be worn on the outside.'[6] It was a small but symbolic step in his transformation of the Royal Choral Society. Within ten years it was the wealthiest and most highly regarded choir in England, making an annual profit of £4,000.

Sargent's success with the Royal Choral Society brought him to the attention of Sir Thomas Beecham, the flamboyant English conductor. Beecham had been involved in many orchestral and operatic ventures by the late 1920s, most of which had ended in failure. On the eve of the First World War his father, Sir Joseph Beecham, had purchased for him the whole of the Covent Garden estate, including the Royal Opera House, from the Duke of Bedford. Sir Joseph then watched in horror as this investment almost bankrupted his pills and potions empire.[7] Anxiety about the debts contributed to his death in 1916. By 1923, the Court of Chancery had found Sir Thomas's liabilities to be £2,131,571.[8] Only the renewed post-war profits of Beecham's potions saved him.

Sir Thomas Beecham had innate musicality but was ill-suited to the increasingly professional musical environment of the twenties and thirties. He had had no comprehensive musical training and notoriously could not write out his own band parts if they needed transposing. He had flourished by a canny combination of charm and cheque-book. Many English orchestral players adored him because he could always be guaranteed to amuse them, often at the expense of choirs – 'Ladies of the chorus, if you will look to your parts, you will see where the gentlemen enter' – and did not work them hard. Results were mixed. If an orchestra knew a work well and needed only an interpretation, the performance might be sublime; in an unknown, under-rehearsed piece, concerts often came close to collapse.

Beecham was never comfortable as a choral conductor. He struggled with complex rhythms and had to make humiliating cuts in contemporary works such as Delius's *Songs of Farewell*. It was the first performance of such a work, *Belshazzar's Feast* by William Walton, at the Leeds Triennial Festival, that brought Beecham and Sargent together. In December 1930 the Festival Committee, seeking to appoint an assistant conductor, asked Beecham, then Chief Conductor, and Sir Hugh Allen for suggestions. Beecham advised that 'the most competent of the young men would be Constant Lambert' but was no match for Allen.[9] 'The question of the Assistant Conductor was discussed and the names suggested were Dr Malcolm Sargent and Mr Constant Lambert,' record the minutes. 'The Committee requested the Secretary to ascertain the terms which Dr Malcolm Sargent would accept for a general retainer to conduct such of the works in the programme as were allotted to him.'[10]

Sargent was already well known in Yorkshire. As Director of the Bradford Festival Choral Society since 1925, he had impressed not just with musical ability but also with his loyalty when the choir suffered financial difficulties. Beecham's test for his young deputy was the most difficult work of the festival; *Belshazzar's Feast*, Beecham thought, was doomed to failure. 'As you'll never hear the thing again, my boy,' he told the composer, 'why not throw in a couple of brass bands' (which Walton promptly did).[11]

Walton was born in Oldham, Lancashire, in 1902 and became a chorister at Christ Church, Oxford, in 1912 where, later, Sacheverell Sitwell befriended him. He lived with the fashionable if louche Sitwells in London for much of the 1920s and 1930s. He wrote *Façade* – a massive society hit – with Edith Sitwell and turned to Osbert Sitwell for the libretto of *Belshazzar's Feast*. The idea began with the BBC, which commissioned a work for small chorus and orchestra in the autumn of 1929. The theme was to be 'something that everyone would know'. At a loss, Walton asked Osbert to come up with an idea. He suggested 'The Writing on the Wall' from the Book of Daniel, although it turned out not to be 'something that everyone would know' when Walton promptly confused kings Belshazzar and Nebuchadnezzar. Once these difficulties were overcome, Sitwell produced an imaginative libretto that was dramatic, concise and highly visual. Walton joined Sitwell in Amalfi to compose the work and it quickly became apparent that he was writing something far bigger than the BBC's commission. Beecham agreed to premiere the oratorio at the 1931 Festival. The BBC commission now withdrawn, Walton dedicated the work to the eccentric composer Lord Berners, who paid him £50.

England as a country had been obsessed by oratorio since the eighteenth century. Works like Handel's *Messiah* and Mendelssohn's *Elijah* became public institutions with huge audiences wherever they were performed. Handel had invented English oratorio with a skilful blend of English anthem and masque, French classical drama, Italian *opera seria* and *oratorio volgare*, and German Protestant oratorio. From them he created something that, even after his death in 1759, was venerated as a perfect expression of the English national spirit. At the commemoration to mark the twenty-fifth anniversary of Handel's death, held in Westminster Abbey in 1784 under the patronage of the King, public rehearsals were so full that an entrance fee of half a guinea was charged, and the concerts were so oversubscribed that repeat performances had to be arranged. Proceeds going to a musicians' charity founded by Handel were close to a staggering 8,000 guineas. 'I have long been watching the operations of good Music on the sensibility of mankind,' wrote Charles Burney after the performance of *Messiah*, 'but never remember, in any part of Europe, where I attended Musical exhibitions, in the church, Theatre, or Chamber, to have observed so much curiosity excited, attention bestowed, or satisfaction glow in the countenances of those present, as on this occasion.'[12] Foreigners attending were astonished at the reverential behaviour on show.[13] Enthusiasm for Handel's oratorio remained undimmed throughout the nineteenth century. In 1857 a choir of 2,000 and an orchestra of 500 performed *Messiah* to 48,000 people at Crystal Palace. In 1859, an audience in excess of 81,000 attended three concerts at the same venue to mark the centenary of Handel's death. The London Handel Festival became a triennial event which saw a chorus of 4,000 mostly amateur singers travel from every part of the country to perform to 87,000 people. Festivals such as the Three Choirs, Leeds and Birmingham matched enthusiasm in the capital, and well-attended choral societies were established in almost every local community.[14]

The popularity of oratorio coincided with an agonising, vitriolic Victorian crisis of religious faith over evolution. 'I would rather be descended from an ape than a bishop,' said Professor T.H. Huxley in an observation that caught the tone of the national debate.[15] Oratorio was successful precisely because it ignored doctrinal complexities in setting well-known Bible stories to music. No demands of faith were made on listeners, who instead could enjoy an evocation of piety that was not dependent on belief in God. Concert halls during performances seemed transformed into places of worship where the aesthetics of religion might be recreated by works using an ecclesiastical tradition in music but now stripped of meaning. 'An evening spent listening to an oratorio may be regarded as a sort of service, and is almost as good as going to church,' observed Richard Wagner after hearing the Sacred Harmonic Society in London.[16] When oratorio was actually performed in the architectural splendour of England's great cathedrals, such as during the Three Choirs Festival in Worcester, Hereford and Gloucester, the emotional resonance was complete (particularly if beforehand the Bishop insisted on saying the universally known Lord's Prayer).

Mendelssohn was the greatest composer of this pseudo-religious genre and second only to Handel in popularity in England. Their example was an inspiration to a generation of English composers and, latterly, William Walton. '*Belshazzar's Feast* has its roots in a long line of English oratorio and, in particular, the rich tradition of choral singing in the North of England,' says conductor Andrew Davis.[17] Walton's skill was in taking a musical form that seemed tired and reinvigorating it. *Belshazzar's Feast* has bold rhythms and instrumentation with the clear influence of jazz in choruses such as 'In Babylon, Belshazzar the King made a great feast'. The use of saxophone, castanets and gongs creates an unusual sound world for a work with a religious subject but within a context that reaffirms the oratorio tradition.

The Leeds Festival had shown a long-standing commitment to

new composition since its inception in 1858. Sir Arthur Sullivan, as Chief Conductor for more than twenty years, had commissioned works from Dvořák, Massenet, Humperdinck, Parry and Elgar. In 1910, the Festival included the first performance of Vaughan Williams's *A Sea Symphony*. The 1931 Festival is remembered just for *Belshazzar's Feast* but it was one of three new commissions performed that day alone. Such highbrow intentions made the Festival a critical if not financial success while causing much friction within the city. 'Musically speaking, Leeds is hopeless,' complained the Chairman of the Festival to the *Yorkshire Evening News*, adding that while 'people come from every part to hear the music in Leeds, the citizens of this city lamentably fail to give the Festival their support'.[18] Visitors from London did not help matters by writing to the local papers to ask why the people of Leeds insisted on lowering the tone of their Festival by wearing lounge suits rather than black tie.

Concerts took place amid the crushed strawberry pillars and stern dictums of Leeds Town Hall. 'Industry Overcomes All Things' emblazoned on the walls served as a fitting call to arms for the Leeds Festival Chorus as it tackled *Belshazzar's Feast*. Members of the choir, having received their vocal parts in March, still could not sing them five months later. The combination of complex intervals and unusual rhythms had proved too difficult to master. Initial excitement about performing the new work had dissipated into, first, hostility and then open rebellion. Influential members of the chorus, complaining that the work was unsingable, began to campaign for its removal. When Malcolm Sargent arrived for the first rehearsals at the end of August 1931, the performance of *Belshazzar's Feast* faced catastrophe.

Sargent's response was simple: he taught the choir to sing Walton's new work bar by bar. Rehearsals, by tradition open to the public, often gave those who could not afford concert tickets the opportunity to hear an informal run-through. 'Dr Sargent has an exceptionally keen ear and it is a real pleasure to work under him,' wrote a member of the chorus in the *Huddersfield Daily Examiner* on 31 August. 'His thoroughness was exemplified on Saturday afternoon when the frequent stoppages and repetition of various passages must have been trying to the public who had attended the rehearsal on a rather fine day. However, when the work was repeated in the evening after its difficulties had been surmounted it was a revelation to the audience. Rarely has one heard such an improvement in such a short space of time.'[19]

'Luckily Malcolm Sargent knew how to control a choir,' writes the composer's wife, Susana. 'William may or may not have liked his conducting but admitted he could deal with choral forces. They ate out of his hand.'[20] The first performance of *Belshazzar's Feast*, with Denis Noble as soloist, was a triumph for composer and conductor. A sense of expectation hung in the air as the audience gathered. Local and national newspapers had reported the threatened choir revolt so that many who attended that night expected 'something' to happen. The choir themselves, sceptical until Sargent's arrival, now seemed convinced that the new work would be the highlight of the festival. The daughter of one choir member remembers her father telling her that *Belshazzar* was 'a very strange piece. He had never sung anything like it before and wasn't sure what he felt about it but as rehearsals progressed, he got quite excited. "Whichever concerts you come to you must come to this one," he told my mum.'[21]

The most disappointed man on the night was poor Eric Fogg. He conducted the premiere of his own work, *The Seasons*, to overwhelming apathy. 'The present work does not amount to much,' reported the *Daily Mail* afterwards.[22] His misfortune was to have his limited talents exposed on the night that his contemporary premiered *Belshazzar's Feast*. The sheer energy of Walton's new work stunned the Leeds audience. Sargent conducted with precision and great energy to produce 'an electrifying result'. This was ' a great performance of a work which bears the indubitable stamp of greatness'. Even critics stood in awe: 'It was a cyclone; and the writer is at the moment of writing still panting a little after the roar and fury and savage whip strokes of this music.'

As the final Alleluias and sustained chords rang out, the audience sat 'dazed by the experience' before jumping to their feet in cheering and furious applause. Walton was brought on to the stage and embraced Sargent. 'The composer was happy in having Dr Malcolm Sargent to conduct his new work for no-one could have put more vitality in the performance or secured a more splendidly forceful interpretation,' reported the *Yorkshire Post*. 'It sounded like nothing on earth,' Walton said of that first performance. 'The audience was mesmerised into accepting it.'[23]

Sargent's mastery with *Belshazzar's Feast* confirmed him as the most exciting choral conductor in the land. Offers from choirs throughout the country flooded in, of which the most important was from Huddersfield. Founded in 1836, the Huddersfield Choral Society was the finest in Yorkshire. They sang at the Town Hall, which was an opulent yet compact monument to Victorian civic values with a magnificent acoustic. 'The Huddersfield Town Hall was for me the finest hall to sing in,' wrote soprano soloist Isobel Baillie.[24]

For thirty years Sir Henry Coward, a highly respected choral conductor in the English cathedral tradition, had trained the 500-strong Huddersfield choir to sing not just with passion but also clear diction and at pianissimo. Subscription tickets for concerts were passed down through generations, while thousands each season entered the ballot for non-subscriptions. 'This choir is second to none in England, second to none in the whole world,' proclaimed Coward at his farewell concert. 'You have a thousand pounds in the hands of your treasurer and a subscription list that is the envy of all other societies in the land and above all you have your singers.'[25]

Members of the Huddersfield Choral Society who sang *Belshazzar's Feast* with Sargent in Leeds in 1931 came back exhilarated by the experience. Sargent's supporters lobbied the sub-committee established to find a successor to Coward. In February 1932, Sargent was appointed to conduct three concerts a year for fifty guineas per concert. The programme for the first season, 1932–3, included *Belshazzar's Feast*.[26] When the Executive Committee confirmed Sargent's appointment on 20 February, it also named a new chorus master, Herbert Bardgett. A temperamental man who never felt his work was given due credit, his appointment would be critical to Sargent's success in Huddersfield. 'Bardgett was a great choirmaster,' concludes Stanley Vann, who before working at Peterborough was Chorus Master of the Leicester Philharmonic Choir under both Sargent and Sir Henry Wood. 'He was a towering figure, acknowledged as the absolute tops as a choir trainer.'[27]

The partnership, which lasted for more than thirty years, would produce some of the best English choral singing of the century. The first concert, on 4 November 1932, was a performance of Bach's *B Minor Mass*, at that time Sargent's favourite work.[28] After the elegance of Coward, subscribers were shocked at the speed and energy that Sargent generated. The *Huddersfield Daily Examiner* proclaimed that 'Dr Malcolm Sargent made a brilliant beginning with the Huddersfield Choral Society in the Bach *B Minor Mass* at the Town Hall last night' and observed that it was taken 'at a pace which few choirs other than the Huddersfield could sustain'.[29] Sargent had found the vehicle with which he could display his mastery of choral repertoire.

Sargent brought not just technical proficiency but inspiration to Huddersfield. 'Choir members would be sitting in the corridor waiting to go on stage and as Sargent walked past, they stood up,' recalls contralto soloist Marjorie Thomas. 'They knew that he was going to draw something out of them that no other conductor could get. They revered him because he made them sing for their lives.'[30] Fascinated by how he achieved such dazzling results, Thomas asked Sargent if she might stand with the choir for the first half of a *Gerontius* performance. 'You could see he inspired choirs and when I stood with the Huddersfield Choral Society, I could actually feel it,' she says. 'There was something magnetic about him.'[31] If singers were not up to the job, however, Sargent was merciless. Choirs were made to learn every note of a piece whatever the frustrations. Soloists were not so lucky. 'A new bass came to sing *Messiah* and made mistake after mistake in the rehearsal,' recollects Thomas. 'Sargent was so patient with him while we were all looking at the floor. When we came back after the break, the man had gone. I felt sorry for him but you did not sing for Sargent if you had not learnt your part properly.'[32]

Both Isobel Baillie[33] and Nancy Evans, who premiered soprano roles for Benjamin Britten, believed Sargent to be without equal.[34] Webster Booth thought him 'outstandingly our greatest conductor and accompanist.'[35] What made Sargent such a sympathetic choral conductor was a judicious blend of clarity and flexibility. He always paid attention to diction, insisting that words had to be clear. 'But his interpretations always had such elasticity,' says Marjorie Thomas.

'He was always prepared to give soloists a great deal of freedom in interpretation and one never felt rushed or dragged back. Performances with Beecham or Boult were very regulated; with Sargent everything was so fluid.'[36] Even Sir Thomas Beecham conceded of young Dr Sargent: 'He is the greatest choirmaster we have ever produced; he makes the buggers sing like the blazes!'[37]

5

Dr Sargent is a Lucky Young Man

Malcolm Sargent's growing reputation brought with it a steady stream of work and enough money in fees to enjoy a more comfortable lifestyle. By 1929, he was able to move his family to London, first into a small house again off Brompton Road and then into bigger premises at Wetherby Place, South Kensington. A brother, Peter, had joined Pamela in 1926. Living in Oakham had proved incompatible with Sargent's conducting schedule and meant him seeing his children for just a few days each month. With them in London, he was often able to spend two or three nights each week at home. Rare days off were spent with the children at London Zoo, already his favourite place to relax. 'Family life depended on whether or not he was there,' reminisces Peter Sargent. 'He was like a meteor that showered everything in sight with sparks and then disappeared as quickly as it arrived. There were tears if his temper blew but most of the time in those early days it was such fun. Pammy and I were just swept along.'[1]

Trips with the children were usually made alone. Sargent had married Eileen in haste in 1922, and rather than repent at leisure, now simply ignored her. 'The infidelities began very early and she knew she had lost him even then,' recollects Peter, aware as a young child that all was not well with his parents' marriage.[2] Aristocratic contacts from Melton and amongst the patrons of the Royal Choral Society had brought Sargent into the social circle of the elite, where he developed a lifelong taste for blue-blooded conquests. As his fame grew, so too did the appeal of well-placed young women, whose advances he found impossible to resist. Often the attraction was more social than sexual. He slept with a number of spectacularly unattractive titled women. Each success was a step away from his humble origins and a reaffirmation of his new-found status in metropolitan society. 'Papa found it impossible to resist the admiration of these women,' muses Peter. 'They found him irresistible and he found that irresistible in itself. He needed to be wanted by as many people as possible and if some nice girl offered herself, it seemed bad manners to refuse.'[3]

Sargent sparkled at parties in a brilliant if nervy way. Raffishly dressed and never dull, he was the toast of the London cocktail party circuit because he could be guaranteed to make an effort to amuse. Even those who felt that he tried too hard or who did not like him agreed that he was rarely less than engaging. Being so was, perhaps, a subtle way of touching his forelock to such well-connected company, but in public at least he appeared not to entertain a moment's self-doubt. Yet for all his apparent confidence, private insecurities lurked.

Malcolm Sargent was a 'working-class boy made good' who preferred to think of himself as perhaps distantly related to the Marquess of Exeter. Stamford provided an acceptable 'county' image to which only his parents and sister offered an unavoidable threat. So he dropped them. 'They made him look jumped up and he was embarrassed by them,' says Peter Sargent. 'They must have realised because we never went down to Stamford. I am ashamed to say that my grandfather lived until 1936 and my grandmother until 1942 but I hardly knew them.'[4] Marjorie Gesior, then in her teens, remembers that Agnes in particular seemed lost without her son. 'Mrs Sargent was a very quiet lady who always dressed in black as if in mourning,' she remarks. 'She never struck me as a particularly happy person. In fact when I look back on it they did not seem a very happy couple.'[5]

The Sargents remained proud of their son and his achievements. As Malcolm's fame spread, their own position in Stamford as 'Dr Sargent's parents' grew. They understood the rules of the game: the Sargents had wanted their son to escape whatever the price. Malcolm had more than fulfilled their expectations but his rejection of them was difficult to endure.

Sargent's parents remained great supporters, but his accomplishments on the Melton and London cocktail circuits had introduced him to more powerful patrons. Included in his new social circle were Elizabeth and Samuel Courtauld, among the most significant artistic benefactors England has known. Samuel Courtauld was an industrialist with a passion for art and millions to spend on it. He was a quiet and courteous man whose artistic aspirations were signalled by the black beret habitually worn since youthful Paris visits. His money came from mass production of rayon but was spent on French Impressionist and post-Impressionist paintings. This magnificent collection of modern art was bequeathed to the nation on his death in 1947.

Elizabeth Courtauld's love of music was enthusiastically and generously indulged by her husband. By the time Sargent met her, she was a 'handsome grey-haired woman [and…] something of a tyrant perhaps: but her keenness on music and the money she has expended on it have gone a long way towards earning her the right to be'.[6] Her first musical pet was the Royal Opera Company, which she rescued from the threat of extinction under Beecham. Between 1925 and 1927 she spent more than £50,000 on opera, but her involvement was not simply financial. She picked programmes, engaged artists, supervised publicity and generally acted on the principle that if Covent Garden wanted her money they would have her tastes as well. She took a musical lead from her friend, the conductor Bruno Walter. The combination of her money and his musicianship produced operas that were regarded as 'the most brilliant that have been held since the war'.[7]

Elizabeth Courtauld had ensured the future of Covent Garden but by 1927 she was tired of the constant political squabbling. Thereafter, she concentrated on a project in which, according to Cicely Stanhope, her secretary, she might 'do *exactly* what she wanted'.[8] Her inspiration came from another friend, the Austrian pianist Artur

Schnabel. Charismatic and with a passing resemblance to Stalin, Schnabel was one of the great Romantic pianists of the age. His controlled technique combined with flexibility of interpretation made him hugely popular and much sought after by concert promoters. But Schnabel was a great pianist who wanted to be remembered as a great man. Fascinated by history, literature and politics, he had advanced views about the social role of music. In late 1927, Schnabel gave a private recital at the Courtaulds' beautiful mansion in Portman Square, impressing the audience not just with his playing but also with an exalted sense of the artist's duty to society. He talked of the workers' concert society of the *Volksbühne* in Germany which block-booked seats at the opera and sold them by subscription. Participation was massive, with Munich having 28,000 members. Courtauld, inspired by what she heard, recognised immediately the potential for a comparable set-up in England. She enlisted Schnabel's support and set about organising her own Concert Club.

Elizabeth Courtauld's elevated aim was to explain modern music to the Common Listener within the context of the traditional canon. She believed that Modernism had revolutionised the arts but failed to galvanise what in literature Virginia Woolf called the Common Reader. 'He is guided by an instinct to create for himself, out of whatever odds and ends he can come by, some kind of whole – a portrait of man, a sketch of an age, a theory of the art of writing,' Woolf wrote in 1925.[9] The Common Listener had been left bewildered by the effects of Modernism in music. Serialism for all its intellectual merit failed to win the hearts of ordinary concertgoers. Compositions were often heckled in performance, with concerts poorly attended. 'I am bored by modern music, it is of no interest to me, much of it I hate and despise,' wrote even Hanns Eisler after studying with Schoenberg in Vienna. 'If possible I avoid hearing or reading it (and, alas, I must include my own efforts of recent years in this).'[10] When in 1926 Schoenberg moved to Berlin, the artistic heartbeat of post-war continental Europe, he was shocked to find his music regarded with little more than academic interest. Musical radicalism in Berlin was not represented by emaciated serialism but by the *gebrauchsmusik* ('use music') of composers such as Weill and Křenek, which was heavily influenced by jazz, music hall and the sounds of everyday life. This *neuezeitmusik* – music for our time – provided an antidote for those who disliked serialism, but its social realism left many yearning for the noble aspirations of eighteenth- and nineteenth-century composers and perplexed about how to approach new music.

Elizabeth Courtauld's first task in addressing this need was to appoint a Music Director who could communicate her vision. Initial thoughts centred on Adrian Boult, who was by now conductor of the City of Birmingham Orchestra. Schnabel persuaded her that Boult lacked flair. He told her about a children's concert earlier in the year at which he had played the Mozart G major piano concerto with Sargent on the podium. The audience, he reported, had 'sat in breathless silence' during the performance. Schnabel persuaded the Courtaulds that Sargent was their man and visited him to warn that the post might be offered.[11]

Courtauld, having gone to see Sargent conduct at the Royal College of Music, immediately gave him the job. He was young, had stage presence and could be expected to do 'what she told him'.[12] It helped that Sargent was so popular with orchestral players. Sidonie Goossens, first harp in the BBC Symphony Orchestra for more than fifty years but a freelance player in the 1920s, recalls that 'he was always extremely popular as a young man, brilliant and clever'.[13] Orchestras that had been used to genial amateurism warmed to his incisive professionalism. The viola player Bernard Shore described Sargent as 'the personification of efficiency [and], in every one of his activities, he is masterly'.[14] 'He was very clear and you could always hear what he said,' agrees Sidonie Goossens. 'You could see what he was beating – there was no swaying around – it was precise and always accurate.' A favourite 'party trick' was to demonstrate how complex rhythms fitted together by beating out with his two hands, tapping his foot and nodding his head in different times. His 'uncanny way of mastering a score' meant that 'not only is he continuously looking at players, but incessantly he clamours for an equal response'.[15] If players had a criticism, it was the familiar one that he invariably talked too much.

Among the three of them – Courtauld, Schnabel and Sargent – the first Concert Club season was pieced together. Before the scheme was launched, a last decision was made. Schnabel told Courtauld that 'the Concert Club' was for publicity purposes too dreary and bland. 'The Courtauld Concerts' was rejected, remembered Cicely Stanhope, lest 'it should be thought that her musical ideals were not serious and that she was only splashing her money about'. So it was agreed that the Music Director's name would also appear on all advertisements, and the Courtauld-Sargent Concerts were born.[16]

On 8 July 1929, Elizabeth Courtauld and Sargent held a meeting at her home in Portman Square for fifteen representatives of large firms including Debenhams, John Lewis and Peter Jones, and professional organisations such as the Civil Service Arts Council and the London Teachers' Association. Sargent and Mrs Courtauld set out their aims, which later were published at the front of programmes: 'We believe in the high value of good music and our object is to serve it by helping the standard of musical taste in this country. There are people, in every class, who love music disinterestedly and for its own sake, and these are the people whose taste is the best. We want to build up regular audiences from them, and to create a tradition which will spread from them, and will demand to be satisfied with *nothing but the best*. This is the surest way of raising a high standard, for it starts with the foundation. It is the only way to ensure the growth of a worthy school of English music − both of composers and executants.'[17]

Each season, they proposed to host six concerts in the Queen's Hall, with ninety per cent of tickets sold by subscription. Their goal was to bring performances of the highest quality at subsidised prices to those who otherwise could not afford London concert tickets. 'There must be people with tastes similar to mine,' Elizabeth Courtauld said, 'and I don't want a concert all to myself. If people are got together who want to hear what I want to hear, we can all enjoy ourselves, and the artists will not be paralysed by the stupidity of a fashionable audience.'[18] Those attending on 8 July combined to take 900 serial tickets immediately; within two months, the number had increased to 1,700 and at the opening concert 1,923 of the 2,260 capacity of the Queen's Hall, the rest being taken by the public. In total, there were 132 Concert Club performances between 1929 and 1940. The subsidy was impressively weighty: Samuel Courtauld realised a loss of over £15,000.[19]

Courtauld's model reflected that of London in the eighteenth century when the range of performances and entrepreneurial patronage had made it an unrivalled musical capital.[20] London, the fastest-growing metropolis in Europe, had then enjoyed a reputation as its most modern city. Visitors were amazed by the marriage of commercial and political energy. After standing in the public gallery of the House of Commons to witness liberty in action, they attended concerts of music by Thomas Arne at the Vauxhall Pleasure Gardens to watch in amazement as aristocrats mingled with 'ordinary' people. From the 1760s onwards, fashionable society thrilled to the newness of progressive and difficult music performed by the best players in Europe. Patrons such as Theresa Cornelys and new concert rooms in Hanover Square and Oxford Street competed in the daring of their programming. Meanwhile, the Concert of Antient Music [sic] was instrumental in establishing a new-found respect for tradition at a time when work by composers other than the living was usually ignored. England 'is the land of opportunity', wrote Joseph Haydn, who in two visits during the 1790s composed twelve symphonies, appeared at more than fifty concerts and cleared 1,000 guineas.[21]

The prospectus prepared by Elizabeth Courtauld and Sargent for the first season of the Concert Club was a worthy successor to its eighteenth-century forebears in its advocacy of modernity and tradition. Internationally renowned soloists performed programmes combining contemporary works with those from the canon. Bruno Walter and Otto Klemperer, Mahler's protégés, conducted two of these opening concerts, with the Club's Music Director taking the remaining four in the series.

The press greeted Sargent's role in the Concert Club with astonishment. 'Dr Sargent is a lucky young man,' observed the *Daily News*, adding, 'It is not everybody who can get a club founded in his honour on lines so sound that crowded houses – if not financial success – is assured beforehand.'[22] The critic of the *New Statesman*, W. J. Turner, launched an astonishing attack on Elizabeth Courtauld for appointing such a youthful director. 'I have nothing against Dr Sargent; he deserves his chance among other young English musicians [but...] a series of concerts backed by Mrs Courtauld is quite sufficient to give Dr Malcolm Sargent a wholly fictitious reputation which will be an obstacle to his own progress and to the progress of music in general,' he wrote. 'Dr Sargent is young, and what Dr Sargent and all other young musicians and amateurs of music need to learn is of the heights in front of them instead of being assisted to crow more loudly on their miniature dung heaps.'[23]

Sargent had learnt at D'Oyly Carte Opera that critics could be excoriating. Criticism is an art not a science; many of its exponents, who are rarely practising musicians, might often prefer a place on the stage to their seat in the stalls. Sargent's difficult position with the critics in 1929 stemmed not just from his relative youth but also from his position as Courtauld's protégé. Sargent on his rise to fame had capitalised on his popularity with the opposite sex. He was a notorious womaniser who from his earliest days also had the knack of flirting with older or well-connected women. He amused and flattered them. They in return promoted him. Other men did not always appreciate that facility. The Concert Club was an important break for Malcolm Sargent but one in which he had to excel to avoid the accusation by critics that he was Mrs Courtauld's lapdog.

The *New Statesman*'s critic was forced to recant by the end of the first season: Sargent had, in fact, 'set a magnificent example to young English musicians'. The reason for Turner's change of heart was the unprecedented quality of preparation that the conductor demanded. The London Symphony Orchestra had been engaged for all six concerts under strict conditions. Each concert had three or four three-hour rehearsals rather than the usual run-through on the day itself. Every player had to attend all rehearsals and the actual performance; this counteracted the outrageous 'deputy' system whereby a player would attend rehearsals, collect a fee and then pay a colleague (less) to play in the concert. When visiting conductors arrived for their first rehearsal, Sargent would have prepared the orchestra. These radical working conditions were central to the pledge to give performances of a quality never before heard in London.

The opening Courtauld–Sargent concert took place on Tuesday 22 October 1929 at the Queen's Hall. For many in the audience it would have been their first experience of this great concert hall beside Nash's elegant church of All Souls, Langham Place. Six double columns framed the entrances above which balconies played host to busts of the great composers. Crossing the road and entering this impressively grand building, those first-time concertgoers descended steps to the underground auditorium. If they were heading for the stalls, down and down they would go until emerging into the arena. And there presented to them was the blue-green, slightly down-at-heel yet still magnificent auditorium of the Queen's Hall, its sensational acoustic alive to a buzz of excited conversation.[24]

The opening Courtauld-Sargent night made little concession to its inexperienced audience. Sargent conducted Beethoven's G major and Brahms's D minor piano concertos with Schnabel as soloist, and Mozart's Symphony No. 40. The impact on the audience was overwhelming. 'You could feel the concentration upon the music,' said the *Saturday Review*, 'and you could gauge its effect from the manner of the applause.'[25] It was, said the *Daily Telegraph*, 'a new chapter in the history of music-making' in England.[26] The six concerts of the first season were suitably diverse. Otto Klemperer conducted the first performance in England of Bruckner's massive Eighth Symphony and Bruno Walter gave only the second English performance of Mahler's *Das Lied von der Erde*. Sargent premiered *Serenade* by Arthur Bliss and conducted the first English performance of Karol Szymanowski's violin concerto with Jelly d'Aranyi. The series ended with the famous operatic soprano Frieda Leider singing extracts from Beethoven's *Fidelio* with Sargent on the rostrum.

The second (1930–1) and third (1931–2) seasons were, if anything, more radical. Mrs Courtauld and Sargent had set out with the expectation that 'those who bought cheaply in order to enjoy Beethoven and Mozart had to accept, and probably learn to enjoy, Stravinsky, Hindemith, Walton and other contemporary composers when their turn came up'.[27] This expectation was more than met: such was the demand for subscriptions in 1930 that each concert had to be repeated to accommodate even a fraction of those who wanted to attend. Performances of Beethoven, Brahms and Mozart were coupled with new works. Sargent conducted the premiere of Delius's complex *Songs of Farewell* for eight-part chorus and the first performances in England of Paul Hindemith's Viola Concerto No.2 and Stravinsky's *Capriccio for Piano and Orchestra*, both with the composers as soloists. On 16 and 17 November 1931, an English audience heard for the first time Stravinsky's *Symphony of Psalms*, conducted by the composer himself, and his Violin Concerto conducted by Sargent with Samuel Dushkin as soloist.

These heady times for London audiences left critics in disarray. While some thought Mahler's *Das Lied von der Erde* 'a great joy' and 'a lovely and inexpressibly moving work', others pilloried its 'false sentiment, sham romanticism and pomposity' and hoped young composers would turn away from 'all this hollow claptrap'.[28] Many critics thought the conductor Otto Klemperer 'not very spontaneous', and 'has not the gift for orchestral conducting'; others thought that 'if we are to have a first-rate orchestra in London, then let the BBC engage Mr Klemperer for three years'.[29] Critics, who could reach no consensus, were galled that the success of the concerts was in no way influenced by their views: subscriptions were sold out throughout the 1930s. These 'people's concerts' were validated by subscribers not critics.

The success of the concerts and Elizabeth Courtauld's apparent imperviousness to any financial deficit made her a threat to London's musical establishment. In the autumn of 1931 a manifesto, signed among others by Sir Hugh Allen, was published in the *Musical Times* denouncing overseas musicians, and Mrs Courtauld for promoting them. They castigated her for apparently believing 'that only a foreigner can possess the true qualities of a musician; that a foreign composer must of necessity be superior to our own musicians'. The signatories demanded to know why 'foreign artists of no repute and of mediocre attainments should be employed in this country when there are so many of our own musicians who lack employment'.[30] Arnold Bax, a composer whose *Nonet for String Quartet* had been given its premiere at a Courtauld-Sargent concert two weeks earlier, ungraciously added fuel to the fire: 'I've got no patience with the snobbery that runs after a foreign name and won't appreciate English musicians because they are English.'[31]

Elizabeth Courtauld was deeply upset by the attack but responded in a measured, factual way. She wrote to the *Daily Telegraph* to point out that in the first seasons of Courtauld-Sargent Concerts, eleven 'foreign' contemporary works had matched the number written by home-grown composers. Her concerts not only sponsored English composers, she argued, but also gave employment to native musicians. The amount paid to English singers, orchestral players and conductors was double that paid to overseas musicians. Money given to foreign performers was less than fourteen per cent of the total expenditure. English talent of the highest quality, like Malcolm Sargent, had been encouraged and integrated with the world's finest. The logic of the 'manifesto' was absurd: should English pianists only play English compositions on English pianos? 'Music is not a trade or a charity,' she concluded. 'It is the purest form of art and it is supranational.'[32]

The tragedy for Elizabeth Courtauld and those who admired her was that the attack on her philanthropy came as she was dying. Her health had been poor for many years and several times she had seemed close to death. On 1 December 1931, she went to the Queen's Hall for the last time to hear her great friend Artur Schnabel play Beethoven's *Choral Fantasy* with Sargent conducting. She died on Christmas Day. Obituaries, many written by those who had condemned her, were now unanimous in praising her contributions to the arts. The composer and conductor Constant Lambert put it best: 'The untimely death of Mrs Samuel Courtauld robbed the musical world of one its great patrons.'[33]

Samuel Courtauld resolved immediately to memorialise his wife. The mansion in Portman Square was dedicated to her as a centre for the study of modern art – the Courtauld Institute – and quickly became one of the most famous art schools in the world. Yet music not art had been her passion, and Samuel Courtauld continued to support the project in which she had invested so much of herself. Sargent, after visiting Courtauld at the smaller Mayfair house into which he had moved, was invited to continue the concerts. Cicely Stanhope would administer the Concert Club but the artistic direction of the concerts would be in Sargent's hands. Only one provision was made: concerts should on no account last longer than two hours (including time for a gin and tonic at the interval). Sargent suggested changing the name of the series to 'The Elizabeth Courtauld Memorial Concerts', but Samuel Courtauld declined: the concerts would continue exactly as his wife had left them. Running until 1940, they offered English audiences varied repertoire of the highest quality. Sargent conducted first performances of works by Bax, Delius, Jean Françaix, Eugene Goossens, Hindemith, Honegger, Kodály, Martinu, Prokofiev, Stravinsky and Vaughan Williams. He invited artists such as Vladimir Horowitz, Nathan Milstein and Georg Szell to make their first appearances in England.

The world's finest conductors – Fritz Busch, Erich Kleiber, Klemperer, Walter – and soloists – Edwin Fischer, Rachmaninov, Carl Flesch, Joseph Szigeti, Pablo Casals, Gregor Piatigorsky and Suggia – continued to perform at the concerts.[34]

Sargent's success was not simply the result of exciting programmes and soloists. A revolution was under way in English orchestras in the early 1930s initiated by the Courtauld-Sargent Concerts. The LSO had been the resident orchestra for the first three concert seasons. Although having promised not to use the 'deputy' system, however, it continued to change personnel during rehearsal periods. The orchestra had been formed in 1904 as a self-governing organisation and had a reputation for being independent-minded. Despite at least three rehearsals for each concert, playing did not meet the demanded standard. Unable to find an established orchestra to meet their expectations, Sargent and Elizabeth Courtauld resolved in 1931 to form their own.

English orchestral playing did not come close to reaching the quality of the best in America and Germany. The inspiration was Toscanini's European tour with the New York Philharmonic Orchestra in 1930. They 'crossed Paris like a meteor' and, in Berlin, the conductor Georg Szell declared himself in 'Toscanini shock'.[35] Sargent had been in the Queen's Hall in June to hear the orchestra play Elgar's *Enigma Variations*. 'The performance left me in such a ferment that I walked by the Thames until three in the morning, absent-mindedly cutting a party at the Courtaulds,' he said afterwards.[36] This performance of Elgar demonstrated in the cruellest possible way the deficiencies of English playing.

The problem was not a lack of good musicians but a stable environment in which they could work. Orchestral musicians were paid for each rehearsal and concert but received nothing when a season ended. The formation of the salaried BBC Symphony Orchestra in 1930 had been a step in the right direction, but the uninspiring platform personality of their Chief Conductor, Adrian Boult, ensured that they failed to capture the public imagination. It was the Courtauld-Sargent Concerts, observed the *Daily Express*, which had accomplished 'what the BBC with its strong educational inclinations might have done', and while these concerts were sold out, 'the BBC Symphony Orchestra plays to row upon row of empty seats'.[37]

The Courtaulds were determined that their own orchestra, drawn from the cream of English orchestral players, would become, in effect, London's 'super orchestra'. They gave Sargent access to a £30,000 start-up fund to hand-pick players for a permanent orchestra and promised to meet any losses the orchestra might sustain each season. A committee of wealthy patrons was formed that included copper millionaire Robert Mayer, who wanted the orchestra for his children's concerts, city banker Frédéric d'Erlanger and Lord Esher. Sargent enlisted further support from Lady Cunard at Covent Garden, the impresario Harold Holt and Louis Sterling at HMV.[38] He believed the Courtauld orchestra might be the final piece in the jigsaw that would re-establish London as a great music capital. The orchestra would be resident at Covent Garden, for the Concert Club, the Royal Philharmonic Society and the Royal Choral Society as well as recording exclusively with HMV. Once such an ensemble was founded, this portfolio of commitments would ensure playing of the highest calibre in all areas of London's musical life. By the summer of 1932, Sargent had put these arrangements in place.

The commitment to Covent Garden belatedly involved Sir Thomas Beecham in the new orchestra. Beecham, despite earlier financial scandal, remained part-owner of the Royal Opera House, and was artistic adviser to the Covent Garden Board, which was dominated by his lover, Emerald Cunard. She insisted that Beecham be invited to join Sargent as conductor.[39]

Sargent maintained an odd relationship with Beecham for almost thirty years. They shared the same birthday, 29 April, separated by sixteen years. Beecham could be scathing of Sargent, such as the time in 1938 when Sargent's car was fired on in Jerusalem: 'I had no idea the Arabs were so musical.'[40] Sargent took these slights in good humour but never really warmed to the rebarbative baronet. By 1932, Beecham, in danger of being marginalised in London's concert life, jumped at the opportunity to conduct the new orchestra. Boards of management in the 1920s found that Beecham's financial and personal unreliability made him a difficult partner. The Royal Philharmonic Society remembered the harsh conditions he had exacted in return for money during the war and kept him at arm's length. The BBC had considered him in 1929 for their new symphony orchestra before deciding he was more trouble than he was worth.

When Sargent approached him, Beecham was fighting a losing battle to take over the London Symphony Orchestra. Sargent deferentially took the title of Auxiliary Music Director, but still took auditions for the new orchestra. He assembled 106 players, blending youthful talent with proven experience. The new organisation, named the London Philharmonic Orchestra, comprised the finest collection of orchestral players in England. The first season was divided equally between the two conductors, with both taking the orchestra into the recording studios for HMV.

Sargent's professionalism ensured that the orchestra was on top form at its public debut. Thirteen rehearsals were called in the early autumn of 1932, with Sargent taking the majority. Sargent conducted the first recordings made by the LPO on 19–21 September at Kingsway Hall. Beecham conducted the opening concert on 7 October 1932. It was immediately apparent that the quality of playing was superior to anything heard before from an English orchestra. At the end of the overture, Berlioz's *Roman Carnival*, the audience rose in ovation, some even standing on their chairs to cheer. Yet the Queen's Hall was only half full, which caused Beecham to rage that London was 'a bloody disgrace'. Three days later, the same hall was sold out for Sargent's first performance with the London Philharmonic Orchestra that opened the 1932–3 Concert Club season.[41]

6

It's a Wonderful Life

The evening of Monday 10 October 1932 was a triumph for Malcolm Sargent. At eight o'clock, he glided on to the stage of the Queen's Hall to open this fourth season of Courtauld-Sargent Concerts. He had chosen a programme of Elgar's *Introduction and Allegro*, Debussy's *La Mer* and Richard Strauss's *Till Eulenspiegel* to show off the London Philharmonic Orchestra's virtuosic qualities.

After the final bars, Concert Club members jumped to their feet and cheered in wild appreciation. Time and time again Sargent was brought back on stage to acknowledge the tumultuous applause. Standing amid the enthusiastic din, Sargent might have reflected on this confirmation of his reputation as the outstanding conductor of his generation. On that night in the Queen's Hall he had every reason to feel very pleased. Or at least he might have done if his temperature had not been running at over 100°F.

Sargent by the autumn of 1932 was a very ill man. For more than six months he had been experiencing increasing abdominal pain. His temperature frequently soared and he was often found doubled over in agony. His appetite was almost non-existent and he had lost over a stone during the summer. The pain was beginning to have an impact on his work, despite his determination to resist. Friends often had physically to restrain him from carrying on. One night during the 1932 *Hiawatha* run with the Royal Choral Society, the organist Arnold Greir insisted during the interval that Sargent must not continue. When he had seen the conductor waiting in the wings before the performance he had been appalled at his physical state. Pulling himself up the rails to get into the arena, Sargent was then transformed once on show; 'Sargent wouldn't have staggered even if dying,' Greir said.[1]

Back in the dressing room, he collapsed. Greir pulled Sargent's pupil, Muir Mathieson, from the audience and sent him on to conduct the second half. Sargent went home, protesting that he should at least stay in the hall, but twenty-four hours later was back for another performance. The pain came and went, blood tests were frustratingly inconclusive, and all the time Sargent continued a punishing schedule. His diary for 1932 had most weeks marked with engagements every day. Concerts in northern England were preceded by overnight rail journeys in rattling sleeper cars, followed by rehearsals at ten o'clock the next morning. The stress was compounded by his commitment to conducting difficult new scores, which often arrived only days before a first rehearsal. The physical and mental strain exacted a heavy price.

Sargent's commitment to pleasure matched his enthusiasm for work. 'My father worked hard and played hard,' his son Peter remembers, 'and he unwound not by resting but by going out to parties and living it up.'[2] After a concert he would vigorously towel himself down – often catching by surprise unsuspecting post-concert visitors who found him naked in his dressing room – and change, perhaps for supper at the Savoy Grill. He would join friends and plunge into a round of parties, always welcomed by grateful hostesses for his ability to amuse. 'He was a real entertainer and wanted to please you,' says Peter Sargent. 'If you live with your foot down hard on the accelerator you tend to attract people, and he always did.'[3] Sargent would talk incessantly, with opinions on almost every subject. At some point in the evening he could be relied upon to take a turn at the piano and persuade his hostess 'reluctantly' to sing for her guests. So he spent night after night talking, playing and drinking copious amounts of champagne. 'Why go to all these parties?' asked his friend, the composer Herbert Howells. 'Because I like them,'

Sargent replied simply.[4] He might have added that each successful outing served to confirm his place in fashionable society and saved him from a night in with the wife.

By New Year 1933, it was apparent that Sargent was close to collapse. His weight was continuing to drop at an alarming rate and the abdominal pain was intense. Three performances of *Belshazzar's Feast* for the Courtauld-Sargent Concerts on 16, 17 and 19 January seemed to push him over the edge. He struggled through the next few weeks and then cancelled all engagements. His doctors confined him to bed at home in Wetherby Place while they tried to pinpoint what was wrong. Blood tests of increasing complexity all came back negative, and while they dithered, Sargent's condition worsened. By early April he had developed a fever and was in and out of consciousness. In desperation and fearing for Sargent's life, his doctor sent him to a clinic at Prince's Gate opposite Hyde Park. Sir Thomas Horder, the King's physician, recognised the symptoms immediately. Malcolm Sargent had tuberculosis. The chances of survival were slim. His family were told to prepare for the worst.

Tuberculosis had reached epidemic proportions during the nineteenth century and afflicted many leading figures in politics and the arts including Cecil Rhodes, John Keats and Robert Louis Stevenson. Great musicians such as Chopin and Paganini had been struck down and Verdi even wrote an opera, *La Traviata*, about the disease. Known popularly as 'consumption', it was often associated in public imagination with tortured genius. In reality, it was no respecter of class, race or talent. By the 1930s, it remained a significant and little-understood killer. The most common way of catching the disease was by inhaling tubercular bacilli coughed into the atmosphere by a careless sufferer, or ingesting it through, for example, unpasteurised milk. Often the immune system would fight off the infection, but in those physically run-down, it could gestate.

Diagnosing tuberculosis was extremely difficult. Patients might appear healthy, off-colour or near death. Symptoms might be light or severe, local or constitutional. Tuberculosis had no clear onset or any distinctive physical evidence. High temperatures, cold sweats and loss of weight gave clues but were inconclusive. In short, a doctor's ability to diagnose tuberculosis was often as much to do with luck as judgement. When the lymph nodes or genito-urinary system were involved, diagnosis was even more elusive. It was Sargent's good fortune to have at his disposal the finest medical attention in England.[5]

Horder operated on Sargent immediately and removed a testicle. The operation on his genito-urinary tract was long and difficult, with only a thirty per cent chance of success. For several days his condition was critical and dependent on his will to live. For nearly thirty-eight years, Malcolm Sargent had been forced to fight for everything he had achieved; the gutter-instinct, which had allowed him to exploit his musical talent, was now called into duty to save his life. For several days the clinic released gloomy press releases that Sargent was 'as well as could be expected'. His body was weak and close to shut-down but somehow he found the strength to pull away from the threshold.

When his life was out of danger the realisation came that he might never be strong enough to conduct again. Sargent tried to be stoical. 'I don't know whether I'm going to conduct any more, but I have no complaints: it has been a wonderful life,' he told his childhood friend, Thomas Armstrong. [6] But what else would he do? His entire life had been dedicated to music. Just weeks previously he had stood on the podium at the Queen's Hall in control of massive choral and orchestral forces conducting *Belshazzar's Feast*. Now unable to get out of bed, his career apparently over, Malcolm Sargent faced a dark, uncertain future.

When Sargent was well enough to be moved, he was taken to a sanatorium in Hampshire to begin several months of slow, painful recuperation. During the summer months, nurses wheeled him out into the walled garden where he stripped to the waist and tried to get some colour back to his skin. Friends would visit, often bringing instruments for impromptu concerts. Neither did fashionable society forget him. Sir Hugh Allen 'went to see The Boy' and complained that 'the room was full of duchesses. I couldn't stand it and came away.'[7] When spring arrived, Sargent was sent to a spa at Montana in Switzerland. Members of the Royal Choral Society turned up at Victoria Station to wish him luck and sing him off.

Sargent was expected to regain his physical and mental equilibrium in this beautiful Valais setting with its spectacular mountain views, sunshine and clean air.[8] The German-Swiss physician Alexander

Spengler had advocated the Alpine cure in the 1850s. He was amazed
to find during a visit to Davos that not only were its inhabitants free
from tuberculosis but victims who came to the village often found
that their symptoms 'miraculously' disappeared. From the 1860s
onwards, consumptive English visitors began to appear in Swiss
mountain villages.[9] Yet for Sargent this lonely foreign cure and the
inactivity that went with it were almost as painful as the illness.
Separated from family and friends, he would lie in bed for endless
days, perhaps reading a little or listening to gramophone records,
getting bored. Only reliving past triumphs while planning a return
kept him sane.[10]

Early relief at survival now turned to frustration when long-term
engagements had to be cancelled. The Australian Broadcasting
Corporation had asked him to visit Melbourne for several months in
1934 to establish an orchestra. His passage was already booked and he
tried to persuade doctors that a sea voyage would aid his recovery.
When told that he was not well enough to go, Sargent threw a
tantrum. Those who visited only had to look at him to realise that it
would be a long time before he was back on the podium. His
complexion was pallid and his cheeks hollow. He had lost almost two
stone during the course of his illness and for a long time lacked even
the strength to leave his bed.

Whatever torments he was enduring about the demise of his
conducting career, Sargent's immediate concern was financial.
Despite his tremendous success, both professional and social, he was
not wealthy or even financially comfortable. He had no private
income but a tendency to live beyond his means. A house in
Wetherby Place that was bigger than he could afford, expensive gifts
and lavish parties had left his bank balance in a parlous condition.
'I've always been extravagant,' he said, 'always gave money away,
threw it away.' Illness made the full implications of that cavalier
attitude frighteningly clear. His income· had stopped without
warning. He was a freelance conductor: if he did not work, he was
not paid. This put a tremendous strain on his family. He had a wife
and young children to support and faced hefty bills for a convalescence that might take years.

The first problem was the house. Artur Schnabel, who had done
so much to promote Sargent's career, offered assistance. He was

looking for a property to let in London and took over the lease until the conductor was able to return.[11] This solved a financial dilemma but left Sargent's wife and children homeless. Eileen, who thought she had left service behind when she married, was forced to accept a friend's offer of a housekeeping post at a girls' school in Bexhill, and took Pamela, aged nine, with her. Six-year-old Peter was sent to a boarding school in Hertfordshire run by friends of the family who waived his fees. He was the youngest boy in the school.[12] 'I was away and used to read about Papa in the newspapers,' he recalls. 'Everyone at school was aware of it and spoilt me rotten.'[13]

Illness might have been expected to bring the Sargents closer together. In reality, it only served to emphasise their emotional dislocation. Sargent probably never loved Eileen but had been able to obscure the fact behind the pressure of work. He only spent a few nights each week at home, which allowed him to conduct his love affairs without too many awkward questions. When illness struck, there was nowhere to hide. Eileen attended Sargent every day while he was in danger. Thereafter, visits provoked only irritation and embarrassment, particularly if she arrived to find a girlfriend already at his bedside. When Sargent went to Switzerland, he did so alone. On his return, days were spent not at home but at London Zoo. Peter Sargent remembers his father spending 'hours in the cages with the wolves or lions and then lunching in the Fellows' dining room. He was very low and the zoo saved him.'[14]

While Sargent talked to the animals, he remained unsure whether he would work again. Tuberculosis is an illness that saps the strength of even the strongest; many sufferers never recover their vitality. Conducting, with its late nights, constant travelling and concert adrenalin, is an occupation that demands huge reserves of energy and stamina. Sargent might have anticipated a return to teaching at the Royal College, but fame and fortune now seemed an impossible dream. With his own hopes apparently dashed, Sargent increasingly came to project them on to his son, Peter.

'I am lucky because my son has perfect pitch,' Sargent told Ralph Vaughan Williams when he came to visit. 'Not bad given that he was cursed at birth.' When Peter Sargent was born in 1926, his mother's gynaecologist, whose own wife had just given him a daughter, slapped the baby's bottom and said, 'Damn, it's a boy.'

Cursed or not, for much of his childhood Peter found being the son of Malcolm Sargent at least something of a mixed blessing. 'He set a terrific standard for his only son,' recalls Peter. Expectation often weighed too heavily on the boy's shoulders and filial nerves manifested themselves in curious ways. Among Peter's earliest memories is being 'shown off' to friends at a drinks party. 'Peter, I want you to take this glass to that man over there. He is a duke and you must call him "your grace" when you give him the glass,' Sargent instructed. Peter took the drink, precariously balanced on a silver tray, and tripped in the middle of the room. The glass flew through the air and shattered into pieces on the wooden floor to general amusement. 'Why did you do it, Peter? There was nothing to trip on,' Sargent later asked his son. 'Yes there was, Papa,' Peter replied. 'I fell over you.'[15]

That Sargent wanted the best both for and from his son was clear, but on occasion this ambition caused lasting damage. Peter had a good voice and in 1934 was sent for voice trials at St George's Chapel, Windsor – a royal choir and one of England's most prestigious. Sargent coached Peter for the auditions himself. Eileen took the boy down to Windsor, where Sir William Harris put him through a series of tests. More than 300 applied to join the choir and Peter was ranked second (the same position that his father had achieved at the Royal College of Organists in 1912). When they got back to the family's London house, Peter rushed straight to his father's study. Sargent was standing at the fireplace with his back to the door and continued to poke at the embers of the fire. Peter could barely contain his delight. 'Papa, I did it. I got in,' he exclaimed. 'Yes, Peter boy, you got in but you were second,' replied Sargent gravely. 'Who was first?'[16]

Sargent enjoyed a reputation as a social butterfly yet his attitude to Peter reveals the narcissism and steeliness that had propelled him from the Stamford gasworks to national renown. The day after the voice trials at St George's, Peter overheard his father reprimanding his mother for ordering a train set to reward the success. 'The boy should have books. Learning is what life is about, not electric train sets,' he told her.[17] There was little doubt that he was proud of Peter's achievement, no more so than when the choir sang at the funeral of George V and the Coronation of George VI. Sargent would often take visiting musicians, including Toscanini, to hear his son sing

Evensong in St George's Chapel ('Cor! It's Toscanini!' blurted out Peter when his father introduced him).

Whatever pleasure Sargent felt at his son's accomplishments, 'well done' remained difficult words to say. Had he been the dilettante that his party-going image conveyed, Sargent could not have risen as he did nor survived the recent threat to his life and career. Now he expected the same hard-nosed ambition from his son. 'He used to tell me when I was at Windsor that you must work all the hours of the day,' says Peter. 'It was part of his nature that you had to be supreme, but to a small boy who just wanted to go fishing it was a little difficult to understand.'[18]

Peter's choral scholarship was important to the family because the bursary paid for his education at a time when Sargent was still reliant on hand-outs from friends. Samuel Courtauld continued to pay Sargent's Concert Club fees and wrote personal cheques that totalled close to £1,000. Robert Mayer made regular payments to settle debts at the Swiss spa which were supplemented by those from wealthy friends in Leicestershire. Personal kindness was mirrored by institutional support from organisations with which Sargent had worked. Huddersfield Choral Society insisted that he take fees for missed concerts and re-elected him as conductor.[19] Local choral societies up and down the country had 'whip-rounds' and posted cheques. The Leeds Triennial Festival appointed him conductor for the 1934 Festival despite the likelihood that he would not be well enough to attend.[20] Orchestral players sent hats round during rehearsals to collect money and made generous donations. The London Philharmonic, 'his' orchestra, made regular and substantial payments over a period of eighteen months.

A focal point of this generosity was the Sargent Fund, established by the Royal Choral Society. Sir Hugh Allen recruited a committee that included Robert Mayer, Lady de la Warr, Lady Snowden and Robin d'Erlanger, who between them combined access to society, newspapers and the City. 'Assistance will have to be forthcoming for some considerable time,' they had concluded in October 1933, and the appeal 'might be needed for a year or two'.[21] They launched the fund with a performance of *Messiah* at the Royal Albert Hall on 6 December. Sir Thomas Beecham conducted and generously donated his fee. The London Philharmonic Orchestra accompanied the

Royal Choral Society and most players waived payment. The soloists followed suit and the Royal Albert Hall charged no hire fee. Even HM Inspector of Taxes seemed moved by 'the distressed circumstances in which Dr Sargent found himself' and gave 'the informal nod' that no entertainment tax would be charged on the concert.[22] The sell-out performance made a profit of £1,168. To this was added a similar figure in personal donations by the likes of Ivor Novello, John Barbirolli, Ethel Smyth and Ralph Vaughan Williams, along with thousands of music-lovers who felt 'the concerts this year are not quite the same'.[23] The extent of Sargent's need was even greater than the committee had at first believed: more than two-thirds of the money was used to pay off arrears in income tax. Sargent's finances had often been close to collapse. Illness had proved his popularity but left him entirely dependent on charity.

Doctors gave Sargent permission to return to work in September 1934 after an absence from the podium of twenty months. His first engagement was Liszt's *Christus* at the Leeds Triennial Festival. Making the long train journey from London to Leeds, Sargent probably wondered if he would have the strength to conduct the huge festival chorus. Friends had helped him prepare by playing to his beat on the piano. Doctors had provided exercises to restore his upper-body strength. Only time would tell what long-term damage tuberculosis had done to his system. No one could doubt that he looked well. Newspapers reported him to be 'in the pink – or rather in the brown – of good health'.[24] He was tanned after another summer in Switzerland and his weight was back at an acceptable level. When he jumped on to the podium at the Leeds Town Hall, the chorus greeted him with a thunderous cheer. He conducted that first rehearsal with great vigour, almost trying too hard and causing concern 'lest his remarkable energy should overtax his strength'.[25] On 2 November, he returned to the Huddersfield Choral Society and received another ovation from both choir and audience. The following week at the Queen's Hall, an enthusiastic Courtauld-Sargent audience stood to welcome back their founder. At the Royal College of Music, his first rehearsal with the Royal Choral Society brought wild clapping and cheering. Organisations that had helped Sargent so generously during his illness now eased him back into work.

Standing on the podium of the Royal Albert Hall in January 1935

Above. Bambino: Mal, aged four, with his parents, Harry and Agnes Sargent, and sister Dorothy.

Right. Stamford choirboy: at St John Baptist with his father, 1905.

Below. Private Sargent (middle row, second from right): Durham Light Infantry, 1918.

Above. 'Hair that stood up like a brush.' Sargent (back row, second right) as organist at a Melton wedding, 1921. On the back row, Mrs Blakeney (second left), Canon Blakeney (centre, in silk hat).

Below. The father of English conducting: Sir Henry Wood.

Above. Malcolm in the middle: Leicester Symphony Orchestra, 1925.

Below. Rising star: Royal Albert Hall, late 1920s.

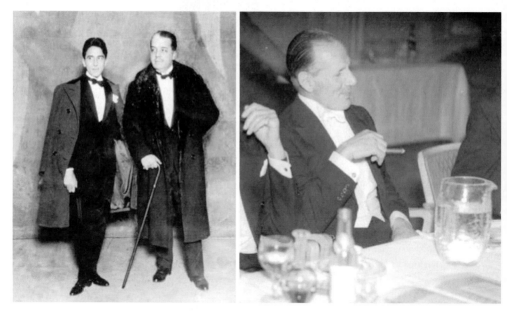

Above left. 'The most extraordinarily frightening man': the impresario Serge Diaghilev (right) with Jean Cocteau in London, 1924.

Above right. Private patronage: Samuel Courtauld, the wealthy industrialist who sponsored Sargent's concerts.

Below. Hiawatha: with Sargent in foreground (right).

Above left. Eileen.

Above right. Daddy's girl: Pamela, aged eight.

Below left. Peter, aged 12, at Eton.

Below right. Lord Horder: the doctor who saved Sargent's life.

Above and opposite top. The Rivals: Sargent and Adrian Boult both photographed by 'Sasha' in 1935.

Opposite bottom left. Sir Thomas, heir to the Beecham empire.

Opposite bottom right. 'Cor, it's Toscanini!': the Italian maestro had donated the photograph for a charity auction and concert in aid of the Battersea Central Mission in 1944. That same year, Toscanini invited Sargent to conduct the NBC Symphony Orchestra.

Above. Blitzed: the Queen's Hall, May 1941.

Below. 'Any Questions?': (left to right) 'Fougasse', Cmdr. A. B. Campbell, Sargent, Donald McCullough, Thomas Woodroffe, Howard Thomas and C. E. M. Joad, recording the Brains Trust for Christmas Day, 1941.

conducting the massed ranks of the Royal Choral Society for *Belshazzar's Feast*, his mind must have drifted back two years. At the Courtauld-Sargent performance, he had been on the verge of physical meltdown. If he had died, the premiere of *Belshazzar* in 1931 should have been his legacy. Friends whose deep pockets matched their generosity had kept him solvent during months of difficult recovery. Now as the thousand voices of the Royal Choral Society declaimed the final Alleluias of Walton's magnificent oratorio, Malcolm Sargent knew for certain that he was back.

7

Bread and Butter

On 3 July 1936 Malcolm Sargent boarded the boat train at Victoria Station to begin a journey that three months later would see him arrive in Sydney Harbour. He had been bitterly disappointed to cancel an Australian tour two years earlier. Now returned to good health and after months that confirmed his ability to work again, Sargent was thrilled at the prospect of a first overseas tour. Newspapers the following day pictured the conductor kissing his wife goodbye. With his beaming smile and immaculate tailoring, readers at breakfast tables across the country might have recognised a happy and relaxed man back at the top of his powers. They were wrong. For all his smiles, Malcolm Sargent was deeply troubled, relieved to leave behind a controversy of his own making. Settling into his first-class compartment as the train pulled away, Sargent was forced to confront the unpleasant truth that he had become almost overnight a hate figure in the English musical world.

Sir Thomas Beecham had capitalised on Sargent's illness in 1933 to assume full control of the London Philharmonic Orchestra, which included responsibility for hiring and firing players. In 1935 he sacked eight members of the orchestra. Sargent not Beecham, however, was condemned for callousness because he made the error of speaking to the press. In June 1936, the *Daily Telegraph* had interviewed him about employment rights for musicians and whether or not they should be entitled to pensions. Sargent told the newspaper that every hard-working employee deserved one, but added that there was 'a snag'. 'As soon as a man thinks he is in his orchestral job for life, with a pension waiting for him at the end of it, he tends to lose something of his supreme fire,' Sargent observed. 'He ought to give of his lifeblood with every bar he plays. Directly a man gets blasé or does not give of his very best he ought to go. It sounds cruel, but it is for the good of the orchestra.' The sacked members of the London Philharmonic Orchestra, he said, were examples of such players. Orchestral musicians should be put on one-year contracts and pensions paid 'only at the end of the musician's life when he has poured out ungrudgingly his whole strength'.[1]

If Sargent had foreseen the decades of abuse he would suffer for these ill-judged comments he would surely have kept his mouth resolutely shut. Musicians throughout the country were outraged. 'Sargent was hated by orchestras overnight,' remembers Jack Brymer, then a college student but later principal clarinet of three London orchestras. 'They had helped in his dark days, clubbed together to send him off to Switzerland to recover from tuberculosis and he repaid them by being thoroughly nasty to them in the press. They never forgave him. Even thirty years later there were players who would not speak to him.'[2] In band rooms up and down the country, disgruntled musicians cut Sargent's remarks from newspapers and pinned them to the notice board. During breaks in his rehearsals, collection boxes went round for a 'Sargent Fund' into which players who had contributed generously in 1933 now deposited fag-ends, sweet wrappers and even 'French letters'.

The LPO took most offence at Sargent's comments. Members had endured sackings and were in the midst of a financial crisis. Beecham, running true to form, had driven out Samuel Courtauld and Robert Mayer but could not balance the books. Some players were owed as much as £300 in wages but Beecham refused to countenance financial backers who might limit his own authority. Thomas Beecham may have taken the orchestra to the abyss but it was Sargent and his inopportune comments that became the focal point of resentment.[3]

Public condemnation of Sargent's demand for the 'lifeblood' of orchestral musicians flowed thick and fast. 'The idea that one must starve to be a great artist is out of date and quite wrong,' said Fritz Kreisler, perhaps the world's most famous violinist. 'Whoever says a man plays better for feeling insecure does not understand musicians.'[4] Sargent's mentor, Sir Hugh Allen, joined the chorus of disapproval, as did Sir Dan Godfrey, Albert Salmons, Sir John McEwen and other leading figures of the musical establishment. Lionel Tertis, the viola player, had frequently worked with Sargent, and seemed to speak for many when he observed that a musician should indeed 'give of his lifeblood' but that 'some conductors reduce him to stone, and from a stone nobody can get blood'.[5]

Illness had affected Sargent's judgement. Where previously he had been possessed of deft political skill, at this important moment he failed to serve his own interests. Perhaps the defiance of death had induced a self-confidence that was beyond censure. Maybe he just thought that everyone should work as hard as he did. Even the torrent of denigration from the press failed to convince Sargent of a strategic error. Rather than deflect the issue, he took the criticism to heart. 'My father always felt that somehow he had been mis-understood and so continued referring to those remarks when really he should have kept quiet,' recalls Peter Sargent.[6] Reporters went back to Sargent for comments on the furore, but attempts to explain only made matters worse. 'Instability about where next year's bread and butter will come from had made many an artist give con-tinuously of their best,' he said. His ideas about establishing civic orchestras for young players leaving music college and a demand for government subsidy went unnoticed. 'Next year's bread and butter' were the words bitterly repeated backstage for years. 'I ventured to say a word about it to Paul Beard [Leader of the BBC SO from 1936] and got back a torrent of measured but obviously deeply felt invective about that young gentleman . . .' reported Adrian Boult later, adding mischievously: 'I am at a loss how to handle a situation of this kind except by simply not engaging him.'[7]

Sargent until the 'bread and butter' dispute had been a respected and well-liked conductor. The fact that he had come back from the brink of death had further enhanced a general sense of admiration for him. That reservoir of goodwill dried up immediately. Orchestras, particularly in London, began to bait him, behaving in a rude and surly fashion. Players made a point of tuning their instruments when he arrived at rehearsals – a discourtesy he detested – and asking impertinent questions. 'The trouble always came from the back, the brass,' remembers Sidonie Goossens. 'They were absolute devils and very unkind. He had been very silly but in the end I got fed up with them. There were some bad moments with the orchestra but it was water off a duck's back to him.'[8]

Sargent could still galvanise players but was now unable to inspire affection. 'At school, we were given tickets for the Manchester Free Trade Hall, right over the orchestra where you could see the face of the conductor and every one of their antics,' reminisces Marjorie Thomas. 'Sargent had a magnetism but the orchestra clearly did not like him. They were not affectionate towards him like they were with John Barbirolli. My goodness he produced the results but there was not that kind of warmth of feeling with them.'[9] Orchestral players began complaining about his 'them and us' attitude. Sargent did not shout in rehearsals, remained courteous in the face of provocation and never lost his temper. Yet he refused to encourage any kind of personal solidarity with players. Sidonie Goossens believes that 'there was always something that got in between. Sargent did not have affection for anybody in the orchestra. We were always "the orchestra". You could be friendly but would never take him to your heart.'[10]

The sense that Sargent was getting too big for his boots was not confined to orchestral musicians.[11] Even friends had noticed a new impatience. He offended Vaughan Williams over the composition of *Dona Nobis Pacem*. Sargent had asked him to compose a work to celebrate the centenary of the Huddersfield Choral Society, and then announced that he would be unavailable to conduct the premiere due to the Australian tour. In a fit of pique, Vaughan Williams withdrew the work, and only the most abject pleading on Sargent's part convinced him to reconsider.[12] Huddersfield now also believed Sargent needed to be cut down to size. When he suggested that the chorus should stand at his entrance on to the concert platform, he received a polite but firm 'no'.[13]

'Little Hitler' was among the many insults thrown at Sargent by unhappy musicians during this period, although he was not unique as a conductor in attracting that tag. [14] The concentration of leadership in one man, bending a huge symphony orchestra to his will, had more sinister overtones in that age. With central European and Italian conductors dominating the orchestral world, it is not surprising to find that a significant number were Fascist or Nazi sympathisers. 'We were all Nazis – Furtwängler, Böhm, me,' said Herbert von Karajan of his contemporaries in 1930s Germany.[15] Wilhelm Mengleberg in Amsterdam made no secret of his admiration for Hitler. In Italy, many musicians, including Mascagni and Puccini, were supporters of the violin-playing Mussolini. 'Everyone who conducts in the Third Reich is a Nazi,' Toscanini shouted at Furtwängler in 1937.[16] He refused to conduct in Germany after 1933, spoke out against Nazi abuses, and conducted the inaugural concert of the Palestine Symphony Orchestra, comprising European refugees. 'If I were capable of killing a man, I would kill Mussolini,' Toscanini wrote as early as 1923.[17]

The authoritarian behaviour and cult of leadership encouraged by these conductors seemed to many a reflection of the times. Wilhelm Furtwängler regularly spat at orchestras. Leopold Stokowski humiliated individual violinists by making them play difficult passages alone in front of the entire orchestra. An assistant to 'Tsar' Serge Koussevitsky observed that 'almost every rehearsal was a nightmare. [...] There were in the Boston Symphony Orchestra 105 players and 106 ulcers (one man had two).'[18] Otto Klemperer and Beecham specialised in cutting sarcasm. Bruno Walter's grace on the podium was underpinned by callousness away from it. The wonderful technical facility of Fritz Reiner and George Szell was matched by their cruelty. Even Toscanini would fly into rages, berating musicians who failed to meet his expectations and audience members who had the temerity to arrive late. In rehearsals he would shout, stamp, throw stands and music, chew his baton and walk out. On one occasion his frustration was such that he took off his jacket, ripped it to pieces and trampled on the remains.

All these tyrants might have argued that the concert halls of Europe and America were littered with the broken batons of conductors who had failed to impose their personality on orchestras. Dimitri Mitropoulos was a fine conductor but his inability to control the New York Philharmonic and the Metropolitan Opera ended in a fatal heart attack. The mild-mannered Pierre Monteux missed out on a top appointment after the First World War despite fame as the conductor who premiered *The Rite of Spring* in 1913. 'I lack what it takes to get to the very top,' said Mahler's protégé Alexander Zemlinsky. 'In this throng, it is not enough to have elbows – you need to know how to use them.'[19]

Malcolm Sargent had understood implicitly from childhood the importance of sharp elbows, but until the 'bread and butter' incident, his natural charm had helped conceal an underlying ruthlessness. Relaxing amid the comfort of his first-class cabin during the long voyage to Australia, Sargent was thankful that at least he had several months away from England during which the furore might die down. As the weeks passed, his thoughts turned to the Australian Broadcasting Commission, which had invited him to conduct in five states and produce a report on the future of music-making. A meandering voyage took him first to Quebec and Vancouver and then to New Zealand, until on 5 September 1936 Sargent arrived in Sydney Harbour aboard the SS *Niagara*.

Sargent's host organisation, the ABC, had been established in 1932 as an independent corporation modelled on the BBC. The wireless was soon extremely popular in Australia and achieved an iconic status in a country of such vast size. The ABC's philosophy of broadcasting as a civilising activity was based on that of the BBC's founding director, John Reith. Throughout the 1930s, the ABC radio news-readers wore dinner jackets and spoke with English-style accents. Reith's ABC counterpart was Charles Moses, an Englishman of urbanity and toughness in equal measures. He became general manager in 1935 and set out to cultivate excellence in all areas of programming to create a schedule that would educate, enlighten and entertain its audience.[20]

The Great Depression of the late 1920s and early 1930s had hit Australia extremely hard, both economically and financially. Un-employment had reached over twenty-eight per cent of the workforce, and a financial crisis including the repayment of debts to Britain had damaged the self-confidence of the middle class. Restoring cultural confidence was almost as important as regaining economic prosperity. The ABC believed that classical music was central to this process of cultural renewal. The Australian

Broadcasting Commission Act (1932) instructed the new organisation to establish 'groups of musicians for the rendition of orchestral, choral and band music of high quality'.[21] In a country without a single professional orchestra, this commitment brought classical music from the periphery to the heart of cultural life with the potential to broadcast into every Australian home. At the ABC's inauguration on 1 July 1932, Charles Lloyd Jones, Chairman of the Commission, spoke of his desire to create 'an Australian National Orchestra'.[22] Orchestras of twenty-four permanent members were formed in Melbourne and Sydney and soon followed by studio orchestras in other states. The Chairman consulted Adrian Boult about conductors. Boult, happy to get a rival out of the way, recommended Sargent.

When Sargent had fallen ill, his Australian work had been offered to Sir Hamilton Harty, who had recently left the Hallé Orchestra. Harty conducted nine concerts with an ABC Symphony Orchestra that combined the orchestras from Melbourne and Sydney. All were broadcast on relay and well received. From California immediately afterwards, Harty wrote to the ABC that 'in spite of the superior material in the orchestras here and in England there was something in the sincerity of the Australian musicians I worked with which in the end I like better than mere technical proficiency'.[23] Harty's genial charm made him a polite guest. Georg Szell, the acerbic Hungarian conductor, in 1936 put it rather differently: 'Between the best they can offer and the least that I am prepared to accept, there is an unbridgeable gap.'[24]

By the time Sargent arrived in that year, the ABC had built up the Sydney Orchestra to forty-five players, Melbourne to thirty-five, and consolidated small orchestras in Brisbane, Adelaide, Perth and Hobart. The best orchestras remained those of Melbourne and Sydney, which continued to combine for large-scale works. The other orchestras were of a much lower standard and could not even fill all their vacancies. No situation could have better suited the talents of Malcolm Sargent.

The orchestras lacked professional discipline and glamour; Sargent gave them both. When he arrived at his first rehearsal with the Sydney orchestra, members were astonished. Immaculate, of course, in double-breasted pinstripe suit with carnation, Sargent made it clear from the outset that he would expect total commitment. Brass players returned from the first break wearing toffee apples in their lapels to mock him. Sargent took this with good grace but later put down a marker by dismissing a horn player for contradicting him. He set about the task almost like a schoolmaster.

Travelling between the orchestras, he taught them how to play and behave with professionalism. New repertoire was approached note by note. Discipline was the key. Talking was not allowed in rehearsals other than by section principals. Players were instructed to sit up straight and not slump in their chairs. Presentation was a crucial component of his regime. Orchestras were shown how to take the stage and acknowledge applause. After rehearsing the music, Sargent would make his orchestra practise their concert routine, ensuring that the choreography of the evening was perfect.

Initial bemusement and irritation quickly passed as it became apparent that Sargent was getting results. By demanding professional standards from Australian orchestras, he showed that he was taking them seriously. 'He did not feel that he should be matey with his players any more than a captain should be matey with his crew,' said Charles Moses of the ABC. 'Australians, who are notoriously matey, might have expected to be irritated by this precise Englishman. They were not. They found in him a painstaking, though never finicky, professional. [He] knew what he wanted from an orchestra and he got it. Australians admired him for this.'[25]

At the end of his visit, Sargent prepared a report for Charles Moses that gave a frank assessment of the orchestras and a blueprint for the future. 'I felt that if you could find, say, 100 of your best performers and place them in the hands of someone really competent to mould them, and then to perform programmes in each State, you would be providing something really creditable to musical Australia,' he concluded.[26]

Sargent's judgement, which echoed that of Charles Lloyd Jones, was impeccable musically but grated with political sensibilities. The six Australian states, each based on a previously self-governing colony, have their own culture and identities; the federal structure of government is a delicate and constantly shifting balance between national and state interests. The ABC was founded as a national broadcaster and remained sensitive to accusations that it was

concerned only with life in Melbourne and Sydney. The creation of
state orchestras was a symbol of the equity of the ABC's commitment. Sargent's plan was further complicated by his suggestion that
foreign players should be employed to raise orchestral standards.
Professional orchestras from Europe and America did not tour
Australia because the Musician's Union imposed harsh conditions on
foreign players. Music schools until 1914 had included many
continental Europeans, particularly Germans, on the staff, but the
First World War had seen them forced out. In the midst now of the
Great Depression, trade unions resisted immigration programmes
and those Europeans who were admitted often suffered blatant
racism. With so many fine Jewish musicians fleeing Germany,
Australia like America might have benefited by welcoming them into
orchestras, but the Musician's Union fought a vehement rearguard
action. 'Once an immigrant, always an immigrant,' ironically
pronounced the high court judge, Sir Isaac Isaacs. He summed up the
attitude of many Australians.[27]

The solution devised by Charles Moses to balance national and
state interests was the retention of an orchestra in each state and the
creation of an ABC 'super-orchestra'. Sargent was invited to return
to Australia in 1938 to see what he could make of the arrangement.
He arrived on 20 July to carry out an arduous schedule: sixteen
orchestral concerts (including three with the new National
Symphony Orchestra), four choral concerts and five special performances for children. 'I am looking forward to this tour,' he told
waiting reporters at an impromptu press conference on the quayside.
'During my last tour I found that there were some weak spots but I
think some of them will have disappeared now. Still you have not
played for very long in Australia. The players have not the musical
tradition but I have reason to believe that on this tour I should expect
much more from them.'[28] Journalists praised his lack of 'side' and
warmed to his 'Magnetic Personality'. The *Sydney Mail* told its
readers unequivocally that Sargent 'is one of the world's greatest
conductors'.[29]

Sargent's first engagements of the season were with the ABC
orchestras in Sydney, Melbourne and Brisbane. When he arrived for
his first rehearsal with the Sydney Symphony Orchestra, he was
given a marvellous opportunity to endear himself to the orchestral

players. The Chairman of the ABC, William Cleary, stood before the orchestra, rebuking them before even a note was played. George Szell, who had conducted just weeks before, had complained that too much time had gone into correcting wrong notes rather than interpretation. They must take their parts home to practise and not waste their eminent conductor's time. 'Of course, I take it for granted that you will do everything possible to master technical difficulties,' Sargent purred after Cleary had left, 'and expect even greater things than you gave me on my last visit.' 'Professor Szell was cranky,' an orchestral player told the press. 'We get on better with Dr Sargent!'[30]

The opening concert with the SSO on 26 July was a triumph. When Sargent emerged on stage, he was given such an ovation that 'the building seemed to quiver from the vibrations'. The main work in the programme was Cesar Franck's Symphony in D Minor in which Sargent showed the qualities of 'energy and poetic feeling' that had made him so popular two years earlier. The most touching story of the evening accompanied the performance of Rachmaninov's Piano Concerto No. 2. Valda Aveling was only seventeen years old and had won a competition in *Women's Weekly*. Her prize was a concerto performance with the Sydney Symphony Orchestra and two years study at the local conservatory. Wearing a simple white chiffon dress, this beautiful young girl had been so nervous before the concert that it seemed she might not be able to go on. Sargent gently coaxed her confidence back and fed her sugar cubes and milk to restore energy levels. On stage, Aveling gave a vigorous performance, after which she leapt up from her piano to kiss Sargent, prompting a huge cheer. 'Dr Sargent is a marvellous person to work for,' she cooed afterwards, munching away on more of his sugar cubes.[31]

Triumph in 'Marvellous Melbourne', Australia's most cosmopolitan city, matched that in Sydney.[32] The late thirties, a time of vibrancy in the arts in Melbourne despite the Great Depression, included a visit by the Ballets Russes to perform Stravinsky, and the *Herald*'s magnificent exhibition of European modernist paintings. Sargent had won warm reviews in 1936 so that his return in 1938 caused much excitement. At his first rehearsal, hundreds turned up to listen as he put the orchestra through its paces. 'He holds together a whole orchestra like a quartet,' said one of the players during the break, 'and after his rehearsals you feel not worn out but polished.' The opening concert of the Sargent season in Melbourne on 6 August seemed more convincing than usual. The Melbourne Symphony Orchestra had 'this season failed to reproduce its acknowledged form' but under Sargent 'the players had recovered old virtues and acquired new refinement'.[33] There was further success in Brisbane where even a minor car crash on a day trip to Mount Donna Buang, from which Sargent emerged unscathed, seemed to confirm a run of good fortune.[34] 'They have improved, I only hope I have not got worse,' he reflected with uncharacteristic modesty on his time with the orchestras.[35]

Sargent remained sure, however, that only radical reform would bring Australia up to international standards. He told the Millions Club in Sydney that the development of orchestral talent in Australia was being held back by insular union regulations preventing the employment of foreign musicians. 'Unions are often right but they sometimes make the mistake of being short-sighted,' he said bluntly. Australian orchestras were 'enthusiastic and extremely inspiring' but if they were to fulfil their potential, he urged, 'the Australian Broadcasting Commission should bring out expert players who could play with the local orchestras and probably teach members at the same time'.[36] The need for overseas players to act as mentors had been a theme of his 1936 report for the ABC. His other recommendation, the formation of a national symphony orchestra, having been tentatively adopted, gave him an opportunity to prove a point.

Three concerts were scheduled for 10, 14 and 17 September in Sydney with an orchestra of a hundred. The pretext for the concerts was the celebration of New South Wales's 150th anniversary. At the first rehearsal, Charles Moses introduced Sargent and begged the musicians to set aside inter-state rivalries. The concertmasters of the Melbourne and Sydney orchestras were appointed co-leaders to symbolise unity of purpose. In reality, this 'national' orchestra mostly comprised players from Melbourne and Sydney. There was muttering in the other states that there were 'some players capable of ousting' many of those from Melbourne and Sydney. 'It is inconceivable,' thundered an indignant writer on the Brisbane *Telegraph*, 'that Mr Eric Hayne (to take but one example from several to be cited from the Brisbane orchestra) is not a better all round violinist than some of the occupiers of back desks in the Sydney component.'[37] Perth and Adelaide complained that unless Sargent heard their players, they had no opportunity to vie for a place in the national orchestra.

Despite this background of dissent, Sargent was able to predict with confidence at the first rehearsal that Australian music stood on the threshold of a new dawn. 'This morning I was present at what may be an historic occasion,' he told reporters afterwards. 'It was the finest collection of 100 players ever gathered in the same room since Australia began to be known to the civilised world. These players were listening to a new sound this morning, I say, a new sound and a new quality, which has never been heard in an orchestra in Australia, because this is the first time that the second flute has been as good as the first flute and so with all the instruments. The three concerts should be the best Australia has yet achieved.'[38]

The inaugural concert of the ABC National Symphony Orchestra on 10 September 1938 was as much a grand social as musical occasion. '*Everyone* was there,' *Woman* magazine reported, '(and every gossip writer knows that the Town Hall can be full to the brim and yet "nobody there, my dear").'[39] As taxis crowded outside the Town Hall in light drizzle, women in beautiful evening gowns and fur wraps, accompanied by men in white tie gathered for cocktails and gossip. The 'House Full' sign had been up all day. Such was the demand for tickets that even the radio announcer had to give up his place once the concert had been introduced. The stage had been decorated with flowers and every member of the orchestra given a buttonhole. The Governor, Lord Wakehurst, arrived to respectful applause shortly before eight o'clock. When his party had taken their seats, the audience settled into a state of hushed expectancy for a programme including Beethoven's Fifth Symphony. The newspapers had been full of speculation about enmity between musicians from different states. Could they set aside conflicting interests to make the experiment work?

When Malcolm Sargent unleashed his orchestra in the explosive opening of Richard Strauss's tone poem *Don Juan*, amongst the most difficult in the repertoire, all doubts vanished. The sheer size and precision of sound was a revelation to Australian ears. After the hush of the final death scene, the audience sat in silence as if stunned by what they had heard, before launching into 'applause that reached the magnitude of an ovation'.[40] At the end of the concert, Sargent was brought back on stage for repeated curtain calls and presented with a laurel wreath to great cheers. Afterwards, when the librarian went to collect Sargent's scores, he found a posse of young women by the podium fighting over his spare baton.

Popular acclamation was matched by critical approval. 'These performances were undoubtedly the finest pieces of orchestral playing that Sydney has ever heard,' proclaimed Australia's leading newspaper, the *Sydney Morning Herald*. The orchestra had combined 'precision' with 'an elegance, a colour, an authority that lit up' every score. 'Dr Sargent obviously inspired the instrumentalists.' His interpretation of 'the Fifth Symphony was as grand a musical utterance as anyone could wish to hear'.[41] The two further National Symphony Orchestra concerts that followed were both greeted with 'an uproar of applause'.[42] When the series with the new ABC orchestra came to its close, critics were united in pronouncing the experiment a success. 'If these players could be kept together by a great conductor,' observed one, 'there is no saying what heights they would climb.'[43] The concerts had been 'THE event' of the year, and 'there'll be a weeping and a wailing when Malcolm Sargent leaves tomorrow'.[44]

An overwhelmed Sargent told Charles Moses at the ABC that he would happily come back each year to conduct the National Symphony Orchestra. He agreed to conduct a two-month season the following year with the orchestra in Sydney and Melbourne, followed by a tour to Brisbane, Perth and Adelaide. 'The plan, I think, would be particularly valuable because it would help to do away with parochial rivalries between Sydney and Melbourne,' Sargent ventured, adding that 'all the players would have continuous symphonic experience and thus would be able to give the best possible results'.[45]

The inaugural series of the ABC National Symphony Orchestra was the high point of Sargent's 1938 visit to Australia but was far from the end of his tour. When he might reasonably have been expected to ease off, he threw himself into two months of touring that included visits to Melbourne, Brisbane, Adelaide and Perth. By

November he had conducted twenty-four concerts, each of which had involved at least three rehearsals. Town halls in five states, each filled to capacity, rewarded him with standing ovations. Hundreds turned out just to watch him rehearse. Even music critics spoke with one voice in acclaiming his work. 'Last time I came [Australian choirs and orchestras] were a little shy of expressing themselves, and were rather amazed at the demands made upon them,' he told reporters gathered at Fremantle to see him board the *Stratheden* on 8 November for the long voyage home. 'This time it was not so.'[46]

A large crowd congregated on the quayside to see Sargent off and he exchanged banter with them from the bridge of the liner. 'I can see all Australia from up here,' he shouted down.[47] As the ship moved slowly away, Sargent returned to his first-class quarters to reflect on his visit and ponder the future. He knew that he would return to Australia the following year.[48] There was also a significant, if unsurprising, offer to contemplate. Charles Moses had informally sounded him out about taking over artistic direction of music at the ABC. A big salary and a permanent National Symphony Orchestra were his for the asking. Settling into his cabin, Malcolm Sargent enjoyed a champagne cocktail and admitted quietly to himself that he was tempted.[49]

'I am happy to say that my tour was a most delightful experience from start to finish and also the concerts were the most tremendous success, every one being sold out,' Sargent wrote to EMI on his return to England.[50] Peter Sargent recalls that his father's conversation after months away was dominated by Australia.[51] The celebrity status that surrounded him there allowed him to play the role of 'Lord' Sargent. By now, Sargent had developed the dandy's image that would remain for the rest of his life. Pristine double-breasted, pin-striped Savile Row suits (grey during the day, dark blue in the evening), slicked jet-black hair and ubiquitous carnation combined to give Sargent a sharp and distinctive look. Many in London's high society sneeringly observed that he was a little too smart to be a real gentleman. Harold Nicolson, official biographer of George V, frequently repeated the spiteful remark of his own secretary that 'Sir Harold, you go to the best tailors and the best shirt-makers but you never look as smart as Malcolm Sargent.'[52] In particular, his country clothes were the subject of derision. 'He

wasn't very good at country clothes,' remembers his friend Robin
Sheepshanks, a Suffolk landowner. 'He always had the wrong
clothes, a townsman's country clothes. He was not a countryman at
all. I remember him coming shooting on one occasion and finding a
pheasant that ran: it was shot but not dead. So he pursued it in the
middle of the drive with a tail stalk and tried to hammer it on the
head, which is certainly not the correct thing.'[53]

The telltale signs of Sargent's origins were less apparent in
Australia, where his status as an English gentleman was taken as read.
He could still occasionally be caught out, such as by the Duke of
Gloucester, who ridiculed him for his refusal to join in the building
of a bonfire in case he spoilt his beautiful clothes.[54] The setting for
most Australian life, however, was the suburbs not the splendour of
the Governor-General's residence. Few Australians understood these
nuances of the English class system; those who did tended to admire
Sargent for his social mobility. 'Whatever Malcolm has that promotes
him to the appeal rank "A" he has got it in a big way,' observed the
Sydney Sunday Sun in 1938. [55]

Celebrity and acceptance were important factors in his love affair
with Australia, but money was perhaps even more significant. By
1938, Sargent was aware of the fame and fortune on offer to
international conductors, with Toscanini leading the way. When
Fortune magazine ran a nationwide poll in 1937, it made the
staggering discovery that 'of all the people in the US – Negroes, poor
whites, farmers, clerks, and millionaires […] more than one-fourth
knows who [Toscanini] is and what he does'. Toscanini, concluded
Fortune, attracted 'a mass audience'.[56] By 1937 his concert fee after tax
was a staggering $3,334.

Sargent had never been a greedy conductor and was often persuaded to perform for considerably less than his market rate. Yet
illness had reinforced an awareness that he worked in a profession
where tragedy might wipe out in an instant his ability to make
money. His magnificent EMI recordings of Beethoven's piano
concertos with Artur Schnabel were considered by the company to
be 'the finest of their kind that we have recorded to date' and yet they
offered him only £17 per session. 'I feel [this] to be too little,'
Sargent told EMI and persuaded them to pay more.[57] When he
received a cheque for twenty-five guineas after conducting the BBC

Symphony Orchestra, he told Boult that 'I was rather surprised to receive the enclosed. I cannot believe this is in line with the BBC's usual fee for conducting a symphony concert. [...] Will you please ask the authorities to adjust this.'[58] Sargent's fees in England increased yet remained paltry in comparison not only with Toscanini's but also with those he could earn in Australia. For each concert of Sargent's 1938 tour the ABC had paid him £115 (sterling), at least a threefold increase on his fees in England.[59]

Sargent's desire to generate more income was not avarice but the response to an appalling family tragedy. His daughter, Pamela, was dying: she needed the best medical attention that money could buy. In August 1937, the Sargent family had travelled to Portofino in Italy for their first family holiday since Sargent's recovery from tuberculosis. Their villa, Casa Signorile, was set on a hillside with magnificent views of the peninsula. They spent the first carefree weeks playing in the sun and sea. 'It was idyllic, just the four of us, everyone relaxed and having fun,' remembers Peter Sargent. 'My parents made a real effort with each other and Pam and I were so incredibly happy.' Sargent telegraphed Adrian Boult and told him, 'It is heavenly here. Blazing sunshine every day.'[60]

In the middle of September, this little piece of heaven was destroyed. The day was spent on the beach in the sunshine. Pamela fell asleep on a lilo in the sea, and when she got back to the villa complained of a sore neck. 'Sunstroke!' laughed Sargent and put her to bed with an ice pack. 'The next morning at five o'clock,' remembers Peter, 'I was shaken awake by my father who told me "You have to come and see Pamela. She is dying."' Peter ran to his sister's room and found her on the bed unable to move, with barely the strength to blink her eyelids. 'What happened next would have been comical if it had not been so dangerous,' says Peter Sargent. The local doctor in Portofino had never seen a case like it and just stood shaking his head. He telephoned a hospital in Rome to be told that Pamela needed an iron lung but that they were all being used.

Sargent made an immediate decision: he had to get his daughter back to England, where the influence of friends would guarantee her the best medical facilities. Accompanied by a rosary-intoning nun from the local convent, she was taken to the railway station, where porters dropped her stretcher. The horrendous journey from

Portofino to Paris lasted seventy-two hours. When they arrived in Paris, the weather was atrocious and all scheduled flights were cancelled. Sargent discovered that a private plane belonging to the King of Greece was at the airport; telephone calls were made to London and the plane was secured. They flew in terrible conditions and arrived to find cameras waiting for them. Pamela was rushed to the clinic where four years earlier Sargent had himself faced death, and her whole body was encased in plaster of Paris. The diagnosis was stark: Pamela Sargent had polio. 'She wasn't in hospital for long because there was nothing they could do for her,' recalls her brother. 'She never once complained and was always smiling, but for the next seven years she became the sole focus of family life.' [61]

Australia was a tempting prospect for Malcolm Sargent because it offered the financial rewards and celebrity that would guarantee Pamela every comfort, as well as a 'fresh start' to his troubled marriage. 'I really believe that when my father left for the tour in 1939,' says Peter Sargent, 'he had made up his mind that the next year we would all be going for good.' [62]

8

The Baton and the Blitz

In May 1939, just weeks before leaving once more for Australia, Malcolm Sargent received public confirmation that he held a place among the great conductors. In a packed Albert Hall he conducted *The Dream of Gerontius* with the combined forces of 'his' Royal, Huddersfield, Bradford and Croydon choral societies as part of the London Music Festival. Sargent's idol, Arturo Toscanini, was in the audience. After the performance, the Italian embraced him. Sargent, he declared, was the finest choral conductor in the world.[1] A benediction from the high priest of conducting sanctified Sargent's position as a maestro of international standing.

Sargent departed with Toscanini's words still resonating, on a month-long voyage that allowed him to sketch a national music plan for Australia. When he sailed into Fremantle on 18 July, he declared his intention to initiate a revolution. The National Symphony Orchestra would be revived and form the centre-piece of an ABC Festival of Music. State orchestras, particularly in Sydney and Melbourne, would be trained to give performances of the highest standards. The world's finest soloists would perform with the orchestras and give recitals. These activities would not be restricted to the wealthy and well connected. Promenade seasons in Melbourne and

Sydney and 'factory concerts' in workers' districts would encourage those who had never before experienced classical music. This was an opportunity, Sargent proclaimed, 'to make Australia very definitely of supreme importance in the world of music'.[2]

A 'Keep Sargent' campaign stretched back to his first tour, in 1936. By 1939 it had reached fever pitch. Questions had been asked in the Australian parliament about how the Postmaster-General, as the minister responsible for the ABC, might ensure that Sargent accepted the post of Director of Music. No other musician had his ability of 'pulling people in', remembered Charles Moses. 'He made music look great as well as sound great.'[3]

Whatever thoughts Sargent had of building a new life in Australia were shattered six weeks after his arrival, when the British Empire declared war on Nazi Germany. This conflict would assume global proportions and cost untold million lives.[4] Sargent was in Melbourne conducting *Belshazzar's Feast* on the day that hostilities broke out. 'Howl ye, howl ye, therefore, for the day of the Lord is at hand,' opens this powerful work about war and conquest, and few could have been unmoved by the grim intimation of events to come.

Only three days after the declaration of war, newspapers clamoured for Sargent to stay in Australia for the duration of the conflict.[5] Charles Moses approached Sargent to ask him to 'consider signing a new contract and staying on in Australia indefinitely'.[6] His family would be brought out and the plans he had already outlined for Australian music implemented. Sargent had decided to accept the challenge of shaping music in Australia. The contract before him was simply the realisation of discussions that had been on-going for more than a year. All it needed was his signature.

The war changed Sargent's mind: his sense of honour would not allow him to sign. He asked to be released immediately from his existing tour and was furious when the ABC refused. Frustratingly, he had to conduct a further sixteen concerts in Australia but put his name down for the first available flight home. He conducted two concerts in aid of the Red Cross and asked only that they use influence to get him a seat on an aeroplane. When a place became available at the end of November he set out on a complicated journey dictated by war strategy, not convenience, with dreadful weather aggravating the already risky trip. Sargent arrived in London on 27 November, unnerved by long and dangerous flights but relieved finally to be home.

On his return Sargent found a country that hardly seemed at war at all. After the initial shock, England had settled down to a period of complacent 'Bore War'. Hitler had consolidated Germany's position in central Europe but seemed reluctant to escalate the conflict into a full European war. Life in England continued with an eerie normality. Music was recovering from the initial war fervour, when concert halls had been shut down. The BBC had merged its channels, leaving the Symphony Orchestra, evacuated from London, with little to do but 'go for long walks exploring the lovely country-side round Bristol'.[7] Sargent took up a familiar routine of pre-war days. Courtauld-Sargent, the Royal Choral Society, Huddersfield and many one-off engagements kept him busy. He continued to conduct German music in his programmes. 'If we place German music under a ban we are showing ourselves to be just as malicious as Hitler,' he warned. 'Haydn and Beethoven have nothing to do with this war. Even where living composers are concerned, I cannot see any advantage in refusing to play their work.'[8]

The Phoney War came to an end in the early summer of 1940 when Hitler, with continental Europe prostrate before him, turned his mind to the invasion of Britain: Operation Sealion. Bombing raids on ports and factories, mostly in the south of England, came as a prelude. Night after night, scores of Heinkel and Junkers bombers operating from northern France and accompanied by packs of Messerschmitt and Focke-Wulf fighters wreaked death and destruction on British cities. The Battle of Britain culminated on 15 September when Reichsmarshal Göring concluded that the Luftwaffe could no longer sustain the heavy losses inflicted by the Royal Air Force. Fighter squadrons of Hurricanes and Spitfires, many flown by young men with only weeks of basic training, had seen off the numerically superior Luftwaffe in what Churchill called Britain's 'Finest Hour'. The threat of invasion had been overcome but the attacks on British cities – the 'Blitz' – continued. Even Buckingham Palace was hit, but in general it was those who lived near ports or manufacturing districts who endured the heaviest casualties and destruction of property. Many chose to take their chances at home rather than sleep in rat-infested shelters.

During the Blitz, the arts boosted morale and expressed the ideals that were at stake in the war. They provided an uplifting alternative narrative to the horrors of urban warfare. The government encouraged the celebration of an English rural idyll that celebrated the pastoral values of a 'green and pleasant land' stretching 'from Hardy's Wessex to Tennyson's Lincolnshire, from Kipling's Sussex to Elgar's Worcestershire'.[9] When war broke out in 1939, the government had established a Council for the Encouragement of Music and the Arts to buttress national cultural values. CEMA's mission was to take the arts to workers in factories and organise performances at prices that anyone could afford. While orchestras lost many of their younger musicians to the armed forces, older members played on. The BBC Symphony Orchestra moved from Bristol to Bedford, where it continued to broadcast on national radio. Other orchestras, particularly in London, Manchester and Liverpool, gave live performances for CEMA in factories, warehouses and aircraft hangars. No one personified the Council's aims better than the pianist Myra Hess, whose 'shilling-a-time' concerts at the National Gallery came to symbolise the still voice of civilisation amid the rubble of war-torn London. 'There were men and women, young and old, rich and poor waiting patiently in the cold up the steps of the Gallery and along the pavements . . . to hear Bach, Beethoven, Brahms, Chopin and Schumann,' observed *Picture Post*. 'Strange things happen in wartime.'[10]

In 1942 Humphrey Jennings celebrated these apparently egalitarian events in a film, *Listen to Britain*, that showed the Queen happily listening to Mozart while surrounded by row after row of 'ordinary' people. The reality was more complicated. Most of those who attended the Hess recitals were bankers on their lunch breaks rather than the celebrated everyday Londoners. Factory employees often reacted badly to the intrusion of classical music, particularly chamber music, into their meal breaks. 'There is increasing evidence that many of the CEMA concerts are failures,' observed one official at the Ministry of Labour.[11] Later in the war, the Entertainments National Service Association (ENSA), paid for by the Ministry of Labour, would offer popular classical performances to supplement its sing-along concert parties. In 1940, however, a gap existed for anyone who could make classical music popular.

Malcolm Sargent failed to anticipate the demands that the war effort would make on him. 'As you will understand, I am not nearly so busy with my ordinary work in the summer months,' he told the BBC talks department that June.[12] He could not have been more wrong. In July a mysterious promoter approached the London Philharmonic Orchestra about a national concert tour. After a great deal of 'cloak and dagger' negotiation, it emerged that the impresario involved was Jack Hylton, one of England's best-known dance band leaders. He wanted the orchestra to undertake a tour of a kind unlike any done before. They would perform twice nightly in musical halls in the large industrial cities, mostly in the north and Midlands. Hylton wanted to rally public spirits but he also wanted to boost the record industry. He had been the best-selling EMI artist of the '78s' period, with the 'Jack Hylton sound' defining popular music for a generation. By 1940 he was looking for new ways to make money as a promoter.[13]

The Second World War would be a boom time for the record industry.[14] During the 1920s, record companies had made huge profits cashing in on the latest dance or music-hall fashions, yet regarded popular music as little more than advertising. The success of the business, they believed, was rooted in producing records of classical music that would provide permanent collections of the great works for successive generations. From the earliest days of radio, experts on records such as Compton Mackenzie and Christopher Stone introduced review programmes that played the latest releases. Stone's Tuesday slot had a huge effect on sales, and record companies lobbied hard to get on air. Stone believed that 'the broadcaster's job is to provide the equivalent of a bath and a change for the tired man's and the tired woman's mind'.[15] His tastes were unashamedly middlebrow and reflected a desire to blur the distinction between classical and popular music. In the 1930s Decca and EMI, both British-run companies, emerged as the most powerful record manufacturers in the world. They were ideally placed to exploit the rise in sales during the War. Best-selling discs were those by radio stars like Hylton, Bing Crosby and Arthur Lewis. Celebrity names guaranteed profits and could ensure the long-term success of a company. When Arthur Lewis created a Decca subsidiary in America and convinced Crosby to sign, he secured the label's future.

Occasionally classical musicians in America, such as Toscanini and Stokowski, crossed over to mass-market fame. They successfully conquered the new broadcasting medium to enjoy an iconic status that translated into prolific sales. Classical music in Britain, however, remained an unexploited commercial opportunity. Jack Hylton had seen a gap in the market-place.[16]

While the three-month tour would offer a financial boost to the LPO, purists were appalled that an orchestra formed in 1932 to be England's elite musical force should be reduced to playing to 'the masses' in variety theatres. Only the obvious morale-boosting effect that the concerts might have on beleaguered urban populations allowed Thomas Russell, the orchestra's manager and a prominent Communist, to claim the 'Blitz Tour' as part of the war effort.[17] Hylton proposed a special set to overcome the acoustical problems of a boxed-in stage. He gave the management of the LPO assurances that the orchestra would not share the 'bill' with any music-hall acts, but was insistent on one point: if the orchestra was to put on a show it needed a conductor with an entertainer's instinct.

Sargent's background with Gilbert and Sullivan and *Hiawatha* made him the obvious choice. 'His svelte figure, incisive manner and conscious showmanship,' observed Russell, made 'audiences feel at once that they are in for a good time.'[18] Sargent thought about more than the music. Even details of lighting and staging interested him. With the war raging, Sargent and the orchestral musicians temporarily put aside their difficult relationship. 'There was still some tension but honestly we were pleased because he was the only famous conductor we could get,' Malcolm Arnold recalls.[19]

On Monday 12 August, just a fortnight after being approached by Jack Hylton, Malcolm Sargent walked on to the stage of the Glasgow Empire to open the Blitz Tour. The previous week he had been summoned to an audience with the Queen, who wished him luck. Pre-war Glasgow had enjoyed a thriving musical life, but when Sargent stepped into the hot auditorium and looked around, it was immediately apparent that this was a more socially diverse audience than usual. Seats had been cheap and, with some costing under a shilling, the Empire was packed. In the audience were workers from Clydebank dockyard who had suffered much during the depression of the 1930s and were now a primary target for German bombing.[20]

Sargent's unashamedly populist programme included short pieces by Berlioz, Tchaikovsky and Sibelius. Thomas Russell found himself astonished at 'the rapt, almost reverent attention' of the audience and believed this to be 'striking proof of the faith I have always had; that music was something for everyone and that its power was in no way restricted to a small coterie of super-sensitive souls'.[21] At the end of a ninety-minute concert the enthusiastic audience cheered and stamped, bringing Sargent back on stage for countless curtain-calls. 'You know, Doc, you're going over real big – George Formby's your only rival,' quipped a stagehand. Sargent was delighted that 'for the first time, hundreds of humble galleryites normally entertained by conjurers, contortionists and red-nosed comedians will listen for an hour to heaven-sent music'. Before the war, classical music had been a privilege; now it had become 'a necessity, a really refreshing food for the ordinary man and woman in the street'.[22] But only, Sargent might justifiably have added, because he knew how to present it.

Sargent's coup also reflected the broadcasting revolution that had swept through Britain after the First World War. The British Broadcasting Company (later Corporation) was formed in 1922 under its General Manager, J.C.W. Reith.[23] In 1923, the first year of broadcasting, there were 125,000 licences in Britain. The number increased to two million in 1926, and three million in 1930, rising to nine million by the outbreak of war in 1939.[24] This amounted to saturation coverage. Reith's own punishing work ethic was matched by a desire to make the BBC a vehicle for national self-improvement. He staffed the company with Oxbridge graduates who radiated an on-air tone of donnish learning worn lightly. Classical music was central to his belief that radio had a role to play in edifying the population. A Music Department, created in 1923, and a Sound Effects Department, established the following year, soon developed a studio technique that enabled engineers to reproduce 'any effect between that of a draped room and that of a cathedral with the full realism of an outside broadcast transmission'.[25] When the Proms faced bankruptcy in 1927, the Corporation took them over and broadcast each concert. The unprecedented step of founding a professional symphony orchestra in 1930 indicated the central role of music at the BBC.

Broadcasting so much music to such a wide audience had a

profound impact on musical appreciation. People who had never been to a concert were introduced to classical music and built up an intimate relationship with their favourite musicians. Sargent had been a fluent, popular radio speaker since 1929, giving regular talks on subjects as diverse as 'twentieth-century composers' and 'how to start a choir or orchestra in your village'.[26] By 1936 the BBC had already identified him as someone who had achieved a 'personality' through broadcasting and was possessed of the 'charm of manner and personal appearance' likely to give him a head start for the new medium of television.[27] During the Blitz Tour, with cheap ticket prices and well-known classics, Sargent utilised those abilities to entertain knowledgeable and dedicated audiences reared on music through broadcasting.

Blitz Tour audiences saw only the flawless presentation of a svelte, carnation-in-buttonhole conductor with his orchestra of seventy musicians in evening dress. Few could imagine the challenges that confronted Sargent and his orchestra. Life on tour for the players was extremely harsh. 'Conditions were absolutely terrible,' remembers Malcolm Arnold. 'We travelled every day and sometimes were away for a whole month. There was great camaraderie and lots of practical jokes but really it was awful.'[28] Each Sunday night they would catch a north-bound sleeper train, huddled together for warmth in unheated carriages with blacked-out windows, on journeys that were long and slow. Arriving early in the morning, the first task was to find somewhere to stay. Accommodation in bombed-out cities was hard to come by, and often players would be forced to sleep on the floor of the band room. Food was always scarce and they rarely managed to eat properly. Factory concerts for CEMA supplemented the two or three concerts at the local theatre.[29]

On Saturday night the exhausted players caught a sleeper train back to London. Arriving around dawn, they would make their way home to their families to sleep. A few hours later, they were back on stage at the Queen's Hall for their Sunday afternoon series. Home afterwards for a brief visit, they would then leave for the railway station to begin the cycle again. Like industrial workers up and down the country, they experienced long hours, meagre rations and miserable nights in air-raid shelters. 'During the winter of 1940–1 with the Blitz at its peak,' records their official historian, 'audiences and players alike found all their physical and mental resources put to the test.'[30]

Malcolm Sargent, classified as a VIP by the War Office, enjoyed privileges that players did without. When in London, he ate at a private club in Orange Street that served black-market eggs, butter and steak, and often joined the fashionable set, sleeping in the Turkish baths of the reinforced-concrete Dorchester Hotel.[31] 'If I can eat well once a week, I can do the work,' he would say.[32] On trains he was always given a sleeping compartment. Cars with uniformed drivers shuttled him between cities. Yet Sargent went wherever the orchestra went and shared the relentlessness of their lives. He told Beecham's secretary of an exhausting schedule that saw him conducting on average more than a concert a day. There was only one missed call during the Blitz Tour, when his car was marooned in a snowdrift on the Yorkshire moors. Sargent's sacrifice was also financial.[33] In contrast to the £115 on offer in Australia, his fee for each of the Hylton concerts was just £20.[34]

Through all the difficulties of war Sargent worked characteristically hard at maintaining his reputation for enthusiasm and elegance – not an easy task when washing powder was limited. Even away from theatres, the image held firm. 'I remember waiting at the railway station for my train home on a foggy day after a wartime concert when I spotted Sargent and the orchestra,' remembers Marjorie Thomas. 'I thought it was too good an opportunity to miss, so I told him that I had been to the concert and asked if he would sign his autograph. Not only did he sign my book but took me round to meet all the orchestra. He must have been exhausted but he made the time.'[35]

The opening night in Glasgow was the first given by Sargent and the London Philharmonic during twelve months from August 1940. In the first ten-week unbroken run, Sargent conducted twice nightly five times a week, with Basil Cameron substituting for him once a week. The orchestra, playing in some of the worst-hit cities, such as London, Birmingham, Liverpool, Sheffield and Manchester, seemed to follow German bombs around the country. The programmes were always accessible. Concert goers who did not like what they heard always seemed willing to say so. 'Play something more cheery,' shouted an Edinburgh woman from the back of the hall after hearing the plaintive slow movement of Dvořák's 'New World' Symphony. 'The next bit *is* more cheery!' Sargent shouted back before launching into the symphony's rumbustious third movement.

Sometimes concerts took place during air-raids and continued until the early hours when the all-clear sounded. Sargent and the orchestra risked their lives playing on while incendiary devices exploded around them and fire-fighters clambered on the roof with hoses, trying to stop flames from spreading to the theatre. 'We played in one town that suffered terrific bombardment after our concert started,' he recalled. 'There was no advance alarm. I announced that anyone who wanted to leave could do so but that we would remain and play something that Hitler could never kill, Beethoven's Seventh [Symphony], and not a person left.'[36]

Sargent's defiance in the face of bombing and destruction captured a popular mood. Box-office takings broke records, and often a third concert at lunchtime had to be scheduled to meet the demand for tickets. 'How shall we explain the queue of more than a hundred people that renews itself all day long at the theatre box-office?' asked one correspondent to the local newspaper.[37] The answer was that Sargent's LPO concerts had become an essential part of the Blitz experience. Even an episode of the BBC's popular wartime soap, *Frontline Family*, took place at a Blitz Tour concert. Sargent himself appeared in cameo, re-enacting a scene when the orchestra played on throughout heavy bombing.[38]

The Blitz involved constant danger for Sargent. On 21 November, conducting the Hallé Orchestra in a Manchester cinema, he warned the audience that such was the ferocity of the bombing that they might not see out the night. Later that year the Free Trade Hall, traditional home to the orchestra, was destroyed. 'I walked down the road to watch the end of one of the greatest concert halls in the world, where I had often sung,' wrote Webster Booth afterwards. 'Among the crowd of watchers I saw Malcolm Sargent, his coat turned up round a white, set face. After so many great triumphs there he had to watch this beastliness of war! I wondered what he felt.'[39]

Sargent had taken over the Hallé Orchestra in 1939 but it was not a happy partnership. The prime mover in Manchester was Philip Godlee, a rude and bullying man who had opposed Sargent's appointment because he wanted a conductor who would live in

Manchester. 'He has many irons in the fire and I doubt whether Manchester would ever be his chief interest,' he told the Executive Committee. 'The conductor of the Hallé Orchestra should not spend half his life in the railway train.'[40]

Sargent had arrived back from Australia to find the Hallé in a state of shambles. The Free Trade Hall had been turned into a war supplies store. The orchestra was reduced to playing in the King's Hall at the Belle Vue amusement park. Yehudi Menuhin remembered arriving to rehearse with Sargent and finding 'that this huge hall had just been vacated by the circus: it smelt very strongly of elephants'.[41] Hallé players were happy to 'double-job' in the BBC Northern Orchestra but when Sargent brought the London Philharmonic to Manchester in 1940 as part of the Blitz Tour, they complained that he was promoting other orchestras. Sargent's 'close connection with and propaganda for the LPO was calculated to damage the interests of the Hallé', they wrote to the Executive Committee, which passed the letter to Sargent with a note indicating that its own sympathies lay with the players.[42] For the next two years, pro- and anti-Sargent factions on the Committee bickered about whether he should be retained. It was no surprise that when David Webster at the Liverpool Philharmonic Orchestra asked Sargent to take over as its principal conductor in 1942, he leapt at the opportunity to leave the Hallé.

The combined flair of Sargent and Webster transformed the fortunes of the Liverpool Philharmonic Orchestra in a matter of months. David Webster was a portly, flamboyant, even louche man. 'He always wore a trilby hat at a rakish angle and smoked a cigar, and liked to think of himself as a latter-day Diaghilev,' remembers Susana Walton. 'Wine and champagne would flow and the artists would feel cared for and could unwind after the anxiety of the performance.'[43] Webster had been general manager at Bon Marché General Stores in Liverpool before the war and would later save Covent Garden from insolvency, transforming it into a world-class company.[44] In 1940 he was persuaded to rescue the Liverpool Philharmonic Society.

His first decision was to keep open the Philharmonic Hall, which ensured that the orchestra avoided the Hallé's embarrassment of sharing venues with elephants. The Philharmonic Hall had been rebuilt in 1939 after the original building was destroyed by fire. The first concert hall to be built with an interior based on scientific acoustical data, it had an unconventional 'megaphone' shape, with the orchestra at the narrow end.[45] In 1942, Webster consolidated the orchestra's position by persuading the Liverpool Corporation to buy the hall, lease it back to the Philharmonic Society free of charge and grant them an annual subsidy of £4,000 in perpetuity. The orchestra's greatest asset among the players was its leader, Henry Holst, who had led the Berlin Philharmonic Orchestra under Wilhelm Furtwängler before emigrating to England in the 1930s. Holst's prestige and contacts enabled Webster to recruit an orchestra to dominate music in the north of England. His most audacious move came when he engaged almost the entire BBC Salon Orchestra after it was disbanded at a month's notice.[46] Webster offered high wages and contracts that guaranteed a weekly salary, with annual holiday entitlement. Armed with civic subsidy, a new hall and salaried musical personnel of high pedigree, David Webster was able to approach Sargent in 1942 confident that he was offering an orchestral force with outstanding potential.

Malcolm Sargent conducted more than a hundred concerts each season with the Liverpool Philharmonic in the following six years. Contemporary works dominated his programmes. He gave the first English performance of Bartok's *Concerto for Orchestra*, regularly conducted Shostakovich and Sibelius symphonies, and frequently included works by living English composers such as Benjamin Britten and William Walton. Sargent and the Liverpool Philharmonic performed more contemporary music than the combined output of all other British orchestras with the exception of the BBC Symphony Orchestra.[47]

Progressive programming was matched by a determination to bring live classical music to Liverpool's industrial working class during the war. The most famous attempt came in Fifteen Popular Orchestral Concerts for the Man in the Street. A Liverpool Holidays at Home committee sponsored the concerts to entertain a civilian workforce that, with wartime travel restrictions, had nowhere to spend vacations. For fifteen consecutive days in the summer of 1944, Sargent conducted concerts at the Philharmonic Hall, blending core repertoire by such diverse composers as Beethoven, Stravinsky and Sibelius. Prices were low, with further discounts for children and those in uniform. Thousands crammed into the hall, with many sitting on the floor. Smoking was allowed during the performances and Spam sandwiches were on sale 'in the foyers from 5.45 p.m. at popular prices'.[48]

By the end of the Second World War, the Liverpool Philharmonic was regarded as the most impressive orchestra in England. Sargent had weeded out sub-standard players and continued to attract musicians from London, not just into principal positions but also to sit in the ranks. Life for tutti string players was made more varied by the introduction of an innovative 'rotation' system that ensured no one was left sitting on the back desk for every concert. There were quarrels with players, particularly those who had come from London and still harboured 'lifeblood' resentment. Sargent always retained his dignity on the podium but afterwards would often retire to David Webster's house to vent his anger and frustration. Webster's impeccable diplomatic skills would always smooth over any difficulties and Sargent did at least attempt to win favour with his players, even paying for the whole orchestra to go to the circus in Blackpool. 'Some of them did try and give Sargent a rough time but it was because he was so very thorough and demanding that they were such a very fine orchestra,' remembered Nancy Evans, who was a soloist at the Man in the Street concerts. 'There were some wonderful players who'd had good solo careers and Sargent made them into a magnificent ensemble that was as good as any in the country.'[49]

Malcolm Sargent's wartime efforts with orchestras on the Blitz Tour and in the Man in the Street concerts were matched by a determination to keep his choirs singing. In Huddersfield, that meant enduring long train journeys to Yorkshire and re-scheduling concerts from Friday evenings to afternoons in order not to break the blackout.[50] In London, matters were more complex. The Battle of Britain and the Blitz had seen the Royal Choral Society almost disbanded in 1940. When Sargent told the committee that he wanted the Society to give its traditional New Year performance of the *Messiah* in 1941, he was told it could not be done. Most of the tenors and basses had been conscripted. Many sopranos and altos had been evacuated to the countryside to avoid the bombing. Even those who remained would be difficult to contact: with so much destruction, it was almost impossible to know where anyone lived. The only chance of getting the choir together would be to put an advertisement in the newspapers, book the hall and hope that enough singers turned up. The advert asked members of the choir to attend a rehearsal in the Queen's Hall at noon on Saturday 4 January, the day of the concert, for a performance at half past two. Three hundred members came and sang scales for an hour. 'You know this work backwards, so take your courage in your hands. I am going to trust you entirely!' Sargent told the choir before sending them off to lunch. The Royal Choral Society repaid his faith. 'Packed house, wonderful performance,' he recorded the following day.[51]

The revived Royal Choral Society provided Sargent's most symbolic performance of the Blitz. On 10 May 1941, the Royal Choral Society and the London Philharmonic Orchestra gathered to rehearse Elgar's *Dream of Gerontius*. Sargent later remembered that 'Hitler was doing his worst as far as London was concerned. We had no choral rehearsal until twelve o'clock that day, but we all knew every note of the work, and the emotional intensity of the situation made an inspired performance inevitable.'[52] London was by now enduring its heaviest period of bombing. One in six Londoners had been made homeless. More than 20,000 had died in twelve months and an additional 25,000 had been wounded. Those who walked down Regent Street to the Queen's Hall that afternoon were badly in need of uplift. The scale of destruction had reached an unprecedented level, and the deprivations of war were beginning to eat away at morale. As the audience gathered, much of the talk comprised a surreal combination of homelessness, rationing and tips on how *The Times* made for more upmarket lavatory paper than the *Daily Herald*. When Sargent emerged into the auditorium he provided a respite from the drudgery of war. Spruce and elegant in crisp white shirt, stiff collar and pressed morning-coat, his appearance was a reminder of pre-war values.

The *Dream of Gerontius* is a work about the transition from death to afterlife. For an hour and a half, an audience of those mourning lost family and friends and each day contemplating their own mortality listened with particular empathy to the priest's prayer for Gerontius: 'By thy Spirit's gracious love, Save him in the day of doom.' Sargent described how 'the hall was packed with people, and as we listened [...] we all felt an uncertain foreboding for the future'.[53] Nancy Evans sang the part of the Angel that day. 'I looked up at that enormous domed ceiling and thought just supposing a bomb hit that,' she remembered.[54]

Hours later, London suffered its worst bombing raid of the war. The tenth of May 1941 was the first anniversary of Churchill becoming Prime Minister: the Germans were determined to give him a night to remember. For five moonlit hours, 300 bombers pounded London with incendiaries and high explosives, killing 1,436 people and injuring 1,792. There were 2,000 fires, and 5,000 houses were destroyed. Every mainline railway station was hit. Westminster Abbey suffered damage, as did the British Museum, the Law Courts, the Mint, the Mansion House and the Tower of London.[55] The debating chamber of the House of Commons was gutted (on which Churchill phlegmatically noted: 'The Huns obligingly chose a time when none of us were there').[56]

In the Queen's Hall, following Sargent's concert, two men – T.J. Evans and Bob Rhodes – were fire-watching. At eleven o'clock they heard the unmistakable thump of an incendiary bomb lodging in the roof. Within seconds, Evans remembered, it sparked and burst into fierce flames 'like an acetylene welding lamp'. The men called the fire brigade who attempted to douse the flames with a fifty-foot hose. Just as they managed to get the fire under control and extinguish the flames, the water ran out. They tried other fire hydrants, to no avail: German bombing had run London's water supplies dry. The flames re-kindled and within half an hour the roof was ablaze. Soon afterwards, burning debris began falling through to the hall on to seats upholstered in highly flammable sorbo. The Queen's Hall became an incinerator, burning out in minutes. Only hours of effort by the fire-fighters managed to save the shell of the building.

James Agate, drama critic for the *Sunday Times*, wrote in his diary the next day: 'Houses of Parliament hit, British Museum also; much more moved by the destruction, all but the wall, of Queen's Hall. This now presents the appearance of a Roman arena, and should be left as a memorial to Hitler.'[57] Cicely Stanhope rushed to the hall that morning and found 'many of those who had played or conducted, there to see their dearly loved hall, some shedding tears'. It was 'a tragic sight'.[58] Sargent made his own visit and wandered amid the rubble. The stage on which he had made his London premiere, conducting *Impressions on a Windy Day*, and enjoyed so many nights of triumph was obliterated.

Sargent was the last man to conduct in the Queen's Hall. 'It is strangely fitting and became prophetic that the last music and poetry heard in that building was what is usually known as the Angel's Farewell,' he reflected. 'The men's voices, as if speaking for a groaning and war-stricken humanity, murmured "Bring us not, Lord, very low. Come back, O Lord, how long," whilst above them the voice of the Angel was singing "farewell but not for ever! Be brave and patient, swiftly shall pass this night of trial here, and I will come and wake thee on the morrow." Then the whole chorus breathed "Amen, Amen". Within a few hours our beloved Queen's Hall met in very truth its night of trial.'[59]

9

Musical Ambassador

The morning after the Queen's Hall bombing, Berta Geissmar, who had been secretary to Wilhelm Furtwängler and Sir Thomas Beecham, walked to Portland Place to survey the damage. Seeing the hall's manager, Charles Taylor, she rushed over to commiserate. 'We shook hands,' recorded Geissmar, 'and although deeply moved, like a true Britisher he did not reveal what this sight must have meant to him personally [but] just said "it looks a bit untidy, doesn't it?" '[1]

Instruments left in the band room after the *Gerontius* performance had been destroyed. That left the London Philharmonic facing an uncertain future. Malcolm Sargent was asked to rally public support. He wrote to *The Times* and appealed on the BBC for spare musical instruments.[2] 'From the moment of that appeal there was no peace,' recorded Geissmar. 'People queued up to the Orchestra's office laden with violins and violas. Cellos were deposited outside the doors. The Orchestra had meanwhile left with borrowed instruments for provincial concerts fixed up long before and wherever they appeared, people turned up with instruments!'[3] In total, the LPO received more than 1,000 musical instruments from the public.

Sargent was able to empathise with those who had suffered during

German bombing, as 'my London house has been completely blasted'.[4] All his belongings, including letters, diaries and papers, were destroyed. Fortunately, music scores and band parts were in Winslow, Buckinghamshire, where his evacuated family lived before a move to Kent.[5] Sargent was forced to rent a small studio flat near Victoria Station. It was in a dark and airless basement with a fold-up bed in the living room and an open kitchen. A secretary worked in the cramped hallway. For the rest of the war, gloomy Chesham Place provided a base while he shuttled around the country's bombed-out cities. 'He really believed himself to be under an obligation,' says Peter Sargent. 'He was not asked to fight and so he wanted to pull his weight. That's why he worked so hard. Even when he was not conducting, he went out as air-raid warden and helped with the fires.'[6]

One night, Sargent and his son were sent to the top of a building to deal with devices on the roof. 'I was terrified,' remembers Peter, 'but he just got on with his job, kicking the things off. Nothing like that seemed to frighten him.' Sometimes after concerts Sargent would visit public shelters to talk to people in sleeping bags and organise informal choruses of 'Rule Britannia'. He was patriotic by nature but his conspicuous bravery during the Blitz provided an opportunity to right a self-perceived wrong. Having been shattered when declared unfit for duty in 1916, Sargent felt somehow cheated in not making it to France with the Durham Light Infantry in 1918. Guilt at surviving the Great War and a sense of debt to the dead were common in Sargent's generation. Harold Macmillan, who fought in the war and was just a year older than the conductor, summed up this attitude when he observed that those who remained had a duty to 'make some decent use of the life that had been spared'.[7]

'Sargent was a great man, there is no doubt about that, a great conductor, the only one here during the Second World War,' suggests Beecham's agent Victor Hochhauser.[8] Declared by Toscanini before the war already to be an esteemed maestro, Sargent showed other noble characteristics during the conflict itself: bravery, a sense of duty, and the ability to use art to transcend despair. The conflict had presented all conductors with similar patriotic and moral choices. Some behaved better than others.

Sir Henry Wood, seventy when war broke out, continued

performing in London. He kept the Proms going, assisted by Basil Cameron and, in 1942, gave the first English performance of Shostakovich's great battle symphony, the 'Leningrad'. Sir Hamilton Harty conducted occasional concerts until mid–1940 despite being diagnosed with a brain tumour.[9] Constant Lambert evacuated the Sadler's Wells ballet to Cardiff and took the company on regular provincial tours until the end of the war.[10] Sir Adrian Boult had not volunteered for active service during the Great War, taking a job in the War Office, but joined the Home Guard – 'Dad's Army' – in the Second World War.[11] He helped move the BBC Symphony Orchestra to Bristol and Bedford, although, according to William Haley, who became Director-General of the BBC in 1944, it went 'completely to pieces [because] Boult didn't like rehearsing very much anyway'.[12]

These conductors were brave to remain in England. The record of others during this international crisis was less distinguished. John Barbirolli had volunteered for service with the Royal Suffolk Regiment in 1917 but like Sargent did not see action. On 29 August 1939, six days before Britain declared war on Germany, he sailed for America to fulfil his contract as Musical Director of the New York Philharmonic. He later said that he went because the orchestra had threatened to sue him for 'thousands of dollars' if he refused. His contract ended in the spring of 1940 but he signed a new one rather than return to England. Hence Barbirolli missed the Battle of Britain and the Blitz. 'I don't know what's going to happen to me if I don't get back to England and see what's happening for myself,' he observed in the spring of 1942 when the Blitz was over.[13] Friendship with A.V. Alexander, a member of Churchill's cabinet, secured his passage across the Atlantic and he stayed for two months to conduct concerts as 'just a little offering'. He returned to America on a banana boat only to find that he had effectively been sacked. Barbirolli's seven-year tenure as Musical Director of the New York Philharmonic had been a tormented one in which he had failed to convince players, critics or audiences that he was a worthy successor to Toscanini.[14] Now their patience had worn out; Artur Rodzinski would replace him from the beginning of the 1943–4 season. Worse was to come: by virtue of his residency in New York, Barbirolli was told that he might expect to be drafted into the United States Army.

'Fine,' he replied, 'I shall be seeing England again.'[15] He returned
home in June 1943 and took up an appointment as conductor of the
Hallé Orchestra.

While Barbirolli's behaviour during the war was ambiguous, that
of Sir Thomas Beecham and Albert Coates was cowardly. Coates
sailed for America at the outbreak of hostilities with Germany and
spent most of the war conducting at the Hollywood Bowl.[16]
Beecham left as soon as the 'Phoney War' ended and did not return
until late 1944 when it was clear the Allies would win. 'It was an
emergency, so I emerged,' he later joked. He spent much of the war
working with second-rate orchestras in the United States of America
and Australia. He had abandoned the London Philharmonic
Orchestra for those he complained 'can only be called an orchestra
by courtesy'. Succeeding the lack-lustre Basil Cameron as conductor
of the Seattle Symphony Orchestra while Cameron himself was on
the Blitz Tour with Sargent and helping Henry Wood at the Proms
completed his humiliation.

Beecham's sudden exit became the butt of public and orchestral
jokes. 'There was tremendous resentment in the LPO against
Beecham who took all the money and did not even let us know
where he was when he had gone,' says Malcolm Arnold. 'I suppose
that made the orchestra more sympathetic towards Sargent because
he stayed.'[17] Adrian Boult recalled turning up at the Queen's Hall
during an air-raid on 30 August 1940 to find Cameron conducting
an impromptu performance of Haydn's 'Farewell' symphony during
which someone impersonated the departing, portly Beecham.[18] The
ultimate irony came on Sunday afternoons in the Queen's Hall: with
Sir Thomas away, Harold Holt and the London Philharmonic
Orchestra continued to present the Beecham Sunday Concerts.

Sargent by 1941 was a well-known figure who for thousands had
come to personify classical music. Three days after the Queen's Hall
bombing he received a letter that would see him transformed from a
minor celebrity to among the most famous men in the British
Empire. The letter, from Howard Thomas, producer of the BBC's
Any Questions?, seemed innocuous enough. Sargent was invited to
join regular panellists at Maida Vale studios on 27 June to record a
radio discussion on questions sent in by BBC listeners. No audience
would be present; Sargent need only speak when he wanted and

there would be no preview of the questions until recording began. The panellists would meet for lunch beforehand at the Hotel Russell in Bloomsbury.[19]

This offer initiated a regular association with *Any Questions?*, later the *Brains Trust*, that would last throughout the war. Donald McCullough, the former spokesman at the Ministry of Agriculture who acted as question master (a term first coined on the show), chaired the waspish discussions. Three panellists were permanent members: Julian Huxley, secretary of the Zoological Society of London; Dr Joad, the popular philosopher; and a retired naval officer, Commander Campbell. Two guests joined them for each programme. Questions ranged from the profound – 'What is civilisation?' 'Should the Empire continue after the war?' – to the ridiculous – 'Why nod your head for yes and shake it for no?' 'Why do women always have cold knees?' Witty, argumentative and often outrageous replies to questions made it an instant hit.

The success of the *Brains Trust* was due at least in part to the fact that the BBC was a national broadcaster speaking to a remarkably united people. The novelist George Orwell remained in London during the Blitz and believed the BBC revealed 'the soundness and homogeneity of England'.[20] John Reith, convinced that the Corporation was central to 'making the nation one man', had pushed it to consolidate a sense of national identity with a calendar of broadcasting that celebrated shared experience.[21] Special programmes aired not just at Christmas and Easter but also on national saints' days, Burns' Night, at the FA and Scottish cup finals, the Derby, the Boat Race, test match cricket, the Lord Mayor's Banquet and the Ceremony of the Keys from the Tower of London. From 1932 onwards, families everywhere took lunch on Christmas Day only after listening to a broadcast by the King.[22]

The *Brains Trust*, first broadcast in January 1941, aired throughout Britain and to the armed services across the world. It soon became the pre-eminent national forum for high-minded debate and witty banter. By April, with a prime-time slot on Sunday evenings, it attracted an audience of almost thirteen million. In 1943, heard by thirty per cent of the adult population, the *Brains Trust* received over 4,000 letters a week. Only *Monday Night at Eight*, a weekly light-entertainment revue, was more popular. BBC Listener Research found that the audience for *Brains Trust* was 'easily the greatest for any regular spoken word programme, other than the News'.[23]

Sargent sparkled from the outset on the *Brains Trust*. He had spent his life preparing for such an opportunity. He was a star of the rostrum but his progress had always involved more than just musical ability. He had glittered at public speaking engagements and private parties for years. Of London's elite clubs the Beefsteak was his favourite because 'you have to defend your head with your tongue'.[24] It was a maxim he applied to life. Quick-witted, opinionated and funny, he had enjoyed since the Melton days a confidence to express forthright views in even the most elevated company. Sargent was not an intellectual, but endless hours spent travelling had afforded time for books. He read mostly non-fiction, particularly on politics, science and religion. He supplemented this with a genuine interest in understanding how things worked; on one occasion he spent almost an hour in the street talking about London's sewers to someone who had popped up from a manhole.[25] Sargent required a certain courage to trust in his verbal and mental dexterity in front of an audience of millions. The countless possibilities for making a fool of himself were obvious. Luckily, he had never lacked self-confidence.

'I do hope you will be able to join us on the nineteenth,' Howard Thomas wrote to him shortly after his first appearance, 'particularly in view of the great success of the programme in which you previously took part.'[26] Another acclaimed outing in September led to more invitations, including a recording on 15 December that was broadcast on Christmas Day. By spring 1942, Sargent was appearing every fortnight. His success was down to a willingness to engage on any subject and provide a lively answer.[27] To the question, for example, 'The man who cuts my hair addresses me as sir, but presumably doesn't call the dustman sir, so am I worth more than the dustman?' Sargent replied: 'I'm all for levelling up politeness – but not impoliteness. It's very convenient for the hairdresser to say sir to anybody who sits in his chair, because he probably doesn't know his name or occupation. He's not in any case going to say Mr Dustman or Mr Solicitor. I'd say when the hairdresser is dressing the dustman's hair he calls the dustman sir and when the dustman is collecting the hairdresser's rubbish, he calls the hairdresser sir.'

Events often showed Sargent's common-sense answers to be more perspicacious than expert opinion. For example, he told Emmanuel Shinwell, who became Minister of Fuel and Power in the 1945 Labour government, that nationalisation would lead to 'endless subsidy'. On other topical questions, Sargent could be provocative. Asked in 1945 if it was possible to re-educate the Japanese and bring them back into the community of nations, he said: 'You can educate fleas to perform quite decently in public. You can educate cats and dogs to be house-trained. I am certain that human beings, the Japanese – if you could get fundamentally at their religion, at their philosophy, you'd make a whole difference. If we can't educate them, then obviously what we do is use lots of atomic bombs, because there's no sense in keeping a race alive who could be a menace in a world which we've got to improve, if we could not believe they would eventually become more decent people.' This reply prompted a deluge of letters to the BBC, some outraged and others supportive. 'I knew why he said that but nobody else did,' says Peter Sargent. 'I had just gone into the Fleet Air Arm – the "Suicide Club" – and he thought I was going to get killed in the Pacific. That's why he said it.'[28]

Listener research showed Sargent's most popular answers were on morality and faith. A typical answer came when asked what attributes he would bestow on a newborn baby. 'There are three things I would be brave enough to ask for,' he said. 'One is simple kindliness, the real art of loving one's neighbour as oneself. Another is a sense of humour, which means placing a relative value on oneself, so that even in one's greatest tragedy there's still something that makes one smile. The third thing is the first thing, really: the gift of faith, ordinary Christian faith. I've discovered that people who have it – there's nothing really in this world that can really affect them at all.'[29]

To a people at war, these homespun truths provided much comfort. Sargent was one of the *Brains Trust*'s best-loved performers, second only to Julian Huxley in popularity with listeners.[30] Howard Thomas later told how he was present when Sargent realised the extent to which his fame had spread. He was walking with the conductor one evening when a grubby-looking girl approached them with an autograph book. 'You Dr Sargent?' she demanded. Sargent smiled and nodded. '*The* Dr Sargent?' she asked sceptically.

He nodded again. 'The Dr Sargent of the *Brains Trust*?' she persisted. He nodded for a third time. 'All right, I'll have your autograph then.'[31] The *Brains Trust* had propelled Malcolm Sargent further into stardom.

With celebrity came trappings including the opportunity to augment an already crowded love life, which put further strain on his rocky marriage. Long tours, the complication of wartime travel and Eileen's evacuation with the children made getting home difficult. Air-raids and the continual destruction by bombing often made it hard to be sure where anyone was at any given time; confusion that played into the hands of a serial philanderer. Assignations were easy to arrange, as Sargent found to his delight that fame encouraged women of all ages to throw themselves at him. 'He rarely turned down an offer and was almost like a machine,' says Peter Sargent. 'Of course, he was inclined to let young girls think that they meant more to him than they actually did.'[32] Curiously, few showed much resentment. Sargent's lovers rarely complained. Even most one-night stands ended amicably. Well-practised in the art, Sargent seemed at least to give physical satisfaction if not emotional guarantees. There were, however, occasional complications when precautions failed. If confronted about paternity, Sargent was cold-blooded. 'The lady concerned is making up the story,' he told a woman from Manchester who claimed that her son was a Sargent.[33] Peter Sargent nevertheless discreetly acknowledged other illegitimate children, whose mothers were often family friends.[34]

Sargent's continuing infidelity sent Eileen spiralling into collapse. 'If Pamela had not been ill the marriage would have struggled on, but as the unfaithfulness became worse the pressure was too much,' says Peter Sargent.[35] In 1942, Eileen finally broke. 'She was examined by a nerve specialist who told me (but did not tell her) that she was suffering from cyclothynia (hysterical, extravagant behaviour, at times leading to physical violence),' Sargent wrote. 'He informed me that he knew these attacks had been frequent in the past, and he gave me [no] hope that they would not occur often in the future.'[36]

The family had moved into part of Knole House, the seat in Kent of the Sackvilles. On Sargent's rare visits home Eileen was scathing about his affairs and even chased him out of the house throwing a steady stream of crockery. Peter and Pamela clung together in their rooms while the arguments raged, unable to comprehend the ferocity of their parents' hatred. Sargent later recounted how 'my daughter at the height of her illness entirely on her own initiative wrote to Lord Horder asking him to take her away from her mother. He told me this was to be done if Pamela's recovery was to be made more sure, and he told me that if I valued my nervous balance I should also separate myself as much as possible from my wife.'[37] 'Actually what was distressing Pamela more was seeing my father coming into the room and my mother getting into a state and having to leave,' says Peter.[38]

On the day that husband and wife decided to part, Sargent seized the initiative. He went immediately to Pamela's room, where Peter sat at her bedside. 'You both have a choice to make but I must point out that if you stay with me I can assure you that you will have butter on your bread,' he told them, and marched out before either could answer. 'Pamela and I looked at each other in horror because it was not what we wanted to hear,' remembers Peter. 'It put us in a terrible position because poor Pam needed so much money spent that we had no choice but to stay with him. He showed a cruel streak and neither of us ever forgot.'[39] Within two hours Sargent and the children had left. Peter soon changed his mind and lived with his mother during Eton vacations.[40] Pamela never saw her again.

Since the Sargents' separation went unreported, it failed to dent the conductor's public image. The *Brains Trust*, broadcast throughout the Empire, had made Sargent a valuable propaganda asset. Having rallied popular spirits at home during the Blitz, in the autumn of 1942 he was called upon to 'show the flag' for the British Council, and was soon dubbed by the press the 'ambassador with a baton'. The British Council had been created in 1934 to counteract the problems caused by the emergence of Nazism on the continent. During the war, it became an instrument of propaganda against 'German cultural penetration'.[41]

The Council was relieved when Sargent accepted the invitation, because few musicians were prepared to endanger themselves. Earlier in the year, Sir Adrian Boult had declined to represent the British Council overseas.[42] On this first trip Sargent was given just twenty-four hours' notice of departure. He cancelled performances with the Hallé and Liverpool Philharmonic orchestras without explanation and caught a train from London to Edinburgh on 4 November. Sargent left from a remote airfield on a Mosquito bomber that took him on an unaccompanied journey over German-occupied Norway to Sweden. He was put face-down into the bomb-rack and watched the ground in terror on take-off and landing. 'They wanted to prove that civilians could get to Sweden without being shot down,' Sargent would later recall. 'People kept whistling "Land of Hope and Glory" in the street and the players of the Swedish Radio Orchestra did "V for Victory" signs under their stands.'[43] His programmes on that and later trips (and also on visits to Portugal) contained a strong English element including works by Walton, Britten and Vaughan Williams. Tickets for his three concerts were sold out. At the Konsertförening, the Crown Prince in the royal box joined the standing ovation. Away from the concert hall, Sargent spent long days at meetings, lectures, cocktail parties and dinners in a diplomatic effort to raise Britain's profile. 'If one considers the hundreds of people who attended his lecture to the Swedish-British Society, the thousands of people who listened to his public concert and the tens of thousands of people who must have listened to his radio concert, it is probable that Dr Sargent must be reckoned to be the most successful visitor the British Council has yet sent out to Sweden,' reported the Council's representative. 'Quite apart from his astonishing success as a conductor Dr Sargent made himself personally most popular by his charm of manner, witty after-dinner speeches and the impression of energy and vitality which he created.'[44] Sargent left on 26 November. The British Minister Plenipotentiary concluded that 'It is not an exaggeration to say that the visit was the best piece of cultural propaganda which we have achieved in Sweden since the outbreak of the war.'[45]

On his return to England it was clear that Sargent had grasped the importance of his role. 'I don't think even yet that enough money is being spent on English music compared with what is being spent by the Germans . . . who visit Sweden regularly, and in this respect British propaganda is weak,' he told reporters.[46] Sargent's trips to neutral countries brought him into direct contact with the enemy in its musical incarnation. Wilhelm Furtwängler, Artistic Director of the Berlin Philharmonic Orchestra, collaborated with Hitler because 'I felt responsible for German music, and it was my task to help it survive this crisis.'[47] Furtwängler's mastery of Beethoven, Brahms,

Bruckner and Wagner, Hitler's favourite composers, ensured that he was the only conductor to enjoy the Führer's unqualified approval.[48]

On 25 November 1942, Sargent attended a concert in Stockholm at which Furtwängler conducted the Swedish Radio Orchestra. Catching sight of Sargent in the audience, the naïve German conductor sent a note during the interval asking to meet afterwards, which the Englishman courteously declined. Furtwängler immediately dispatched another note assuring him that he was not a Nazi. 'I had always admired you as a man and musician but now I only admire you as a musician,' came back Sargent's cutting reply.[49] In his more reserved English fashion, Sargent had echoed the sentiments of Toscanini that 'Everyone who conducts in the Third Reich is a Nazi.'[50] To add to the German's discomfort, 'Without doubt the applause which Dr Sargent received in Stockholm was considerably warmer than that at Dr Furtwängler's first concert,' observed a gleeful British Council representative.[51]

The German government recognised that culture was important to the propaganda war. Furtwängler was sent to Lisbon in January 1942 to follow immediately a Sargent concert series. When Sargent returned to Stockholm in September 1943, he discovered that the Germans had upped the ante by dispatching not just Furtwängler but the entire Berlin Philharmonic Orchestra to follow him.[52] During a later trip, Sargent found himself at a formal reception with Herbert von Karajan, the Austrian conductor. Karajan had been a member of the Nazi Party since at least 1935. A protégé of Reichsmarshal Hermann Göring, he had conducted throughout the German occupied territories.[53] Karajan now delivered a personal threat to Sargent: 'When the Führer gets to London, you'll be shot.' 'Thank you,' replied Sargent. 'How gratifying to be on the wanted list of the SS.'[54]

Even as Karajan spoke, the war had turned decisively in favour of the Allies. The Red Army had won a titanic battle at Stalingrad and Anglo-American forces landed in Italy. This was the beginning of a general offensive that would see Allied ground troops push towards Berlin from east and west while bomber aircraft reduced German cities to rubble. The terminal phase of the war in Europe, the Siege of Berlin, began on 20 April 1945 and resulted in the surrender of Germany three weeks later. On 30 April, Hitler committed suicide with Soviet troops only 200 yards from his bunker. During these weeks of destruction and ultimate victory, Malcolm Sargent, celebrating his fiftieth birthday, made a recording that distilled his wartime experience.

Buoyed by a recent visit to America to conduct the NBC Symphony Orchestra at the behest of Toscanini, Sargent went to Huddersfield that April to record Elgar's *The Dream of Gerontius*.[55] He had loved *Gerontius* ever since Dr Keeton at Peterborough flung the score at him with the words: 'You can have this. I can't make head nor tail of it.'[56] When he first heard the work, conducted by Thomas Armstrong's father in Peterborough Cathedral, he told his friend: 'I'm going to be a composer; I am going to be a second Elgar.'[57] Sargent had first conducted the work in 1922 in Leicester with the Melton Mowbray Choral Society, and after the leader of the orchestra had written to Elgar, the composer invited Sargent to meet to discuss the score. 'We spent the morning and the afternoon with *Gerontius*,' Sargent later remembered, 'he playing the piano and singing, or tapping my shoulder while I played, going through every bar with the greatest care, pointing out to me every little difficulty in performance, or interrupting to recall some incident which occurred when he was composing it.'[58]

That day initiated a friendship that would last until the composer's death in 1934: 'From the first moment of our meeting we were obviously friends with an accepted mutual understanding,' Sargent later wrote.[59] Elgar proposed Sargent for membership of the Beefsteak, saying, 'We ought to have another musician to follow me.'[60] Sargent championed Elgar's music during the 1920s and 1930s when it was deeply unfashionable. 'Many things have been written of Elgar's character,' he once said, 'but to anyone who knew him or had eyes to see the real Elgar, both in his music and in himself, Elgar was a mystic.'[61]

Sargent had a strong personal reason for giving so much of himself to the recording of *Gerontius*: he would dedicate it to his daughter. 'My father absolutely worshipped Pammy and could not do enough,' remembers her brother, Peter. 'She adored him although – I never told him this – she was a little frightened of him.'[62] Pamela was a naturally cheerful girl and throughout her illness tried her best to resume a normal life. She persuaded Sargent after the split with

Eileen to send her to Hartland Abbey, country outpost in Devon of the famous 'Monkey Club' finishing school for girls. For two years she seemed to rally and was integrated into the life of the school. In early 1944 she had a relapse and doctors told Sargent his daughter would be dead within the year.

The next months were appallingly difficult. Pamela became increasingly frail and often seemed close to death. 'How I envy you,' Sargent told the composer Herbert Howells, whose own son had died of polio. 'Mick died after three days; Pamela is in the seventh year of her suffering.'[63] Sargent gave instructions to his son and staff that he be informed immediately should his daughter die. On 22 May, he was performing with the Royal Choral Society in the Albert Hall while Peter entertained his father's guests in his box, loggia 21. During the first half, while Sargent was conducting Brahms's *'Haydn' Variations*, there was a discreet knock at the door. An Albert Hall official entered and told Peter: 'I am very sorry, sir, but Miss Sargent has passed away.' When Malcolm Sargent came off stage, he found his ashen-faced son waiting for him with the news. He collected himself and walked on stage to conduct *The Dream of Gerontius* as a poignant memorial to his beloved daughter. After the performance, Peter was waiting for him. 'Papa, there's been a terrible mistake,' he said, 'Pammy is not dead.' The following morning at the clinic, to her amusement, Sargent showed his daughter the first and second editions of newspapers that carried the reports and subsequent retractions of her demise.

Pamela's life force gradually slipped away during the next months. Sargent spent hours at her bedside, catching sleeper trains before and after concerts so that he might sit with her in the day, playing the piano, reading or just holding hands. While genuinely moved by his daughter's plight, Sargent also discovered a hitherto unseen guilt. The combination of his hedonistic lifestyle and demanding work schedule had left no time for family life. His marriage was finished, the relationship with Peter tense, and his daughter dying: whichever way he looked at it, Sargent's personal life was a mess. 'Malcolm never really forgave himself for his failure as a parent,' remembers his god-daughter, Lilias Sheepshanks. 'That's why he was so devoted while she was dying.'[64] Sargent began to seek comfort by attending church. He avoided Sunday services, at which he would have been on show, preferring instead to slip into Brompton Oratory or St Stephen's, Gloucester Road, during the week.

Sargent poured his fears into music with a new orchestration of Brahms's *Four Serious Songs*. These songs of meditation on death range in mood from bitterness to a sense of the nobility of God. Sargent made this arrangement for Kathleen Ferrier, who would also die at an early age. Discovered by Sargent, Ferrier believed that he wove much of his personal tragedy into the orchestrations. The third song, 'O Death, How Bitter', she found almost impossible to sing without choking emotion.[65] Marjorie Thomas, who often performed the songs with Sargent after the war, knew that he 'was thinking of his daughter when he wrote it'.[66] Ferrier gave the first BBC broadcast of the *Four Serious Songs* in August 1944, while Nancy Evans sang the first live performance at a Man in the Street concert in Liverpool. 'I remember that concert so well because his daughter was dying,' Evans recalled. 'Sargent was moved and so was I. Tears were streaming down his face while we were doing it. It was heartbreaking to see such emotion in a man who was usually so controlled.'[67]

On Monday 14 August Peter Sargent drove his father down to Hartland Abbey. Sargent had taken the unusual step of cancelling all concerts for the week. Half a mile from the school Peter pulled the car into a lay-by so that his father could drive up to the house himself. Pamela was bedridden and clearly had only days to live. Sargent decided immediately to take her away alone for a few days, ignoring medical advice that she should not be moved. 'Everyone criticised him for it, saying he had made her worse but the one thing she really wanted was to be alone with her daddy for one last time,' recalls Lilias Sheepshanks.[68] Father and daughter returned to Hartland for a few more days during which Sargent hardly left her bedside. As he prepared to leave on Saturday evening Pamela said to him: 'I do so miss dancing: will you put on a waltz and dance with me?' Sargent held his daughter in his arms, lifted her from the bed and they danced. 'He held her off the floor, of course, but to my amazement she actually moved her legs and danced,' remembers Peter. 'She used all her remaining strength to have that dying wish.'[69]

Four days later, on 23 August 1944, Pamela Sargent died. Sargent was conducting in Leicester when he received the news. He travelled back to London by train to be met by Anne Chapman, his secretary. 'Pamela's dead, all is lost,' he told her.[70] Pamela was buried at Hartland Abbey where she had been so happy in her last years. 'Her death was the greatest tragedy of his life,' says Peter Sargent. 'I don't think he ever recovered emotionally.'[71]

Because *The Dream of Gerontius* was Pamela's favourite work, Sargent was determined that his recording in April 1945 would be a fitting testament. The British Council sponsored this HMV recording, which was the first complete performance of *Gerontius* set down on disc.[72] The Council was keen to record the work for its propaganda benefits, aware that 'it has a far wider recognition than any other [English] work produced in the last fifty years on the continent' and 'has a special appeal in Roman Catholic countries'.[73]

Sargent was the obvious choice to conduct the work, but Walter Legge at EMI had other plans. Legge was, in his own words, 'the Pope of recording' and perhaps the outstanding producer of his generation.[74] After the war he became close to German artists with Nazi sympathies, particularly Elisabeth Schwarzkopf (who became his second wife) and Herbert von Karajan. Myopic, badly co-ordinated and overweight, with a cigarette perpetually in the corner of his mouth, Legge was the antithesis of Sargent's elegance and loathed him. Writing to his friend Beecham in San Francisco at the height of the Blitz, he reported characteristically that 'for their [Hylton] music-hall concerts the LPO are quite appropriately in the charge of Flash Harry'.[75] Legge attempted everything possible to convince the British Council to engage Boult, who he argued had 'intense vitality, sensitiveness and [a] deep understanding of Elgar's mind'.[76]

Against him stood William Walton, a committee member, who insisted that 'it should be done as soon as possible with Malcolm S, the Liv Phil and Hudd choir'.[77] Ernest Makower, Chairman of the Music Panel, who believed that Sargent had the more famous name and choral expertise, settled the matter.[78] 'I am not prepared to reopen the question,' he wrote in September 1944.[79] Legge grudgingly agreed that 'if your Music Committee is of the view that this choice of Orchestra and Conductor is final our only remaining job is to make records of the work as good as possible with those forces'.[80]

The role of Gerontius was taken by Heddle Nash, perhaps its finest exponent. 'Heddle Nash was a truly great singer,' remembers Nancy Evans, Legge's first wife. 'He had so much flair and just loved singing. It was a beautiful sound – breathtaking, in fact.'[81] Elgar had written to Nash in 1930 that 'I hope to hear you sing *Gerontius* some day.' When he did the following year, the composer wrote on his score: 'Many thanks to Heddle Nash★ Edward Elgar, Croydon, 10 November 1931 (★ Good).'[82] Nash was an instinctive singer whose beauty of tone had a searching quality ideal for *Gerontius*. 'One Three Choirs festival performance of *Gerontius* will stay with me all my life,' remembered Isobel Baillie. 'I sat in the back stalls, the entire length of the cathedral away, and heard a truly inspired performance. I have only to close my eyes to hear his highly individual voice ringing out in the *Sanctus fortis* or achieving an exquisite pianissimo in "I went to sleep". His recording of *Gerontius* should be studied by all students of singing.'[83]

Gladys Ripley, Dennis Noble and Norman Walker joined Nash for the recording. Behind them stood the Huddersfield Choral Society. Unlike choirs such as the Royal Choral, many of the Society's men had not gone abroad because they worked in important reserved professions such as coal mining. Huddersfield had been chosen by Walton in 1943 to make the first recording of *Belshazzar's Feast*. 'If the choir can see their way to help, they will be doing a great service to me personally, and to British music in general in showing what a wonderful choir they are,' he wrote beforehand.[84] Shortly after the end of the war, the *Daily Telegraph* proclaimed the choir as 'undoubtedly the finest choral instrument in Britain. It has the precision and elasticity of a great orchestra and its tone is as extraordinary in dynamic range as its quality is beautiful.'[85]

For five days in April 1945, Sargent worked from ten o'clock in the morning until ten o'clock at night to record *Gerontius*. Choral sections were sung in the evenings to facilitate those singers only available after work. Passages for soloists and orchestra were recorded during the mornings. Afternoons were spent in the recording van with Walter Legge working on technical details. Hugh Maguire, who later led the BBC Symphony Orchestra, remembers that 'Sargent was very good at making records. He was very smart and paid great attention to getting the cut absolutely right; people forget that making records is a mechanical as well as musical business.'[86] The combination of technical proficiency and emotional intensity produced a recording that ranks as Sargent's finest. *Gramophone* in 1999 judged it in the top seventy-five recordings ever made.[87]

EMI immediately recognised in Sargent a winning commercial artist. The success of *Gerontius* prompted a contract offer to record a major choral work each year with the Huddersfield Choral Society and the Liverpool Philharmonic.[88] The first recording of this new contract did not disappoint. They recorded a spectacular *Messiah* in just four days in July 1946 under the demanding conditions of post-war austerity.[89] Isobel Baillie, the soprano soloist, remembered the exhaustion of recording all her solos in one day. 'I can still picture myself now, standing on the stage and singing out into the empty hall as if it were full of people,' she recalled. 'If ever I put my heart into anything it was that recording.'[90] Sargent felt the same and could hardly contain his glee when the recording was a best-seller: '83,000 sold in a few weeks,' he boasted.[91] Within six months of release, 120,000 sets had been sold: Sargent was confirmed as England's best-loved conductor. Few were surprised when his name appeared in the King's Birthday Honours list in 1947. Dr Sargent was to become Sir Malcolm.

10

Knight Errant

On the morning of Tuesday 8 July 1947, Malcolm Sargent surveyed himself in the mirror as he prepared to leave for his investiture as a Knight Bachelor at Buckingham Palace. Oliver, his new valet who was on a month's trial, had dressed him. Looking himself up and down in black morning coat, moleskin hat and yellow chamois gloves, Sargent had a rare moment of self-doubt. 'This is ridiculous – I look like a damn bank clerk,' said the boy from Wharf Road to his reflection. 'A bank *director*, Sir Malcolm,' purred Oliver smoothly, brushing fluff from the shoulders of his master's jacket. 'You've got the job!' laughed Sargent and left for his appointment with the King.[1]

The employment of a manservant was one of many changes that Sargent introduced that year. He had received news of his knighthood at a rather seedy apartment in Brompton Square referred to only half-jokingly as 'my hovel'. It was another dark basement flat with a small upright piano, bed and desk, and a spare fold-up bed in the damp hallway where Peter had slept when on leave. 'Although he loved other people's lifestyles with town houses, places in the country and all that, he didn't seek it for himself and could not really afford it,' remembers Peter Sargent. 'But then Edwina took hold of him and moved him into Albert Hall Mansions.'[2]

Edwina was married to 'Dickie' Mountbatten, the King's cousin. Her great wealth came from the estate of her grandfather, Sir Ernest Cassel, confidant of Edward VII. The combination of Lord Mountbatten's royal but penniless lineage and her money made them one of the smartest couples in English society. During the hedonistic 1920s Lady Mountbatten had won notoriety in elite circles for behaviour that saw her labelled a nymphomaniac. It was said that the butler at their Park Lane house 'would be hard put to keep "Hugh", "Laddie" and "Bunny" unaware of each other's presence when the three happened to call simultaneously'.[3] Her most infamous relationship was with the cabaret singer Hutch for whom she had commissioned from Cartier a jewelled phallic sheath.[4]

Edwina met Sargent in 1941; by the end of the war they had become occasional lovers (although he was given only cuff-links). 'Who couldn't love her?' asks Peter Sargent, who often stayed at Broadlands, the Mountbattens' Hampshire home. 'She had the most terrific charisma. My father and Edwina were obviously attracted to each other in every way, I am sure. I don't think Dickie worried too much. He was accustomed to the fact that Edwina was attractive and attracted to other people.'[5]

By 1947, Lord Mountbatten was an extremely powerful man. His left-wing sympathies had been known for many years – 'I'm Socialist but I think my butler votes for you,' he was reputed to have told a Tory canvasser who called at his house – and after Labour's crushing election victory in 1945 he was appointed Viceroy of India to oversee the difficult task of British withdrawal. Mountbatten disliked Sargent, finding him too smooth, but tolerated the conductor to appease his wife. He left for Asia with Edwina in March 1947, having, at her behest, advised the Prime Minister that Sargent deserved a knighthood for his war work. When the knighthood was announced, Lady Mountbatten insisted that Sargent's dignity and reputation demanded more salubrious living quarters than a dingy flat. She found him an apartment opposite the Royal Albert Hall and had it furnished. Persian carpets, mahogany tables, china, silver, paintings and golden-thread armchairs were taken from Broadlands to Albert Hall Mansions, where they remained until Sargent's death.[6]

No. IX Albert Hall Mansions had the elegance and gentlemanly air that London society expected of a man of Sir Malcolm Sargent's stature. The Mansions had been built off Kensington Gore in 1879 to accommodate the well-to-do when land for houses ran out in London's smartest areas, (defined as 'within a short cab ride of Piccadilly'). The architect, Norman Shaw, designed these mansion flats in red brick with Dutch motifs and built them as high as the regulations would allow. Inside, wood, brass and plasterwork abounded. The main staircase dominated the entrance, but most visitors to No. IX took the coffin-like lift. The apartment was a duplex, with a double-height hallway, winding staircase and stained-glass skylight. The public rooms were on the lower level, with stairs that led to private quarters and a panelled study. The apartment enjoyed wonderful views of Hyde Park and the Royal Albert Hall. The music room was large enough to house, at last, a grand piano. Secretarial staff had their own office. A small staff flat accommodated Oliver. 'No one ever went in there,' remembers a secretary. 'When Oliver finally retired, we had to burn every-thing!'[7]

For the next twenty years, whenever Sargent was photographed at home in Albert Hall Mansions, he always seemed to exude such an air of confirmed bachelordom that many assumed he had never married. When he had moved there in 1947, he arrived not as a bachelor but a divorcee. On 25 February 1946, Eileen Sargent had been granted a divorce on the grounds of her husband's desertion. After his investiture in July 1947, Sargent had posed with Laurence Olivier for photographers outside Buckingham Palace, the first divorcees to be knighted by the King.

Sargent, enjoying fame but not fortune, remained a punishingly busy conductor. A glance at any of his diaries shows continuous months of work with barely a day off. 'Eventually it would become so ridiculous that I would mark in a day's holiday in an indecipherable scrawl and say nothing until it was too late for him to change it,' remembers a member of his staff.[8] Occasional young conducting assistants such as Maurice Miles, who in turn taught Sir Simon Rattle, helped ease the strain. The burden of organising this hectic timetable rested with the secretaries. 'The stress of their work was enormous,' recalls Peter Sargent. 'He demanded a hundred per cent all the time and was a very hard taskmaster. He was a martinet and he knew it.'[9]

Sargent had employed typists for most of the 1930s but the first secretary to take on the complicated task of running his life after the marital breakdown was Anne Chapman. Sargent had arrived back from Portugal in January 1943 to find that his temporary secretary had left, able neither to organise his complex diary nor tolerate working in the cramped hallway of the Chesham Place flat. When Sargent put the key into the door of the apartment, letters were piled so high that he had to shoulder-barge his way in.

Sargent immediately telephoned friends in desperation to see if they might recommend a secretary. Anne Chapman, 'attractive, charming and well spoken', arrived the next day.[10] She had never worked before and Sargent gave her quick tests in shorthand and typing. 'Congratulations,' he told her. 'When do I start?' she asked. 'Take a letter,' he replied. Chapman stayed until early 1947 when the intensity of their working relationship saw her leave 'before I have a nervous breakdown'.[11] She understood his demand for total dedication, which she had provided for more than four years before burning out. The woman who replaced her had an even closer working relationship. Sylvia Darley ran Malcolm Sargent's life for two decades and, in the words of Sargent's executor, 'knows everything'.[12]

Sylvia Darley's relationship with Sargent did not get off to a good start. One dreary May morning, he sat waiting to interview a prospective secretary, who was late. A friend had recommended the girl, then working in an art gallery in Bond Street, who wanted to be secretary to a musician (if possible, Sir Adrian Boult). When the doorbell rang twenty minutes later, an indignant Sargent answered the door to a woman drenched by rain. The bus had broken down, leaving her to run all the way. 'Why do you want the job, anyway?' Sargent asked her. 'Free concert tickets,' she replied. He laughed and told her: 'The job's yours. Here's my diary. I'm off to a rehearsal.'[13]

Sylvia Darley was a striking twenty-one-year-old with flame-red hair. She had been in the WRNS during the war and had a self-possession that came from tours of duty in Norway, India and Australia. Her slim, almost waif-like figure and delicate bone structure combined to make her a quintessential English rose. This gracefulness captivated the English painter Anthony Devas, who painted five portraits of her during the 1950s. She was pursued by countless admirers but from 1947 devoted her life to 'the Maestro' and never married. 'Sylvia certainly had a love for Malcolm and I know that he loved her,' says Lilias Sheepshanks, who observed her over many years.[14] Sargent quickly became possessive about this new secretary and on more than one occasion warned off suitors. Friends urged him to marry Sylvia, but his sense of propriety always got in the way. Having already married a girl in service, it somehow did not seem quite 'the done thing' for Sir Malcolm now to wed his secretary. He guarded against loose talk by delegating his son to take her out for 'petty cash' lunches, fearing that 'if I am seen people are bound to gossip'.[15]

For twenty years, Sylvia Darley ran Sargent's life with military attention to detail. 'Oh dear, here comes Nanny!' he would cry if he had disrupted the day's schedule.[16] No two days were the same but many were alike. Oliver called Sargent at half past seven and served him a cooked breakfast in bed (the only meal the conductor ate with enthusiasm). He would take a bath (with Hughie the budgerigar) and dress either in a Harrow jacket with formal striped trousers or a Hogg and Johnstone pinstripe suit. Sylvia, having arrived shortly after eight, would be waiting at the bottom of the stairs at nine to secure the red carnation into his buttonhole. A car would be standing by at the front door to take them to rehearsal. Sargent read his letters on the journey and 'always got cross that I could not take shorthand in the car because it made me sick'.[17] If a rehearsal began at ten o'clock he would arrive at a quarter to the hour, Sylvia walking two paces behind, to spend a few moments with the orchestral management.

At precisely three minutes before ten, Sargent would enter the rehearsal room. Clasping the leader's hand in a firm lock, he might utter some pleasantries about 'how delighted' he was to work again with 'this splendid orchestra'. He would remove his coat and pass it to Sylvia, who in turn gave him the black alpaca jacket he habitually wore for rehearsing. The carnation was removed and placed in a small glass of water. Sargent would say a few words of greeting to the orchestra before lifting his baton to begin. When the rehearsal came to its conclusion, Sylvia immediately reappeared at his shoulder. Off came the smoking-jacket to be replaced by his morning-coat. The red carnation was restored to its buttonhole. One or two section principals might be invited to join Sargent for lunch at London Zoo. 'They buy the best possible food for the animals – no tinned food for them,' he told them. 'The Fellows get what's left.'[18]

Later Sylvia would collect Sargent and drive him back to No. IX. In the afternoon he might look at scores and catnap for a couple of hours. Oliver always woke him at half past five for an egg flip. Changed into full evening dress with white carnation, Sargent left for that night's concert to arrive with half an hour to spare. If it was the Royal Albert Hall, having ensured that everything was order, Sylvia would be responsible for organising Sargent's private box. Guests went afterwards to the Green Room to see Sargent and then over the road for drinks or supper. 'He always said "join us for a drink" but however grand they were I always excused myself,' recalls Sylvia. 'It was midnight by the time I'd finished and I had to get to bed sometime.'[19]

Working in the office with Sylvia Darley was a succession of invariably well-bred assistant secretaries. 'It was great fun but very, very pressured,' remembers Lady de Zulueta, who was an assistant during the early fifties. 'He worked so incredibly hard – sometimes too much so. Sylvia would say to him "you ought to have a day to rest" but she rarely took a day off herself.'[20] Assistant secretaries would type letters, answer the telephone and organise scores. After concerts they would be called into service at supper, much to the amusement of guests. 'It was bizarre,' says Kenneth Rose, the *Sunday Telegraph*'s diary columnist. 'All these high-born girls – a Waldegrave, the Bowes-Lyons, Sylvia, Venetia Fane, Marie-Louise de Zulueta – that he had working for him never sat down to supper but just brought in the drinks. I mean they were called Librarian and that sort of thing but in the evening they were his waitresses.'[21]

If it was odd that scores of 'high-born girls' were serving the drinks at supper parties, it was less surprising that others were considerably closer to Sargent.[22] As his celebrity grew during the forties, what Sargent euphemistically called his 'social list' came to read like a copy of *Debrett's Guide to the Peerage*. Cousins of the Queen, duchesses, countesses and ladies-in-waiting fell before him. He would take them to supper at the Savoy Grill after concerts and whisk them off for holidays in the sun. 'We were taken along as the married couple to make the whole thing "proper",' recalls Robin Sheepshanks of a holiday with Sargent and Diana Bowes-Lyon in Bermuda.[23]

Sargent's advances were not always welcomed. It was known in London society that certain families would not receive 'the Maestro' after unfortunate incidents involving women of the house. On one occasion, a peer threatened Sargent with a horsewhipping when it was discovered that he had seduced the man's under-age daughter.[24] Occasionally, Sargent could be persistent. 'After rehearsals I often drove Malcolm back to his flat near the Albert Hall,' recorded Susana Walton. 'On the way I had to fend off the advances of this incorrigible womaniser, who insisted on fumbling under my skirt, by steering with one hand and determinedly but politely removing his hand when it went beyond my knee.'[25] Whatever the truth of her allegations – 'They are nonsense,' says Sylvia Darley. 'Susana Walton was not to Sir Malcolm's tastes'[26] – their plausibility lies in the fact that similar tales of Sargent's advances are legion. As Robin Sheepshanks pithily observes: 'Malcolm always had his hand up some girl's skirt.'

Sargent's attraction to blue-blooded women often drew accusations of snobbery. 'Yes, they are social climbers, aren't they,' he would riposte.[27] Even friends thought that his attitude to royalty came too close to sycophancy. 'I think the Royal Family considered him a little flash – the nickname – that's how they regarded him,' recalls Kenneth Rose. He noted in his diary a revealing detail at IX Albert Hall Mansions: 'Malcolm's Christmas cards. All from the Royal Family. There are only two spaces left, so he fills one with the Duke of Buccleuch and the other with the Earl of Dalkeith.'[28]

Sargent's upwardly mobile tastes certainly account for a number of his relationships. 'Obbie', Countess Fitzwilliam, was an ordinary-looking woman who enjoyed a reputation for promiscuity. 'If she had not had a title he would not have been so keen,' suggests Peter Sargent.[29] Her heavy social programme ensured occasional hiccups, such as the time when father and son arrived at the Ritz, where she kept a permanent suite, to find her *in flagrante delicto*. 'Another time, perhaps,' Sargent observed coolly and headed for the door.[30]

His most elevated social conquest was Princess Marina, dowager Duchess of Kent, who, like Edwina Mountbatten, favoured both Sargent and Hutch. The conductor was a regular guest at Iver and rarely missed an opportunity for a flamboyant gesture. On one occasion he arrived wearing goggles and flying leathers in a Tiger Moth piloted by his son, who performed aerial acrobatics over the beautiful formal gardens. Sargent's affair with Princess Marina was well known in London society. As patron of the Royal Choral Society she was a frequent visitor to the Royal Albert Hall for his concerts. Neville Marriner, then Principal Second Violin in the London Symphony Orchestra, recalls mischievously complimenting Sargent on a rather grand pair of cuff-links. 'Sshh, they were given to me by a princess,' he whispered back.[31] Peter Sargent was 'never very happy about Marina but my father's awareness of behaviour at court means that any seduction must have come from her. Even he would not have chanced his arm there.'[32]

Malcolm Sargent's reputation as a lady's man was common knowledge, but there were other rumours. Gossip abounded, more by association than verifiable evidence, that Sargent was as likely to find his hand in a man's trousers as up a woman's skirt. 'I know it has been said that my father was bisexual, which was a shock because he was the most heterosexual man I ever met and I've been defending him for it ever since, but it is just "what the butler saw",' says Peter Sargent. 'Mountbatten's valet said that Mountbatten and my father were bisexual and Edwina, my father and Mountbatten were lovers.'[33] Sargent's friendship with the Earl and other prominent figures of questionable sexuality, including Bob Boothby and Bernard Montgomery, laid him open to enquiries about his own preferences. He was certainly sensitive to the scandal of homosexuality, which remained illegal. In 1953 at the Haymarket Theatre he would refuse to meet Sir John Gielgud, recently arrested in a Chelsea public lavatory whilst 'persistently importuning male persons for immoral purposes', telling Dame Sybil Thorndike that 'I don't think I can; you see, I mix with royalty.'[34]

There is no evidence in Sargent's private papers of homosexual liaisons. None of his many male friends have spoken of or even implied physical intimacy. 'I spent many late nights at Albert Hall Mansions talking into the early hours,' says a contemporary who was propositioned by Noel Coward (but politely declined) and might reasonably therefore have expected a similar invitation from Sargent. 'There was no hint that anything other than friendship was on offer.'[35] The same could not be said of the many women whose names appear alone against the frequent entry in Sargent's diary: 'Supper, 10 p.m.'[36]

11

Olympian

Thursday 29 July 1948 brought blazing sunshine and sultry heat. Malcolm Sargent sat in the Royal Box at Wembley Stadium exchanging pleasantries with other VIPs including Stamford's Lord Burghley. The roof of the grandstand provided some shade from the searing sun, but with temperatures close to 30°C it was a day better spent in the garden than at work. Sargent was dressed in morning coat underneath the cream silk gown and purple hood of Durham University (chosen ahead of the honorary Oxford doctoral robes to which he had been entitled since 1942).[1] Below, on Wembley's 'hallowed turf', two guardsmen, resplendent in bearskins and scarlet tunics, marched to the Royal Box and presented arms. Sargent stood, bowed to the King, and was escorted to the middle of the pitch. There he mounted a rostrum to face a choir of 3,000 voices and the massed bands of the Grenadier Guards. Sargent lifted his baton and led the crowd in a stirring rendition of the National Anthem. This was the ceremonial opening of the Olympic Games. To those watching him harnessing such vast forces at Wembley that day, Sargent must have seemed like a man standing on the Olympian heights.

The official opening of the Olympic Games was, in fact, quite trying for Sargent. Roasting like a chestnut in his heavy clothes, he was confronted by a choir that could not hear itself sing and a band whose instruments had gone out of tune in the hot sun. Having been marched to the podium under the eyes of many thousands, he discovered that his son had dropped his baton and sent him scurrying back towards the Royal Box to find it. After Quilter's setting of Kipling's *Non nobis domine*, Sargent remarkably led the crowd in the 'Hallelujah' chorus. 'What's it like conducting a crowd in such a vast arena?' he was asked in the Royal Box afterwards. 'Like taking a jellyfish for a walk on an elastic lead,' Sargent replied.[2] Yet whatever difficulties he encountered that day, he conducted with customary panache and gave the occasion the visual spectacle it demanded. Malcolm Sargent was a man at the peak of his powers: knighted for his services to music and his country, a celebrity of national and international proportions recognised far beyond classical music's boundaries, and acknowledged as the finest choral conductor in the world.

That same year Sargent was honoured by his home town. He returned in triumph to Stamford to be granted the freedom of the borough. The ceremony in the hall at his old school 'was carried through with all the pageantry of a more gracious age', observed the *Stamfordian*.[3] The Town Council in full array passed a unanimous motion conferring the honour on Sargent, and the Mayor presented him with a casket containing the scroll of Freedom. After the ceremony, Sargent conducted Parry's festal song *England* with the Stamford Choral and Orchestral Society. Watching from the front row was his childhood piano teacher, Frances Tinkler. She stood with tears in her eyes applauding her protégé. When Sargent climbed off his rostrum and embraced her, it drew the biggest cheer of the night. Her prediction forty years earlier that 'one day he'll be a knight' had been fulfilled.

Sargent's happy homecoming was recognition that 'their boy' was now the most popular conductor in England. He could fill 10,000 seats on successive nights at such unlikely venues as the Haringey Arena, where other conductors might attract only hundreds.[4] It came as no surprise when the BBC asked him to conduct at the most successful music festival in the world, the Promenade Concerts: only in the fact that the invitation was so late in coming. When Sir Henry

Wood had died in 1944, the BBC had snubbed Sargent in favour of Adrian Boult. Jessie Wood, Sir Henry's widow, had been furious. 'If it is a fact that our dear ones are always with us, then what must [Henry's] sorrow be now, and how he will grieve for the foolishness which besets these people to render to shreds the edifice he has helped to build in this strange old country,' she wrote to Sargent in 1945. 'We shall always remember that Henry said many years ago that you could follow him, if you would.'[5]

Sargent made an immediate impact at his first Prom season in 1947. 'Sir Malcolm has made, in our opinion, a brilliant debut in the Proms,' wrote K.A. Wright, acting Director of Music.[6] Even Adrian Boult, an unhappy rival, admitted that Sargent's energy and boundless enthusiasm were precisely what a Proms audience needed. Sargent himself was delighted at the enthusiastic reception he was given by the Promenaders. 'I shall always remember it as one of the happiest seasons of music that I have been fortunate enough to take part in,' he wrote afterwards.[7]

Henry Wood and Robert Newman, manager of the Queen's Hall, had founded the Promenade Season in 1895. Previously once the concert season closed for the summer, there had been no music in London. This meant the recently built Queen's Hall went unused for two months of the year; idleness threatened its financial viability. The Proms filled the gap in the concert programme to make use of the empty hall during its fallow period from late July to early September. Tickets were cheap and costs were kept to a minimum by engaging the orchestra for only one rehearsal on the day of the concert. After Newman's death in 1926, the BBC took over responsibility for the concerts, and from 1931 used its own symphony orchestra. The destruction of the Queen's Hall in May 1941 saw the concerts transferred to the much bigger Royal Albert Hall, where they attracted huge wartime audiences. Following Wood's death, the BBC Symphony Orchestra's Chief Conductor, Sir Adrian Boult, also became Chief Conductor of the BBC Henry Wood Promenade Concerts.

The Proms provided music-making for those who could not otherwise afford to attend concerts. Through them all music-lovers had the opportunity to attend concerts during the otherwise barren summer period. The problem, however, was that Promenade concerts were not very good. Sir Edward Heath, later British Prime Minister, was Organ Scholar at Balliol College, Oxford, during the thirties. 'I went to the Proms before the war and they were pretty poor,' he remembers. 'I used to cycle from Broadstairs and stay in London for the week, going to a Prom each night. Sir Henry Wood was kind enough to let me sit at the back of the hall for rehearsals, which were always very rushed and at the evening concert they often did things unrehearsed.'[8]

When Adrian Boult became Chief Conductor of the Proms, he sought to introduce a 'fundamental overhaul' by engaging assistant conductors and other London orchestras to spread the workload. Yet Boult never warmed to the Proms concept, and his lack of enthusiasm showed on the podium. 'I like at least several days to prepare an important performance and I cannot help feeling that nightly work of this kind is in danger of becoming very superficial,' he wrote. 'This applies to the orchestra, which, as a rule, gets only one single rehearsal for everything it does.'[9] By 1946 he was desperate to offload this commitment. 'This is not only an absurd situation,' he told the BBC, 'it is dishonest, for the slipshod nature of our performances cannot be understood by most of that young audience, and even our professional critics seem to assume that we have three rehearsals for every concert.'[10] Boult suggested engaging Sargent for the 1947 season and pushed for his appointment as Chief Conductor of the Proms in 1948.

This was no act of generosity. Adrian Boult disliked Sargent so much that he even tried to have him removed as a guest conductor of the BBC Symphony Orchestra during the war.[11] 'There was real hostility there and he was no friend of Malcolm's,' remembers Sir Neville Marriner. 'Celebrity sells tickets and influences newspapers which Malcolm could do in a way that Boult could not. The *Brains Trust* made Malcolm more famous than Adrian, who was ostensibly the prime figure in English music-making, and quite frankly it stuck in his throat.'[12] Boult gave Sargent the Proms because he viewed them with contempt. This vengeful deed proved another tactical blunder. In 1947 the BBC had begun televising the Last Night of the Proms; presiding over these annual festivities made Sargent the most recognisable musical figure in England. Just as the *Brains Trust* had given him fame through radio, so the Proms made him a television star.

The BBC had broadcast a television service between 1936 and 1939 to 23,000 people living near London's Alexandra Palace. In 1946 television broadcasting was resumed with new transmitters, so that after ten years almost the entire population was within range. Radio was quickly eclipsed. In 1947, radio's primetime programmes reached thirty-five per cent of the population; within twenty years that had collapsed to just four per cent. The crossover year was 1955, when radio and television both enjoyed a fifteen per cent audience share.[13] The 1954 Television Act challenged the virtual monopoly of the BBC. An Independent Television Authority watched over ITV stations, which were organised regionally not nationally. A golden age of wireless was over and the Reithian concept of 'making the nation one man' declined.

Classical concerts did not translate easily from radio to television. The Sound Effects unit for a radio broadcast had been able to reproduce the sense of a concert hall even if the performance was taking place in a recording studio. Listeners at home could without difficulty imagine themselves at the Royal Albert Hall or Covent Garden because their own sense of aural and spatial awareness coincided with that of the broadcast. With television this was impossible. Whatever the quality of sound, concerts broadcast on television had an audio-visual conflict that was impossible to correct. The passive TV viewer could never achieve what for the radio listener seemed easy: a genuinely interactive sense of being present at a concert. Producers often struggled to find interesting shots to fill out a full concert programme. The BBC, in particular, was reluctant to follow the example set by NBC, which concentrated almost entirely on Toscanini's face and upper body throughout broadcasts.[14]

Television also took away much of the mystique of concerts by showing the mechanics of performance, including musicians sweating under the powerful lights required for broadcasting. 'Malcolm said that he had always sweated heartily on his conductor's rostrum but the long-distance camera with its close-ups had added a new terror,' recorded the journalist Collin Brooks in his diary. 'You know how the eyebrows channel the sweat so that a drop forms on the nose, than which nothing is more revolting,' Sargent told him. 'I invented a way of seeming to wipe my forehead lightly which enabled me to wipe my nose with my thumb – but the cameras have stopped that.'[15]

The Last Night of the Proms was the one concert that successfully made the transition from radio to television. Sargent understood that the new medium required spectacle and introduced a greater emphasis on audience participation, including his own dazzling arrangement of 'Rule Britannia'. Pictures of young Promenaders stamping, cheering and singing with patriotic fervour, coupled with Sargent's stage presence and witty speeches, made the Last Night tremendous viewing. He quickly established these end-of-term festivities as part of the national annual television diary, joining events such as the FA Cup Final and the monarch's Christmas message.[16]

The Last Night was not alone in enjoying an overhaul. Sir Edward Heath remembers that 'from the beginning Sargent's Proms were remarkable. He increased the variety without getting away from the Prom shape. They were significantly better under Sargent.'[17] Where Boult had been unable to adapt his languid style to a punishing Proms schedule, Sargent excelled. 'When he was doing the Proms they had not reached the luxurious stage of three rehearsals for every concert,' says Sir Neville Marriner. 'Malcolm was getting through an awful lot of repertoire on a three-hour rehearsal. He was meticulous and you knew exactly what was expected. That was a great virtue.'[18] At the end of the 1948 Proms, the BBC's Director of Home Broadcasting, Basil Nicolls, wrote of his impression that the symphony orchestra was settling down and beginning to play really well again under Sargent.[19] EMI was enjoying massive sales of *Messiah* and *Elijah*, and was delighted by the further publicity that the Proms brought. 'From first to last the concerts seem to have met with quite unusual appreciation and I am sure that this is largely due to your personal skill and enthusiasm,' wrote Brenchley Mittell, head of recording at EMI, to Sargent. 'Long may it continue!'[20]

Sargent's first season in charge of the Proms had brought plaudits but little in the way of financial reward. The BBC, it seemed, was generous with praise but less enthusiastic about paying him well. As Sargent resumed his life of hotel rooms and sleeper trains, it began to rankle that he did not seem to be getting enough money for his efforts. When in autumn 1948 the BBC invited him to conduct ten winter Proms (which each had the luxury of two rather than one rehearsal) and offered an insultingly low fee of fifty guineas per concert, his patience snapped. 'I do not enjoy discussing money matters over the lunch table, and I frankly hated our last meeting with its usual business angle of "you suggest one thing, I'll suggest another and we will split the difference"!' Sargent told Bill Streeton, BBC Head of Programme Contracts. 'I think it is more straight-forward if for the winter proms I tell you definitely what I wish my fee to be, believing this will not seriously incommode the finances of the BBC, nor be in any way unreasonable.'[21] His request was for a sum of seventy-five guineas per concert. When Streeton countered with an offer of sixty-five guineas, Sargent decided to be intransigent. 'I am sorry to be firm but this is quite definitely my fee and if you do not approve of it, I am asking you to make other plans for the winter Proms, and will be grateful if you will let me know as soon as possible.'[22]

Unable to sacrifice Sargent's obvious box-office pull, the BBC capitulated, but with such bad grace that a nasty row broke out. Streeton sent Sargent a churlish letter agreeing to the fee but noted that he had done so only because time would not allow him to find a replacement. He then provocatively offered a lower fee – sixty-five guineas per concert – for the summer Proms and stated explicitly that if Sargent felt unable to accept these terms, the BBC would feel obliged to make other arrangements.[23]

'Before making the obvious reply to this letter, I am writing to ask you if this really is an official letter from the BBC,' Sargent wrote to Basil Nicolls, going over Streeton's head, and finally releasing years of resentment. 'Always the fee paid has been lower than that I have been getting from other concert organisations of an established financial position and considerably less than fees given to other conductors of your BBC Symphony concerts whom, in all modesty, I feel to be of more or less equal public appeal, i.e. box-office draw.'[24] Nicolls immediately apologised for the unnecessarily belligerent tone of Streeton's letter, which did not reflect the BBC's attitude to Sargent. Would he be prepared to regard the letter as not having been written? 'So happy to receive your letter,' Sargent replied. 'May our pleasant relationship continue.'[25] The civility of Nicolls's corre-spondence was in marked contrast to the scorching dressing-down given to Streeton for issuing an ultimatum to the 'mainstay conductor' of the Proms.[26] To appease Sargent further, the BBC offered a concert fee of eighty guineas.[27]

Sargent's concern that he was being underpaid in England was not paranoia. His pre-war fees in Australia had been handsome and by 1949 he was in a position to negotiate a tour to South America that would see him paid more than 300 guineas per concert.[28] In comparison, his desultory English fees were often considerably below those of less popular conductors. Although commercially successful for those who employed him, Sargent was not a well-paid artist. The BBC's list of conductors' fees for 1948 shows the disparity: 'Victor de Sabata, 185gns; Sir Thomas Beecham, 175gns; Sir John Barbirolli, 150gns; Rafael Kubelik, 100gns; Albert Wolff, 95gns; Ernest Ansermet, 80gns; Sir Malcolm Sargent, 65gns; Basil Cameron, 35gns and Constant Lambert, 35gns.'[29] These fees paled in comparison to the $3,334 per concert that NBC gave Toscanini, the $1,000 given to Serge Koussevitzky in Boston or the $500 to Eugene Ormandy in Philadelphia. Yet the figures illustrate that each time Sir Thomas Beecham or Sir John Barbirolli stood in front of the BBC Symphony Orchestra, they were paid at least two and a half times more than Sargent for their efforts.[30]

Sargent's poor pay shows a foolish business sense. Impresario Victor Hochhauser remembers that if he wanted Sargent to conduct a concert, he would simply telephone Albert Hall Mansions. 'I would speak to Sylvia because Sargent did not have an agent,' he recalls. 'He had his office and knew all the concerts people, so Sylvia did it and he kept the ten per cent!'[31] Although Sylvia Darley would often sign letters to contracts departments 'S. Darley, Manager' and ran his daily affairs, she could not give the kind of financial advice that Hochhauser might give Beecham.

Being a cheapskate cost Sargent money. His market price as a conductor, slashed during the war, failed afterwards to rise in line with his eminence or box-office appeal. A good agent would have told him that something was amiss and organised his diary to secure fewer concerts for more money, just as Kenneth Crickmore did for Barbirolli with the Hallé Orchestra in 1948. 'My father always said, "I am worth what people will pay me", and so undersold himself for years,' says Peter Sargent. 'An agent would have sorted him out but he would not hear of it. He thought it was somehow demeaning.'[32]

Sargent often found it difficult to say 'no' to poorly paid work from an innate sense of loyalty to the institutions which had supported him during tuberculosis. Organisations such as the Royal Choral Society, Huddersfield Choral Society, Leeds Philharmonic Chorus and Liverpool Welsh Choral Union had underpaid him for years. Between 1946 and 1965, for example, Sargent conducted ten or eleven concerts each season for the Royal Choral Society, which paid him just £40 for each performance.[33] He worked with these groups out of affection and because he understood that his small fee was not a result of meanness but an attempt to balance books at a time when radio and television had eaten into concert audiences. Sargent never wavered in his commitment to them, but after 1948 he also gave renewed attention to lucrative foreign tours that might help maintain the lifestyle demanded by his status.

Sargent's reputation as the 'ambassador with a baton' was never higher than in the immediate post-war years. His heroic efforts during the Second World War had given him an important profile abroad. '[A] better representative of British musical life . . . could not possibly have been found,' wrote an EMI representative from Copenhagen in October 1948, expressing a view that was echoed round the world.[34] Sargent had turned down many well-paid tours during the war due to his 'many commitments in this country'.[35] Afterwards, so many invitations flooded in that some had to be refused. 'It must have been irksome to hear that Malcolm Sargent could not make it after all,' wrote the British Council to the British Political Mission in Hungary in 1946. 'He is a very busy person and between the time we laid our plans and your confirmatory cable he had got himself signed up elsewhere.'[36] Between June 1948 and June 1950, Sargent undertook tours of South Africa, Denmark, Norway, Spain, Portugal, Switzerland, Austria, Gibraltar, Italy, Greece, Argentina, Chile, Uruguay and Brazil, some of which lasted more than two months.

Even Britain's new Cold War opponent paid Sargent the back-handed compliment of harassing him. Travelling through the Soviet-occupied zone of Austria on his way to conduct both the Vienna Philharmonic and Symphony orchestras, Sargent was woken by Russian soldiers in the middle of the night, taken off the train and held for alleged 'irregularities' in travel documents.[37] When released, Sargent was made to walk with his luggage through deep snow across a temporary Danube bridge to the American sector. 'It is very important that there should be no ill-feelings about it,' he told reporters afterwards, although it did not stop questions being asked in the House of Commons about the matter.[38] Other inconveniences at border controls were self-inflicted. On receiving his knighthood, he had enthusiastically scratched out 'Dr Malcolm Sargent' in his passport and inked in 'Sir Malcolm Sargent', only to find himself detained for an hour by officials at London Airport for defacing a legal document.[39] Sargent's Viennese concerts inspired acclaim. 'Malcolm Sargent is not only one of the greatest English conductors, he is counted among the few international musical leaders,' wrote one critic. 'The Vienna Philharmonic made music from real enthusiasm which made the "goodbye" to Dr Sargent very hard. We have only one wish, that he should come again soon.'[40]

Another European trip gave Sargent a prestigious debut with the orchestra at La Scala, Milan. He conducted the opening performance of the Symphony Concert Season in October 1949 to become the first English conductor of the orchestra in its own theatre. Sargent's trip to Rome the previous year had been a sensation, causing severe embarrassment to Adrian Boult, whose own visit had been such a flop that the ambassador complained about him to the British Council.[41] Sargent began provocatively at La Scala with the first performance of Elgar's *Cockaigne*, which went down well, and finished with another premiere, Sibelius's First Symphony, which did not. 'At the end they all started walking out and it looked as if I wasn't going to have a call,' he recalled. The showman in him rallied. 'I decided to deal with the situation. Instead of going off through the wings, I halted among the last fiddle desks and came back. This set off clapping among a handful. I walked back to the wings and came back again. More clapping, this time a bit louder and longer. It was heard by people out in the corridors and foyer. "Ah, a success!" they thought. "We must be in on this!" and back they came. At the finish I got something like an ovation but they didn't understand Sibelius.'[42]

Sargent's triumphant visits to South Africa and South America matched in popular enthusiasm his pre-war trips to Australia. He had first visited South Africa in 1946 to conduct the inaugural season of the Johannesburg City Orchestra. 'I want people to go away from this concert feeling they have enjoyed a wonderful spiritual experience,' he had told players, but he achieved results with the newly formed ensemble by hard work and his usual attention to precision. 'Believe it or not, we all had more energy at the finish than when we began,' said a violinist after the first rehearsal.[43]

Johannesburg in the 1940s, at the heart of the system that would become apartheid, lacked the sophistication of Cape Town or Durban. At this opening concert, the all-white audience crammed into the City Hall while their black chauffeurs mingled outside. The only opportunity that members of the black community had to hear the orchestra was if they happened to be cleaners scrubbing the floors at the hall. Amid the crackling of sweet papers and the fug of cigarette smoke, Sargent and the City Orchestra gave a performance that won a standing ovation. He had hatched yet another orchestra. 'It has turned out to be a songbird of no mean proportions,' he said.[44]

On his return to South Africa in June 1948, Sargent conducted five concerts to universal acclaim. Before leaving England he had been concerned that Beecham, who was conducting in South Africa in August, might get star billing. 'Sir Malcolm has received letters from friends in Johannesburg complaining there is no publicity for his concerts but any amount for another conductor later on,' complained Sylvia Darley to Johannesburg City Hall.[45] Sargent need not have worried. 'If all the great conductors now living had brought the combined Vienna Philharmonic, London Philharmonic and Philadelphia orchestras to Johannesburg, the praise in some quarters could not have been more effusive,' observed the music critic of the Johannesburg *Star*.[46] Concerts all sold out and programmes of his usual blend drew popular approval. 'You are a charming people,' observed Sargent with a trace of irony at Victoria Falls shortly before his departure. 'A stranger feels he is welcome and appreciated here and forgiven his differences of behaviour and speech. That is not always so, even in our Commonwealth of Nations.'[47]

The conductor's South African success was eclipsed in South America: a two-month tour that perfectly illustrates the phenomenon of the ambassador with a baton. He left London on 8 May 1950, the fifth anniversary of VE Day, and did not return until 14 July. He was not a man much given to recording his thoughts in a diary, but this tour is a rare, instructive exception. He flew to the Argentine capital, Buenos Aires, which he found 'very hot and noisy', for concerts at the magnificent Teatro Colón.[48] The schedule of rehearsals and performances might have been designed for a man of Sargent's temperament. Rehearsals, of which there were six for each concert, and performances took place from half past nine in the evening until half past midnight. Sargent did not get back to his residence until almost two o'clock each morning and even then stayed up 'talking with F'.[49] Frances Balfour was wife of Sir Jock Balfour, British Ambassador to Argentina, and a long-term friend. The Balfours had been active in initiating Sargent's visit and Frances travelled with him often during the tour.[50]

Sargent's timetable was packed with music, parties, official visits and press conferences. His first meeting with the press was 'a very happy conference' but provoked some tough questioning about the main work of the tour: Ralph Vaughan Williams's Sixth Symphony. This work, written between 1944 and 1947, and often described as a war symphony, is the composer's symphonic masterpiece. 'Here we have the complete testament of a man who, in his seventies, looks back on the human sufferings of his time,' Sargent told the Argentine press. 'I never conduct the Sixth without feeling that I am walking across bomb sites; chaos, despair, desolation and the peace that flows from desolation.'[51] Surely such a work was beyond the comprehension of a Buenos Aires audience which had no experience of such things? asked a journalist. 'A city which can't understand the Sixth Symphony of Vaughan Williams deserves to be bombed,' Sargent answered, adding that he was confident that Buenos Aires would grasp the message easily enough. 'British Council delighted,' he recorded in his diary.[52] The country's Fascist 'Líder', Juan Perón, was less impressed and the comments led to Sargent not being paid, 'thanks to Evita Perón, I hear'.[53]

If Sargent's observations irritated the Perón regime, they did nothing to dim public enthusiasm for his concerts. 'The Colón concert was an outstanding success – orchestra, audience and press being enthusiastic,' he recorded, a popular triumph gratifyingly witnessed by an eminent rival. 'Furtwängler visited me during the interval. A fantastic success – the traffic had to be stopped in the streets afterwards.'[54] Sargent's concerts had been sold initially at a much lower rate than those of the German, but 'after my first rehearsal they raised the price of tickets and after my second rehearsal raised the prices again', Sargent noted proudly.[55] He conducted four concerts in Argentina, the last of which saw 4,000 people packed into a giant cinema to hear music by Beethoven and Walton. Afterwards crowds thronged in the streets and lined Sargent's departure route for more than a mile, throwing flowers at the conductor's snail-paced car. Sargent left Buenos Aires for Montevideo on 22 May without his concert fees but confident that he had made both a political and a musical impression in Argentina's capital.

His reception in Uruguay was just as enthusiastic. 'No sooner had he reached the robust climax of this work [*The Young Person's Guide to the Orchestra* by Benjamin Britten] than the audience rose as one man and cheered him to the echo for many minutes,' reported the British Ambassador, Douglas Howard. 'I am assured that a visiting conductor, particularly one so new to this country, has seldom obtained so warm a welcome.'[56] Sargent on visiting the President at the end of his tour was told that 'We Uruguayans are fond of all English people, Sir Malcolm, but we are especially fond of you.'[57]

Sargent left Montevideo for Brazil on 4 June. 'Rio Bay incredibly lovely,' he observed. 'Like Sydney but the foreground is spoilt by huge tenements, dirty buildings.' When he met the Brazilian Symphony Orchestra, he was gratified to find among these 'charming and gentle people, many women and coloured players' including 'a big black violinist!'[58] When he was not working with the orchestra, Sargent entered into his usual 'leg-wearying' routine. He made speeches at dinners, gave several interviews to Brazilian radio and attended cocktail receptions given in his honour. The Brazilian composer, Heitor Villa-Lobos, darling of the Parisian avant-garde during the 1920s, invited him to tea at the Brazilian Academy of Music. Sargent was charming but unimpressed. 'V-L played his very bad records to me, accompanied by much conversation in the room and many motor horns outside,' Sargent wrote. 'Very dull modern music.'[59] More enjoyable were drives into the mountains and 'a delightful steam yacht trip round the bay'.[60] Sargent's concert in Brazil enjoyed similar popular approval to those in Argentina and Uruguay with 'great shouting at the end' and 'many autograph hunters'.[61]

Sargent returned to Buenos Aires on 11 June to join up again with Frances Balfour, who had left him in Montevideo. The following day he travelled to Chile, where he stayed for a month to conduct six concerts with the University of Santiago Symphony Orchestra. His flight across the snow-capped Andes, in magnificent sunshine, offered among the most spectacular views of his life. Chile gave Sargent 'the most happy orchestral experience in all S.A.'. Each concert at the Institute of Music sold out. Eager, respectful students filled the hall to watch rehearsals. Performances of Vaughan Williams's Sixth Symphony, Britten's *Young Person's Guide*, Sibelius's Fifth Symphony and new works by Chilean composers were all acclaimed. 'Great enthusiasm afterwards, many other people seatless and crowd in the street,' Sargent recorded after the first performance. His last saw him conduct Brahms's Fourth Symphony. 'Again an overwhelming success,' he recorded. 'Countless recalls, orchestra cheering and autograph hunters by hundreds. The bar was decorated with carnations!'[62]

When Sargent left the hall by the stage door, he was mobbed by an enthusiastic crowd and for a moment events got out of hand. Concert-goers pushed forward, carrying Sargent along and towards a busy road. As the crowds spilled on to the highway, the driver of an oncoming lorry skidded to halt but not before delivering a glancing blow to Sargent on the shoulder. It was not a serious injury but the lesson had been salutary: public adoration could be life-threatening.

Over-enthusiastic crowds were not the only danger. The tour, covering many thousands of miles and with a continual sense of being 'on duty', had left Sargent exhausted. By the Chilean leg, the physical symptoms were already beginning to show. He complained uncharacteristically of being 'rather too tired to dance' at a 'very gay' party at which he might normally have been in his element. Towards the end of the trip he 'suddenly broke out in cramps and spots' before being 'put back to bed in agony of irritations and nervous twitchings until midnight'.[63] His anxious hosts at the British Embassy, perhaps unaware of his reputation, organised a restful trip to the mountains in the Ambassador's Rolls-Royce with a diplomat's wife to help him recover.

Sargent left Chile feeling 'very tired'.[64] He was invited into the cockpit for the spectacular flight across the Andes before landing in Buenos Aires. Frances Balfour was there to meet him and the following afternoon they spent hours together at the zoo where, bizarrely, they 'saw an elephant kill and eat a pigeon!'[65] The Balfours took him back to the airport that evening and Sargent began the long journey to Lisbon, with stops at Montevideo, Rio and Natal for refuelling. 'Spent a lot of time in the cockpit, by starlight,' he wrote.[66] On Friday 14 July, Sargent left Lisbon, arriving back at London Airport at six o'clock in the evening. He had been away for more than two months and had earned £3,500.

The South American tour, popular and lucrative, underlined Sargent's status as an ambassador but did not bring with it musical prestige. Wilhelm Furtwängler might happily tour South America confident that his international name rested on his position as Artistic Director of the Berlin Philharmonic Orchestra. Sargent understood that if he wanted to be regarded as a great symphonic conductor then he must stand at the head of a leading orchestra. Touching down at London Airport, exhausted by his exertions abroad, he was confident that the final piece of the jigsaw was about to be slotted into place. A London orchestra with a name known around the globe, once described by Toscanini as the finest in the world, had invited him to take charge from 22 July 1950.[67]

Sir Malcolm Sargent was the new Chief Conductor of the BBC Symphony Orchestra.

12

God's Gift to BBC Music

'Received by the King and Queen in the morning, had luncheon with Mr Churchill and tea with Mr Attlee – all on the same day,' Sargent recorded proudly on the day he signed to become Chief Conductor of the BBC Symphony Orchestra.[1] On 28 April 1950, shortly before leaving for South America, Sargent had met the Director-General, Sir William Haley, at Broadcasting House. Haley had formally offered him the appointment with just one instruction: turn the symphony orchestra into a world-class ensemble.[2] Sargent was exultant. 'It is a position with such a first-class orchestra that anyone would like to have,' he told reporters at a press conference on 4 May.[3] The fact that the orchestra enjoyed the initials 'BBC' was another bonus. That name, having come to represent the defence of freedom during the war, was respected throughout the world. If the BBC was a cultural representation of English values abroad, it seemed only natural that 'the ambassador with a baton' should head its orchestra.

Despite its international reputation, the orchestra that Sargent inherited from Sir Adrian Boult in July was in an extremely poor state. 'The BBC was bedevilled by the fact that before the war Toscanini had conducted it and said "The BBC Symphony

Orchestra is the finest in the world",' observed Haley. By 1950, the DG believed that it had gone 'completely to pieces'.[4] Morale within the orchestra was low. Players were deserting for other London orchestras that offered better pay and conditions. Vacancies often went to replacements of lower quality.

Of those who remained, many were well past their best. The leader, Paul Beard, personified the orchestra's faded glory. He had been appointed by Sargent and Beecham as inaugural leader of the London Philharmonic Orchestra in 1932 and joined the BBC Symphony Orchestra in 1936. By 1950 Beard's gruff, unfriendly manner was mirrored by his playing. Hugh Maguire, who would replace him as leader in 1962, sat as his 'no. 2' for a brief period during Sargent's tenure. 'I got quite a shock because I thought he was very crude and raw,' remembers Maguire. 'Paul played with a spade, really. Rather rough and tough. He had ability but no finesse at all. His solos were dreadful, painful. An awful thing to say but he was past it.'[5] Sitting on the other side of Maguire was Bernard Andrews, Principal Second Violin, who was even cruder. 'They played violins like trombones, really,' concludes Maguire.[6] This lack of sophistication at the front of the string sections established the pattern for playing in the ranks. The standard of wind playing was no better. 'It was not very high at all,' recalls Jack Brymer, Principal Clarinet of the Royal Philharmonic Orchestra in 1950. 'Even before the war it did not compare with the London Philharmonic – they were like chalk and cheese. Boult was in charge and a pretty sloppy job he did too.'[7]

Adrian Boult had been Chief Conductor of the BBC Symphony Orchestra since its inception in 1930. A diffident man, his languid approach had left the orchestra in a parlous state. According to Sir Neville Marriner, Boult had 'a loose floppy technique which I always found hard to follow – a small beat with an enormous stick – and no vitality at all'.[8] His platform persona was dreary, but away from the public gaze he was known for his ruthlessness and astonishing fits of pique. 'Adrian had an extraordinarily strong temper and became quite violent at times,' recalls Marriner. 'He would walk out of studios, slam doors and even hurled someone down some steps.'[9] Boult had been directing a Brahms symphony in Walthamstow Town Hall. As he waited to begin the second movement, voices resonated off stage. The conductor began to colour and, still waiting for silence, eventually flushed full red in the face. While the talking continued, he climbed off his podium and walked into the wings to throw the offending orchestral attendant down a flight of stairs before returning to continue the symphony. 'Malcolm would never have done that,' says Neville Marriner.[10]

Boult enjoyed playing office politics, but he had more than met his match in Steuart Wilson, who became Head of Music at the BBC in 1948. Wilson had an impeccable musical background and was somewhat Machiavellian. As a student at Cambridge, he had sung Vaughan Williams's *On Wenlock Edge* in the presence of the composer, who then dedicated *Four Hymns* to him. In the twenties and thirties he had made a name for himself in the title role of *The Dream of Gerontius* (performing often with Sargent), and after the war proved a fine administrator at the newly formed Arts Council. The defining experience of Wilson's life was the First World War. He had fought with the King's Royal Rifle Corps in France between 1914 and 1916 before taking a bullet through the lung at the Battle of the Somme that almost cost him his life. 'I could not have stuck out and done nothing,' he had written to his Cambridge tutor, E.J. Dent, in 1914. 'I believe that war really calls out a lot of people's best faculties.'[11]

Boult had spent the war as a translator at the War Office, but a youthful friendship with Wilson transcended the fact that he had declined to volunteer for action. The two men were separated in age by just three months and had met in Oxford where Boult had been an undergraduate. In the early 1920s they had organised a festival at Petersfield, where Wilson lived with his wife, Ann, and regularly enlisted Sargent to act as a competition judge. Boult was godfather to the Wilsons' son, Richard. He even stayed at their London home when receiving psychological help to overcome chronic shyness. It therefore came as a terrible shock to Wilson when he discovered that Boult was having an affair with his wife. After Ann Wilson divorced her husband in November 1932, she married Boult the following summer. Steuart Wilson never forgave them.[12]

Wilson's position as Head of Music lasted only two years. During this brief time, his most significant act was to remove Boult as Chief Conductor of the BBC Symphony Orchestra. Wilson's game plan was as clever as it was simple. Boult was due to reach the BBC's official retirement age of sixty in April 1949 and Wilson insisted on enforcing it, despite being the same age himself. John Reith, Director-General when the BBC Symphony Orchestra was inaugurated in 1930, had told Boult that when he reached sixty a new contract would be drawn up to accommodate him. Yet by 1948 Reith was gone. Boult attempted to ignore the problem by moving his office from the BBC Music Department at Yalding House, in Great Portland Street near Broadcasting House, to the orchestra's base at Maida Vale.

On 26 May 1948, just weeks into the job, Wilson told Sir William Haley that his 'first priority' was to find a new conductor for the symphony orchestra.[13] Haley, mired in parliamentary committees, for the next two years endured 'a stiff harrowing time – the most arduous I have ever gone through'.[14] He had brought Wilson in to reform music at the BBC and was too busy to worry about Boult. Shortly afterwards, a clerk in the Programme Contracts department sent Boult a two-line chit informing him that he was due to retire on 8 April 1949. 'They have sacked me,' the conductor blurted out to Princess Elizabeth during a concert interval shortly afterwards. 'Then I hope they've given you a pension,' fired back Prince Philip.[15]

Finding a successor as Chief Conductor of the BBCSO was a more complicated task for Wilson than sacking Boult. His first choice was always Sargent. 'You know as well as I do all the difficulties there are, and you also know that we can look to each other for what the Prayer Book calls loving and cherishing in difficult circumstances,' Wilson had written to Sargent on 6 January 1948. Six days later, the two men had taken tea at Albert Hall Mansions to discuss the position of Chief Conductor. At the beginning of June, Wilson formally offered him the job.[16] After a week's deliberation, Sargent refused because it would restrict his foreign tours without a salary that would compensate for lost income. Wilson responded by suggesting the idea of a 'condominium' with Sir John Barbirolli, to which Sargent agreed because it would allow him to maintain these other commitments. 'I note with great pleasure Malcolm's willingness to enter into the scheme,' Barbirolli wrote to Wilson in August 1948, adding that he too was 'most willing to give full consideration' to the proposal.[17] Negotiations dragged on for four months. Even though the Corporation agreed to all his terms, Barbirolli turned down the job in December. 'May I . . . tender to you and your associates my most sincere thanks for all your kindness during this, for me, rather trying time,' Barbirolli wrote to Wilson. In reality, Barbirolli had ruthlessly exploited negotiations with the BBC, which his agent leaked to the press, to secure better terms and conditions at the Hallé Orchestra. 'Barbirolli's off,' Basil Nicolls told the Director-General. 'All he did was to go to the Hallé Society and squeeze more money and fewer performances out of them.'[18]

Publicly humiliated by Barbirolli's rejection, Wilson immediately proposed that the BBC make Sargent Chief Conductor, with Rafael Kubelik as Associate.[19] The following week, when Sargent was rehearsing the BBCSO at Maida Vale, Wilson implored him to accept the Chief Conductorship. Sargent still held out, unsure that his commitment would be sufficient to meet the orchestra's wide-ranging needs. Rejected by Sargent twice and Barbirolli once, the BBC decided to offer the post to the younger man, Kubelik, who had already expressed an interest.

Rafael Kubelik had been Chief Conductor of the Czech Philharmonic Orchestra since 1936 but after the Communist take-over defected at the 1948 Edinburgh Festival. Negotiations with the BBC Symphony Orchestra, which began in February 1949, ended ten months later in farce. In the midst of the talks Kubelik had left to conduct a series of concerts in America, promising to return at Christmas to sign a finalised contract. On 12 December he telephoned Wilson apparently in some distress to say that he was unable to accept the BBC job. 'He wouldn't come because his wife was terrified,' William Haley recalled. 'She said that England was too near Europe and she feared that they might again be over-run and she would go nowhere but America.'[20]

In reality, Mrs Kubelik's worries provided a convenient smokescreen for her husband's ambition. He had been happy enough to take sanctuary in London after leaving Czechoslovakia and recognised that the BBC post would smooth the way to British citizenship. When at the last moment the Chicago Symphony Orchestra asked him to be Musical Director after it sacked Artur Rodzinski, Kubelik dropped the BBC. 'What particularly distresses him is the boundless affection for and sense of indebtedness to

England, the BBC and you,' wrote Kubelik's agent disingenuously to Wilson shortly afterwards. 'He is grieved to have to go against all that.'[21]

Steuart Wilson had spent two years trying to replace Boult as Chief Conductor of the BBC Symphony Orchestra: his first, second and third choices had all declined. In desperation, he pleaded with Sargent to take the job in order to save a great orchestra from public humiliation. At lunch on Friday 6 January 1950 Wilson offered the post on any condition. Over the weekend, he formalised his proposal, recognising that Sargent could not make a full-time commitment but hoping he might still accept.[22] On 18 January, at Albert Hall Mansions, Basil Nicolls told Sargent in frank terms that without him those within the Corporation who sought to disband the orchestra would use the failure to secure a new conductor as evidence of its decline. This was an SOS signal.

Pressure on Sargent to accept the BBC post coincided with a month spent in London by Edwina Mountbatten, home from Malta where her husband was Commander-in Chief of the Mediterranean Fleet. Sargent was by inclination a Tory but Lady Mountbatten was, like her husband, a committed socialist. When Labour won a massive landslide victory at the 1945 general election, she had used access to the highest levels of government to obtain Sargent's knighthood. The euphoria of the immediate post-war years had by 1950 given way to popular disillusionment with the government. Economic austerity, the continuation of rationing and problems implementing the welfare state had left the 'New Jerusalem' crumbling at its foundations.

Only a promised 'Festival of Britain' in 1951 seemed to stand between Labour and a crushing election defeat.[23] The aim of the festival was 'to declare our belief in the British way of life' and 'recover our hold on all that is best in our national life'.[24] Herbert Morrison, the government minister responsible, explained its purpose more simply: 'I want to see the people happy. I want to hear the people sing.'[25] Happy, singing people made happy electors; this was the government's last chance to convince the country to vote Labour.

The cultural centrepiece of the Festival of Britain was a new concert hall to replace the Queen's Hall. The BBC Symphony

Orchestra was to give the opening three concerts under the direction of Arturo Toscanini. The government had recognised by late 1949 that the failure to secure a Chief Conductor for the orchestra was a political as well as cultural embarrassment that might undermine the festival. The government informed William Haley that it would be awkward if questions were asked in the House of Commons about why Sargent had not been appointed as Chief Conductor of the BBC Symphony Orchestra.[26] When the BBC renewed its offer to Sargent in January 1950, Lady Mountbatten told him that he owed it to her to take the job as a matter of loyalty to Attlee. With the BBC pleading and Lady Mountbatten insisting, Sargent set aside his reservations. By 26 January, the Board of Governors heard that Sargent was willing to negotiate a contract to become the new Chief Conductor of the BBC Symphony Orchestra.[27] A month later he accepted the post in principle. 'I have a great interest in, and admiration for, the musical work of the BBC,' he told Nicolls. 'It would give me great pleasure to be definitely associated with you by accepting this post.'[28] Having pursued him for two years, the BBC finally had its man.

Sargent had an extremely modern view of the role of Chief Conductor. He made clear from the outset that he wanted to be involved in every aspect of planning the orchestra's musical activity, including programming, invitations to guest conductors and the hiring of players. He had an additional interest in the BBC chorus, which might combine with the orchestra for choral concerts. 'As you know, I am much more interested in that angle than was Adrian Boult,' he told Nicolls frankly, 'and feel that although England is the most renowned country in the world for choral singing, the BBC have not perhaps fully exploited this possibility.'[29] Sargent was being tactful: under Leslie Woodgate, the BBC Choral Society had gained notoriety for poor ensemble mixed with an inability to sing in tune. Astonishingly Nicolls told Sargent, the finest choral conductor in the world, that his services were only required with the orchestra.

Sargent's principal concern was not the BBC choir but a determination not to find himself beholden to a bureaucrat. Steuart Wilson had given notice and a new Head of Music was yet to be appointed. Sargent proposed a change in the hierarchy of the Music Department, suggesting that the Head of Music and Chief

Conductor should be equal in status. 'I hope I made it clear that my desire was not so much to be in any way a head of department as it was to protect myself from the disadvantage which might occur from being under a junior,' he wrote to Nicolls. 'If you feel sure that difficulties can be avoided without defining my position more clearly than that of "Chief Conductor, no more, no less" I must rely on good will and your protection if needs be.'[30]

Sargent's contract was finally settled. At a meeting with the Director-General on 28 April 1950, Sargent agreed to terms that made him answerable to the Head of Music but that his influence and advice would be welcome at all times; more significantly, he was given the right to decline to conduct any work. Sargent was obliged to give twenty-three weeks of the year to the BBC. No age limit was put on his contract, which could be severed by a year's notice on either side. He would not receive a salary but continue as a freelance conductor at a rate of £84 per concert, an increase on his standard concert fee of £78.[31]

The negotiations had been long and unexpectedly difficult. 'His tactics give one a growing feeling that a definition of duties is more necessary in his case than it might be in others,' wrote Dick Howgill, Controller, Entertainment. 'Any laxity which strengthens his idea that he is God's gift to BBC music will make life intolerable not only to Head of Music and myself but to programme Controllers.'[32] The fact that Sargent had saved the BBC from humiliation by accepting the job had been quickly forgotten by apparatchiks concerned with preserving administrative hierarchy.

The range of material that the BBC expected of its symphony orchestra suited a conductor of Sargent's strengths and tastes. The orchestra's appearances combined ten 'showcase' concerts with the more populist Promenade season. Most public performances were broadcast and, along with those in the studio, provided the backbone of the BBC's classical musical output. The orchestra made an important contribution to three channels: the Third Programme, the Light Programme and the Home Service. The Third Programme (later Radio 3) by 1950 held only 0.15 per cent of the total British listening audience but enjoyed a disproportional influence on the Music Department. Lindsay Wellington, Controller, Home Service, between 1945 and 1952, frequently complained that the concerts broadcast by his channel did not provide enough standard classics and criticised the Music Department for concentrating on the Third Programme to which, statistically speaking, no one was listening.[33]

The Music Department in the early 1950s was home to the dispossessed of English musical life, a place where frustrated composers and academics unable to win tenured appointments at universities licked their wounds and passed judgement over their more successful contemporaries. There were honourable exceptions: Lennox Berkeley and Robert Simpson continued to compose with some success whilst at the BBC, but most had aspired and failed to create work of any significance.[34] The atmosphere at Yalding House was conservative, introspective and smug. Tweedy music staff would discuss over morning coffee the 'alpha minus' qualities of one English composer against the distinctly 'beta plus query minus' efforts of another. Whilst they might disagree about the relative merits of individual contemporary composers or performers, most agreed that anything enjoyed by the vast majority of the population was, by definition, crass. Yet their brand of elitism, which perversely had tired of the Great Tradition, was neither radical nor geographically wide-ranging. The programmes that they planned were 'safe and perhaps rather dull', said the *Musical Times*. [35]

Senior officials at the BBC had employed Steuart Wilson in 1948 to rid the Music Department of its complacency. He had none of the associations with failure that afflicted so many in the department and, as such, was despised by its staff. They baulked at his abrupt manner and willingness to offend sensitivities. He left for Covent Garden after two years, despairing of the BBC's conservatism. Wilson's replacement, Herbert Murrill, was a typical Yalding House figure. He had been Organ Scholar at Worcester College, Oxford, during the late 1920s and turned to schoolteaching after failure as a composer. After joining the BBC in 1936 he was an uncooperative Assistant Head of Music to Wilson in 1948. His appointment as Head of Music in 1950 was a triumph for Music Department insiders.

Relations between Malcolm Sargent and Yalding House were unhappy almost from the beginning. Only eight months into the post, Sargent wrote to Dick Howgill complaining that the Music Department was ignoring him: 'I am supposed to be a member of the music panel and when taking on the post of Chief Conductor it was understood that I should be invited to all meetings.'[36] As the first anniversary of his appointment drew close, he asked for a meeting with Sir William Haley to thrash out problems with the department. It was reiterated that in the future Sargent would be brought into the decision-making structure and, in particular, would be consulted on programme building.[37] 'They are carrying on exactly as if I were Adrian Boult,' he complained.[38]

Boult's career at the BBC had offered a cautionary example to Sargent, one of which he rarely lost sight. Working with the BBC Symphony Orchestra for twenty years, presenting works for which he had no sympathy, almost destroyed Boult's reputation as a conductor. Too often his performances were safe but uninspired. The English composer E.J. Moeran spoke for many contemporaries when he observed after the premiere of his *Sinfonietta* by the BBC Symphony Orchestra under Barbirolli in 1944: 'Thank God, we have escaped Boult for it!'[39] Boult's unwillingness to stand up for himself at the BBC had caused Beecham to christen him 'Dame Adrian'. It is no coincidence that Boult only blossomed as a conductor after leaving. 'I am afraid he is a bit of a yes man,' said Moeran of Boult; Sargent was determined that no one would think the same of him.[40] 'As things are now worked it would seem that [Head of Music] can stop any suggestions from moving any further . . . by saying "I think it cannot be done" or "I do not want it to be done" which at present seems to be the same thing,' Sargent wrote to Haley at the end of his first year. 'I hate being a nuisance but under the present arrangements I can only make my voice heard if I become one.'[41]

Sargent's relations with Murrill reached crisis point the following autumn when the two men had a blazing row at Albert Hall Mansions which cut to the essence of the problem: hierarchy versus status. Before accepting the BBC appointment Sargent had expressed concerns about protecting himself from 'the disadvantage which might occur from being under a junior'.[42] After more than a year 'the situation now seems exactly that which I was afraid of before joining your corporation. I find it difficult to fulfil your "elder statesman" role when I am not informed as to what is going on,' he told Basil Nicolls.[43] Sargent complained that he was kept outside the policy-making loop of the Music Department and that the BBC was not doing enough to promote its orchestra. He believed that without enough public performances and international tours, the prestige of the orchestra would continue to slip. When Murrill reluctantly visited Albert Hall Mansions on 6 November, he criticised Sargent for not using his office or secretary in Yalding House and told him that he had little right to complain about plans made there if he was never in. 'I do not think it necessary for me to sit in my office at the BBC waiting for something to turn up when it is quite easy for a secretary's telephone message to bring me pretty quickly into the building,' Sargent retorted.[44] 'I do not see how any senior official of the BBC can hope effectively to work in close collaboration with his colleagues by telephone,' Murrill spat back.[45] After several minutes of argument before an astonished BBC concerts manager, W.W. Thompson, Sargent peremptorily dismissed Murrill mid-sentence and disappeared into his study.

Murrill, apoplectic after this meeting, set down four pages of invective against the conductor, which he sent to Basil Nicolls. He restated his disgust that Sargent was never at Yalding House and still conducted orchestras other than the BBC Symphony. The tone of the memorandum was belligerent, desperate and a little hysterical. Herbert Murrill was a man losing his grip, but not without cause: he was dying of cancer.[46] By Christmas he had left the BBC, soon to be replaced by Dick Howgill as Controller of a reorganised Music Division. Howgill was not a musician but an able administrator with a more sophisticated understanding of bureaucratic politics than Murrill. 'I am too old a man to wish to bother to maintain a job by avoiding intrigues or combating resistance, passive or otherwise,' observed Sargent.[47] Dick Howgill, it was hoped, would initiate a quieter, more competent era for BBC Music. Sargent even began weekly visits to Yalding House. 'I have spent my first day "*in officio*" and enjoyed it very much,' he told Nicolls. 'I do hope you are pleased with me!'[48]

Murrill had believed that Sargent failed 'to dispose his work [so] that his Corporation duty came first'. Amid such acrimonious charges, it is surprising to find the BBC Symphony Orchestra transformed during Sargent's first two years in charge. 'We were pleased when Sargent was appointed,' recalls principal harpist Sidonie Goossens. 'I already knew him and was quite happy about it; we wanted to work with him regularly because he was so precise and accurate which was a change from Adrian.'[49] Sargent's first concert as Chief Conductor came on 22 July at the opening night of the 1950 Proms. His impact on the orchestra was immediate. Steuart Wilson reported that the BBCSO responded so wholeheartedly to the personal excitement and incentive that Sargent brought that the Proms' other orchestra, the LSO, complained about being given Basil Cameron not Sargent. The season broke all attendance records. After the Last Night, William Haley hosted a party for Sargent at which the Prime Minister, Clement Attlee, made a brief appearance. Praise was drawn from all quarters. 'I am writing to let you know how contented and happy I have been throughout the whole season,' Sargent told Haley shortly afterwards. 'Certain changes will have to be made but I do not want to rush this situation. My relationship with them [the orchestra] has been completely happy and they have done magnificent work.'[50]

The success of the 1950 Proms season had not hidden that the BBC Symphony Orchestra needed a thorough overhaul. 'It was not rated by London players,' recalls violinist Brian Smith, later Chairman of the Royal Philharmonic Orchestra. 'If you just wanted to work from ten until five and then go home to prune the roses, you joined the Beeb. It was the orchestra then for people who just wanted to sit and vegetate.'[51] As he had done in Liverpool, Sargent immediately brought in progressive reform to improve quality and motivation in the orchestra. Rotational seating was introduced; a system that was more equitable and stimulating, and helped foster an even sound quality throughout a section. After an initial bedding-in period, Sargent's idea improved ensemble to such an extent that other orchestras in London copied it.

Progressive seating, standard practice today, was an attempt by Sargent to get the best out of the players; other reforms showed a ruthless determination to sack those who were not up to the job. He had commented in the 1930s that 'as soon as a man thinks he is in his orchestral job for life, with a pension waiting for him at the end of it, he tends to lose something of his supreme fire'.[52] Sargent always believed his only crime had been to speak an unpalatable truth. He concerned himself simply with the quality of playing, not how mortgages were to be paid on low orchestral wages. At lunch with Haley on 2 July 1951, he suggested that contracts for members of the

BBC Symphony Orchestra should be reviewed annually rather than every three years and that notice of dismissal should be reduced.

The BBC resisted these changes but did accede to his demand to re-audition most rank-and-file string players. This took place in the spring of 1952. A number of retirements and voluntary redundancies helped to soften the process, but after rigorous assessment, eight players were sacked with others put on 'probation'.[53] Musical considerations were Sargent's primary if not sole rationale when looking to improve the orchestra. 'There was one poor girl, a viola player,' recalls Sidonie Goossens, 'and when he was sacking people he said, "She's ugly; I can't stand her in front of me" and so they pensioned her off.'[54]

Sargent gave the BBC Symphony Orchestra a new lease of life. According to its official historian, Nicholas Kenyon, later Controller of Radio 3, Sargent's 'arrival at the BBC was a breath of fresh air, a welcome change, and for a couple of seasons his dynamism, inexhaustible energy and lively style injected a spark into the orchestra's playing which had previously been missing'.[55] In a display of affection for the orchestra, Sargent organised during each Proms season a cocktail party on the Fellows' Lawn at London Zoo and invited celebrities along to add glamour to the occasion. He arranged for keepers to show animals and, at the first party in the summer of 1950, drew gasps when leading in a cheetah on a chain. Chimps, bears and snakes were handed round with the drinks. 'It's a bit startling to have a boa constrictor flipped round your neck by a member of the house of peers when you have a glass of burgundy in your hand and a mouth full of chicken sandwich,' recalled one player.[56] Sargent was always jovial at such occasions and busied himself with ensuring that everyone was having 'fun' (one of his favourite words). One side of his character, however, was kept in abeyance. He never made advances to women in the orchestra and was unusually careful in avoiding even harmless physical contact.

Having revived the orchestra's fortunes and raised spirits, Sargent was determined to show it off. Part of the reason why the BBC Symphony Orchestra had slumped after the Second World War was that, despite the security the Corporation offered, many quickly became bored of its routine. The work, centred at Maida Vale studios, often involved the performance of undistinguished contemporary works for the minuscule audience that tuned in to the Third Programme. Orchestral musicians thrive on the adrenaline of performance and studio recordings of mediocre works did not set pulses racing. Sargent understood that keeping his players holed up in Maida Vale was detrimental to their development as an orchestra and thought that, like a maiden aunt, they really should try to get out more often. It is typical of Sargent's enthusiasm for the modern that he should have wanted the BBC to take advantage of publicity surrounding a new concert hall in London to enhance its profile. The Festival Hall, completed in 1951, overnight became an icon of contemporary British architecture. It stood on the south bank of the Thames near Waterloo Station and, when lit at night, shone across London as a beacon to the capital's cultural life. Beecham derided it as 'a monumental piece of imbecility and iniquity' but Sargent, who had been an adviser to the design team, argued that 'there is no doubt about it being better for music than the Albert Hall'.[57] Yet despite his advice, the department decided not to involve itself in the hall's opening season beyond the Festival of Britain, signalling an unwillingness to compete with London's premier orchestras.

The BBC Symphony Orchestra had been invited for the Festival of Britain to give three out of six concerts in the opening series organised at the Festival Hall. In these, with Sargent triumphant, the orchestra proved the equal of any in London. Members also participated in the dedication ceremony on 3 May conducted by Sargent and Boult, in which they joined a composite orchestra. The King, in the final year of his reign, unveiled a commemorative stone before listening from the royal box to music that included *Zadok the Priest*, the 'Hallelujah' chorus, *Pomp and Circumstance March No.1*, 'Rule Britannia' and 'Jerusalem'. Everyone who was anyone in the British Establishment seemed to be there that day. The monarch and his heir, Princess Elizabeth, the Prime Minister and the government and leading figures from the arts toasted the new hall with champagne.

The event could have been made for Sargent. His sense of glamour and panache helped produce a performance that generated an ecstatic audience response. The highlight of the evening was Sargent's arrangement of 'Rule Britannia'. State trumpeters joined the orchestra and choir, drawn from seven London choral societies.

Brilliant in gold-braided scarlet uniform and black velvet caps, they ceremonially joined the final chorus with exhilarating effect. When the music stopped, the King led the audience in a standing ovation. 'Even you stood up,' Sargent later mocked the left-wing MP Aneurin Bevan. It was several minutes before Adrian Boult, who did not enjoy the occasion, could get on stage to conduct Vaughan Williams's *Serenade to Music*.

Afterwards, Sargent was summoned by the King only to find this normally reserved man in a state of excitement. 'You know I am not very musical,' George VI told him. 'Sir, you are teasing,' replied Sargent diplomatically. 'No, I am serious,' continued the King. 'I have never been moved by any music as much as your arrangement of "Rule Britannia". Do remember this: whenever I come to another of your concerts I will ask you beforehand, no, I will *command* you [laughs] to perform it again.' 'That is very kind, sir, but it may be difficult if we have been performing Bach's *B Minor Mass* or the *St Matthew Passion*,' answered Sargent delicately. 'It won't be difficult,' the King retorted. 'I shan't be there!'[58]

Even though the official opening of the Festival Hall showed Sargent at his charismatic and dashing best, his significant musical contribution came later in the opening week. Toscanini, having been invited to perform at the hall, had insisted on conducting the BBC Symphony Orchestra, with which he had worked so successfully before the war. Two months before the concerts, the Italian maestro, already in mourning for his wife, cancelled his visit after suffering a minor stroke brought on by pedalling too hard on his exercise bicycle. The Festival of Britain Council and London County Council, which administered the Festival Hall, went into an immediate panic that only subsided when Sargent coolly accepted their invitation to take over.

Music for the concerts had already been advertised but it caused Sargent little inconvenience because Toscanini's repertoire was so similar to his own: Beethoven's symphonies 1 and 9, Debussy's *La Mer*, Strauss's *Don Juan* and Vaughan Williams's Sixth Symphony. For three nights Sargent conducted magnificent, deeply felt concert performances that were his finest since the pre-war Courtauld-Sargent series. During the Second World War, Sargent had often sacrificed high musical ideals to give popular concerts on little rehearsal to rally the spirits of those who had suffered most from bombing. Standing on the rostrum of the gleaming Festival Hall conducting a revived BBC Symphony Orchestra in Toscanini's place, he understood that he had returned to older values. Far from feeling a poor substitute for the Italian he so admired, Sargent welcomed the comparison. Like Toscanini, he was Chief Conductor of an orchestra run by a broadcasting organisation that could put his vision of classical music into every living room in the country and many beyond. After the exultant sounds of Beethoven's Choral Symphony had washed over him on Friday 4 May and he returned to take his ovation, Malcolm Sargent could justifiably have regarded himself as England's Toscanini.

13

Malta Dog

Malcolm Sargent was the most famous English conductor in the world. Only one familiar detail seemed to threaten a claim to greatness: money. When he stood on the podium of the Festival Hall at the three inaugural concerts of the Festival of Britain, he was given £157 for each performance. When Toscanini came the following year to conduct the Philharmonia Orchestra, the Italian cleared more than a £1,000 for one concert, a lower-than-usual fee negotiated with his friend Walter Legge, who ran the orchestra. In 1937, NBC had paid Toscanini $40,000 to conduct twelve concerts in ten weeks; after the war, his (undisclosed) fees were reported to have trebled.[1] In comparison, Sargent's domestic fee was an insult.

One consequence of Sargent's low pay was that despite being the most famous English conductor, he had to be the hardest-working. He had scaled down commitments outside London and used well-paid foreign tours to boost his income but his diary was still extraordinarily full. During the Festival of Britain and the subsequent Promenade season, his commitments were such to break even a younger man. Between 5 April and 5 August, Sargent had just three days off. During the Festival, almost every day offered diary entries for work from ten in the morning until eleven at night. He conducted concerts for the BBC Symphony, London Symphony and Philharmonia orchestras. EMI recorded Mozart violin concertos with Sargent and Jascha Heifetz. He conducted Gilbert and Sullivan for D'Oyly Carte at the Savoy Theatre. There were three Festival concerts with the Royal Choral Society and another with the Huddersfield. Concerts for the Festival in Liverpool and Manchester meant more uncomfortable nights on bumpy sleeper trains. 'I don't think the Maestro liked starting his night journeys back to Liverpool again,' noted Sylvia Darley.[2] No sooner was the Festival of Britain over than Sargent plunged into the Proms seasons to conduct three concerts a week with rehearsals every day. No one could sustain such a punishing timetable and it came as no surprise when, on 5 August 1951, he collapsed whilst conducting in Brighton.

Sargent was rushed back to a London clinic. Lord Horder arrived to examine him, looking grave. Almost two decades after the long and complex tuberculosis operation, the King's doctor found Sargent weak and breathing shallowly. Initial fears that consumption had returned proved unfounded; Sargent had pleurisy but Horder was taking no chances. Tuberculosis is never cured but only in remission. Since any lung infection was dangerous, Horder ordered Sargent to take three weeks off. He travelled to Ireland to recuperate with the Mountbattens, returning to the Proms only at the end of August. Lord Horder was in attendance backstage to give Sargent a medical during the interval. Promenaders used to the Chief Conductor's energy and vitality were shocked when he emerged slowly down the bull-run to the podium, where he sat on a high stool to direct Stravinsky's *Firebird* suite. There were ten further concerts to conduct that season; Horder insisted on a check-up after each. Following the Last Night on 22 September, he ordered Sargent to take a month's holiday in the sun and regain his strength.

Sargent went first to Scotland before flying to Gibraltar and motoring with Diana Bowes-Lyon to 'a perfect little house in a garden on the seashore' near Marbella. The house belonged to Frances Balfour whose husband had that year been appointed British Ambassador to Madrid. As always in the sunshine, Sargent was relaxed and happy. 'The weather was perfect all holiday,' he wrote in his diary. 'Hot and we did nothing but sunbathe and seabathe and occasionally motored into Marbella or Malaga.'[3] There were trips to the covered market full of 'dirty people and strong smells' and fishing trips in an open boat when 'I caught an octopus'. After months of enduring an intolerable workload, Sargent finally relaxed. 'We ate, drank and slept well and did nothing else,' he wrote contentedly on the last day. 'A perfect rest for me and I got very tanned in the sun.'[4]

When Sargent returned to work in October, he resumed the unyielding schedule that had made him so ill over the summer. Between 18 October and Christmas Eve 1951, Sargent again took just three days off work. He travelled north to conduct in Leeds, Bradford, Huddersfield, Hull, Manchester and Liverpool; he went west to Cardiff and Swansea; in London he directed his own BBC Symphony Orchestra and the London Symphony Orchestra, gave concerts with the Royal Choral Society that included performances of *Hiawatha* in aid of the Battersea Central Mission for Children, and presided over the *Daily Herald* National Brass Band Championships, for which he had made arrangements of orchestral works. In the studio, he made recordings for HMV and Decca that included a new piano concerto by Alan Rawsthorne. He was paid £78 for most concerts, £100 for recording sessions and £157 for the brass band championships.[5]

The frantic pace of Sargent's life was a matter of concern to his staff, who urged him to slow down. 'He worked incredibly hard, sometimes too much so,' remembers Lady de Zulueta. 'He was very slight – thin – and the diary would be so full.'[6] Sargent's obsessional attitude to work was a psychological product of his youth. Inside that elegant Savile Row suit remained the insecurities of a little boy who had come from nothing and grown up suspecting his illegitimacy. Peter Sargent remembers how 'when people talked about the working class, he would say, "I am the working man" and he meant it'. Sargent had always been a workaholic. Overburden had almost killed him in the 1930s. Now his health was again at risk. He ignored the symptoms because he believed that only by driving himself to the limits of his physical and mental powers could he retain his status. 'It was simple,' says his son. 'God had given him a talent for which he thought he had to pay by working twenty-five hours a day.'[7]

Sargent's load was further increased by his sense of obligation to the wider activities of the music community. He served on the Music Panel of the Arts Council, advised the British Council and was official Music Adviser to the Chairman of EMI. Away from music, he used his celebrity to support charities and sat on committees for the RSPCA and London Zoo. He entered into all these commitments with his usual vigour, never complaining of the drain on his time and energy. Some even turned out to be tremendous fun, none more so than his post as honorary adviser in music to the Royal Marines.

As Commander-in-Chief, Mediterranean, Dickie Mountbatten took a close interest in the Royal Marine Band Service, which had been founded by his father, Prince Louis of Battenberg, in 1903. He must have been galled, therefore, when his wife used the service to facilitate her affair with Sargent. The relationship had cooled during the Mountbattens time in India, when Edwina had been close to Jawaharlal (Pandit) Nehru, but the affair picked up again as soon as she returned.[8] Using her influence, and knowing of Sargent's love of brass bands, Edwina suggested to her husband in 1949 that a post be invented to give the conductor a role in the life of the Royal Marines.

Sargent was the first and last musical adviser to the navy since the post lapsed on his death in 1967. His opening concert for the Royal Marines was a magnificent affair. On 29 March 1950 he conducted the bands and orchestra of the Portsmouth Command in their barracks gymnasium to raise money for the Queen of the Hellenes Fund for Greek refugee children.[9] The programme included extracts from Vaughan Williams's *Sea Symphony* and Sargent's arrangement of 'Rule Britannia'. Afterwards, Admiral of the Fleet Sir Algernon Willis hosted a reception for Sargent on Nelson's flagship, HMS *Victory*. Sargent was thrilled with his new position. The meticulous arrangements, splendour of the uniforms and brightness of the playing, with all the accompanying deference of piping, saluting and 'sir'-ing, appealed to both his pride and sense of occasion. It also offered a wonderful excuse to spend more time with Edwina Mountbatten.

In September 1952 Sargent joined the Mountbattens in Naples for a cruise with the fleet, ostensibly to discuss arrangements for the following year's coronation concerts. 'The House of Mountbatten now reigns,' boasted Dickie of the new Queen, who was married to his nephew, Prince Philip.[10] Sargent had arrived in Naples exhausted by another arduous Promenade season but still played characteristically hard in the Mediterranean. On his first day on HMS *Surprise*, he was startled by early morning 'deck-scrubbing, bugling, bands playing, etc!' He was awake when 'Edwina called upon me at 8.30' and 'breakfasted in bed at 9.00'.[11] They spent 'hours of bliss, lolling in the sunshine' on the C-in-C's private deck and took out barges from which to swim and fish. In the waters off Capri, they played with dolphins, which almost led to catastrophe. 'I put on feet flippers and a mask but I soon got into breathing difficulties,' he recorded in his diary. Only two alert Italian divers saved him from drowning. Sargent hated to fail at anything, so 'again tried to wear a mask and breathe thro' the snorkel tube but only half-drowned myself and took to the lilo'.[12]

Days spent lazing in the sun were complemented by trips on land when the ship docked. There was a 'thrilling' climb to the top of Mount Vesuvius, which had had 'no eruption since 1944 but one expected next year!'. Sargent and Mountbatten often took a sports car for breakneck drives through mountain passes with 'Dickie driving magnificently (as we still live)'. More adventures were offered in the brothel district of Algiers, which he toured with Edwina. 'Outside each door was a highly painted middle-aged woman – very amiable and pleased to see us,' he wrote. 'Through the bars of a grid in the door we first saw two or three highly made up girls who then opened the door and cheerfully accepted cigarettes – some were obviously very far gone which did not deter them in the least – a few were attractive but most look very hard-bitten! I asked the price of the nicest one!'[13]

Wherever Mountbatten's party went ashore, sumptuous banquets and glittering cocktail parties were given in their honour. During one visit, Sargent heard Gracie Fields sing for hundreds of sailors in 'a stupendous show of artistry'. Yet the highlight of the voyage came when he stood beside Mountbatten on the bridge of the flagship, HMS *Glasgow*, while the C-in-C directed manoeuvres. Twenty-six ships performed quadrilles and 'grid irons', culminating in two lines of ships meeting at forty knots and 'passing through'. Afterwards, HMS *Surprise* was brought alongside and a high line fixed between the two. Sargent was fitted with a lifebelt, put his foot in a stirrup and was winched from one to the other to cheers from the assembled crew. 'Found it not in the least bit frightening or uncomfortable,' he wrote in his diary. 'I am told that I made a good impression on the crew – glad to hear it!' All in all it had been the most 'incredible day – impossible to describe'.[14]

After two weeks cruising, Sargent arrived in Malta, where the Mediterranean fleet had its headquarters. With his holiday almost over, he began to think again about work. He went to hear the Commander-in-Chief's orchestra and gave an impromptu rehearsal. On his last night, he dined alone with the Mountbattens and played the piano for them. After Edwina saw him fly off the next day, he was back at work by ten o'clock the following morning.

The Queen's Coronation in 1953 added a royal dimension to an already gruelling workload. Sargent attended the service at Westminster Abbey on 2 June before conducting the film soundtrack of the event that was shown in cinemas throughout the world. In London he led Coronation concerts that ranged from a performance of Benjamin Britten's *Spring Symphony* at the Festival Hall the day after the service to a thousand-voice *Messiah* at the Albert Hall. For the BBC, he gave first performances of Rubbra's *Ode to the Queen* and Berkeley's *Suite for Orchestra*, both commissioned to mark the occasion.

Sargent returned to Malta to conduct the Royal Marines bands' Coronation concerts. Again he spent long, lazy days in the sunshine with Edwina on HMS *Surprise* or swimming off the island of Gozo with Dickie. Afterwards, they lay on lilos in the sun until Sargent got heat stroke. No sooner had he recovered than a particularly unpleasant strain of dysentery known locally as 'Malta Dog' put him in bed for four days. He spent an uncomfortable time in his cabin while Edwina applied cold compresses and naval staff scurried around.

With his Maltese concerts fast approaching, Sargent insisted stoically that he was well enough to conduct. He made a disagreeable journey ashore but once in front of a band of a hundred men never faltered. Ignoring physical discomfort, or perhaps not even noticing it, he rehearsed for five full days in searing heat. The concerts on 10 and 11 July began with *Pomp and Circumstance March No. 1* and ended with 'Rule Britannia', with thirteen other 'crowd-pleasers' in between. Humidity in the hall was so overpowering that many in the audience fainted. Sargent showered and changed into new clothes during the interval to maintain his crisp appearance. An ovation followed the end of each performance, and when Sargent came on for his call after the second concert, bandsmen in their white uniforms stood to call 'three cheers for Sir Malcolm'. When he left the hall afterwards in Mountbatten's Rolls-Royce, with its silver naval signalman on the bonnet, hundreds who had attended the concert threw flowers in its path. The ambassador with the baton had scored another hit.

His duty done, Sargent returned to HMS *Surprise*, which left on 13 July for another cruise of the Mediterranean. 'If you'd like to stay on for a bit of the cruise you could either come with me in the *Glasgow* or with Edwina in the *Surprise*,' Mountbatten had written to Sargent beforehand. 'I gather *Surprise* moves off on the 13th to Greece,' Sargent quickly wrote to Edwina. 'I would love to stay with you.'[15] Mountbatten put the entire fleet into Naples, where massed bands 'beat the retreat' on the jetty. They marched in quick and slow time and lowered the white ensign to the yearning sounds of 'Sunset'.[16]

Sargent returned to London on 19 July, his week with Edwina having done much to revitalise his spirits for the coming hectic months. The pressure of another Promenade season included the first concert performance of William Walton's *Coronation Te Deum*. The following year Sargent would reluctantly accept another Walton first – the opera *Troilus and Cressida*. Events leading up to that premiere on 3 December were as turbulent as those of *Belshazzar's Feast* in 1931. Sargent had not wanted to conduct *Troilus* but was prevailed upon by the composer and by David Webster, who now ran the Royal Opera. Sargent had not often been in the pit since the 1920s. He had conducted at Covent Garden only once before, for Charpentier's *Louise* in 1936; it had at other times been a closed shop ruled over by Sir Thomas Beecham. 'Do you know the English word jealousy?' replied Sir Adrian Boult when asked why he too did not conduct at Covent Garden. 'He [Beecham] wouldn't let anyone near him who was of comparable stature and education.'[17]

The BBC had commissioned *Troilus* in 1947 in the warm afterglow of Britten's success in 1945 with *Peter Grimes*. It took Walton seven difficult years to compose a work that even his official biographer dismisses as 'a failure'.[18] Walton, basing the opera on Chaucer's *Troilus and Criseyde*, tried to initiate a neo-Romantic style of opera. Where Chaucer's story is passionate and compelling, Christopher Hassal's libretto is leaden. The characters are so weakly drawn that we can hardly care less what happens to them. Walton's self-conscious, affected music provides a desiccated imitation of the passion of Puccini and Verdi. 'Part of the trouble was that I didn't know enough about the mechanics of opera writing to be able to say what I really wanted,' confessed Walton later. 'Nor did I know enough about the theatre or what might work theatrically.'[19] *Troilus and Cressida*, Walton's first opera, caused a serious reverse in his reputation.

Preparations for *Troilus* were dogged by incompetence, bad luck and recriminations. The leading role, Cressida, had been written for Elisabeth Schwarzkopf, but her husband, Walter Legge, ruthlessly pulled her out of the first production, despite his long friendship with the composer, when he realised the opera was inadequate. Her replacement, the Hungarian Magda Laszlò, spoke almost no English and sang the words incomprehensibly. Conductor and singers, who had received their scores only in September, were hesitant and uncertain five weeks later at rehearsals. Sargent normally thrived on such difficulties but the opera pit was not his environment. He struggled to instil discipline. Peter Pears, who sang Pandarus, demanded that ensemble passages be conducted, but Sargent, like Toscanini, refused to conduct singers when the orchestra was not playing.

Walton railed against Sargent's 'shameful and unprofessional behaviour towards [the] opera' and, despite his poor reputation as a conductor, even asked to take over the podium.[20] Matters were not helped by an Oxford University Press score that was difficult to read and riddled with errors. The first orchestral rehearsal ended in confusion after 238 mistakes were found in the band parts. Much time was wasted at later rehearsals trying to purge errors of notation. Sargent's own thoughts on changes to the score did not always meet with the composer's approval. 'I'm not making any more alterations,' Walton shrieked at him. 'It's my fucking opera.'[21]

Gossip about rows at the Garden spread through London society with malicious pleasure. Many who arrived for the opening night did so expecting 'something' to happen. 'I ask Malcolm Sargent whether the music profession is as mean and jealous as the acting profession,' recorded Harold Nicolson in his diary. 'He says it is far worse.'[22] If admirers and enemies alike wondered if Sargent was about to make a fool of himself, they underestimated his unerring ability, in the words of Walton's wife, to pull 'rabbits out of hats'.[23] *The Times* observed that 'Sir Malcolm Sargent, who has not been at an operatic desk for years, was vigilant, served the singers with tact and elicited from the orchestra that stringency which is one of the marks of Walton's orchestral writing.'[24] Both conductor and composer received an ovation and together enjoyed a spectacular first-night champagne party that went on into the early hours.

Critics praised Sargent but the opera won few admirers. Compared to the dramatic contemporary operas of Britten and Tippett (whose *Midsummer Marriage* was premiered the following month), Walton's disjointed Romantic efforts seemed disappointingly old-hat. 'The failure of this opera haunted Walton for the rest of his life,' says John Tooley, assistant to David Webster.[25] The composer's acolytes blamed the cool reception for the opera on Sargent, but Walton knew better. 'You wouldn't have been displeased with the Cov Gar performance by comparison,' he later wrote to Sargent after being booed at La Scala, Milan. 'Life is full of disappointments!'[26]

14

The Gospel According
to St Malcolm

'The object of his ingenious and somewhat deceitful manipulation of our machine is to get his own way over orchestral musicians, the choice of programme items and various other things that would enable the BBC Symphony Orchestra to be a vehicle for his own personal vanity,' had complained Dick Howgill of Sargent to the new Director-General, Sir Ian Jacob, as early as the 1953 Promenade season.[1] Sargent's political technique was as old as it was successful: divide and rule. He played senior BBC officials off against each other by winning agreement to a proposal from one when another had already rejected it. Higher and higher up the chain of command he would take rejected suggestions until, when necessary, Ian Jacob was given lunch at the Garrick and smoothly won over. 'What it all amounts to is a perpetual failure to see himself in the correct perspective as an instrument of BBC policy,' wearily concluded Howgill. The only truth Sargent understood was 'the gospel according to St Malcolm'.[2]

Sargent's first years working with the Music Department had not been happy, but when Murrill died in 1952, the conductor had been hopeful of a fresh start. The BBC, recognising that the department was performing unsatisfactorily, had tried to introduce radical reform. A new Music Division had been created under Dick Howgill as the first Controller of Music. He streamlined administration but followed a 'safety first' policy and deferred to Maurice Johnstone, the forceful Head of Music Programmes (Radio). Johnstone, another failed composer, had been private secretary to Sir Thomas Beecham before joining the BBC in 1938. His bluff common-room sociability fitted in well at Yalding House. His frighteningly narrow musical preferences centred on minor English composers such as Rubbra, Alwyn and Bliss. William Glock, a prominent writer on music during the 1950s and later Controller of Music, was astonished to discover that Johnstone not only rejected most contemporary European composition 'in a spirit of moral indignation' but 'also informed me, without apparent regret, that he had never heard the *St Matthew Passion* and that he did not set much store by chamber music'.[3]

At the heart of the relationship between Sargent and the BBC was still a fundamental disagreement about the function of the Chief Conductor. Sargent was on the cusp of modern trends: he envisaged his role as that of Music Director of the BBC Symphony Orchestra, responsible for every aspect of its artistic life. It was in a very real sense, he believed, 'my orchestra'.[4] Howgill, like Murrill, sought to control the musical direction of the orchestra; Sargent was simply the conductor and expected to lead the orchestra when and where he was told. But Sargent, unlike Boult, did not meekly submit when his ideas were dropped.

Tensions that had simmered ominously for months finally gave way to the first eruption of open hostility between Sargent and Howgill. The BBC had invited Bruno Walter to conduct the orchestra in May 1955 at the Festival Hall. Sargent had been friends with Walter since the 1930s when the two had worked so happily together in the Courtauld-Sargent Concerts. He had encouraged the Music Division to engage Walter and wrote to him personally to say, 'I am so happy to hear that there is a possibility of you coming to work with my orchestra in May 1955.' He also suggested that Walter might consider performing Mahler and Bruckner symphonies, 'which you do so magnificently'.[5] Days later, Sargent received a letter from Howgill that denounced him for undermining his authority by writing to Walter.[6]

Sargent was furious. 'If Bruno Walter thinks poorly of the BBC organisation it is *your* fault, not mine,' he told Howgill. 'As you know, when I joined the BBC the terms of reference were made quite clear and your own instructions state that "Sir Malcolm is to be consulted on all matters, etc., including programmes, conductors, soloists." The situation is farcical and [...] quite honestly, the grievance is mine.'[7] On receiving a charming reply from Walter, Sargent gleefully sent a copy to Howgill to which he appended his own damning assessment: 'You obviously wish me to be out of the news.'[8]

The first serious heave against Sargent by the Music Division followed soon after. At Albert Hall Mansions, Sargent bawled Johnstone out 'fortissimo con fuoco' for engaging guest conductors, allocating Proms programmes and reorganising the orchestra's schedule without consultation. 'You are just the conductor,' Johnstone responded. 'The Controller is the BBC's musical director and you have no official jurisdiction over the symphony orchestra's work beyond the work you conduct.'[9] A flabbergasted Sargent told him that 'one or other of us will have to go'.[10] Johnstone, resolving that it would not be him, told Howgill immediately afterwards that he was happy to lead the charge on Sargent's dismissal. For six months, he worked on a long memorandum headed 'The BBC and Sir Malcolm Sargent'. Vitriol and spite leak from every paragraph of a document which argued that Sargent was uncommitted to the BBC and should be replaced by Rudolph Schwarz. 'A strong tree will carry a cankerous branch for many years,' Johnstone concluded, 'but its natural growth is crippled.'[11]

Johnstone's memorandum was the beginning of the end for the Chief Conductor. The HMP (Radio) constantly briefed against Sargent and goaded him into criticism of the Music Division. In February 1955, Sargent took up the orchestra's complaints about having to work too hard. 'We must note that almost every conductor who has been with us lately has complained of the amount of work that has to be done each week by the orchestra,' he reported. The distinguished conductor Eugene Ormandy had told him that 'he could take it for one week but that he certainly would not dream of conducting that sort of work for one month'. The orchestra, Sargent observed, 'had to do it for some eleven months in the year'.[12] Mind your own business, Johnstone replied, adding that players always grumbled in the winter and usually took matters into their own hands by pretending to be ill.[13]

Sargent was forced to complain to Howgill that 'his first sentence has a sting in it which I do not altogether enjoy, the point being that it was not a concern of mine. The whole thing is that I am responsible to you for the personnel, happiness and well-being of the orchestra.' The problem, Sargent concluded, was that he was 'less and less' involved in policy-making. 'The whole present problem with the orchestra arises from the fact that the policy was settled without any reference to me,' he observed. 'I could have pointed out at the outset, and indeed did as soon as I knew of it, that the present difficulties would arise.'[14] Sargent might have expected protection from Dick Howgill as Controller, but got none. Howgill was happy to let Johnstone wield the knife against Sargent whilst keeping his own hands clean. He refused to reprimand his deputy, who continued to send Sargent abrasive letters and dismissed the Chief Conductor's claims that he was out of touch with the familiar suggestion that he should spend more time behind a desk at Yalding House.[15]

The final breakdown in Sargent's relationship with the Music Division came on a matter so personal that Maurice Johnstone's intentions can have been nothing short of vicious. Sargent was to conduct Alfredo Campoli and the BBC Symphony Orchestra at the Royal Festival Hall on 11 May 1955 in the first performance of a violin concerto by Sir Arthur Bliss. A studio recording of the same work was scheduled for the next day to be broadcast on the Third Programme but no one had bothered to inform Sargent. The previous August he had told Dick Howgill that he was to conduct a concert at the Festival Hall on 12 May with Pierre Fournier performing three cello concertos with the LPO. The performance was in aid of research into polio, the illness from which his daughter had died.

Two months before the concert, Sargent received an extraordinary letter from Johnstone demanding that he withdraw from the 'rival' concert and seek permission in writing before taking future outside engagements.[16] 'I cannot work against enmity and misrepresentation,' Sargent complained to Howgill, adding that the letter was nothing short of 'a defamation of character'.[17] When Howgill countered that his strictures were too harsh, Sargent gave full vent to his frustration. 'At heart I get a feeling, which is not only personal but is suggested to me by people who should know, that MJ really would like me out of the BBC,' Sargent wrote, concluding that 'I am obviously not the ideal appointment for those in the BBC, who would like a "yes man" completely at their beck and call, but frankly I feel that you will never obtain this and at the same time get other qualities and a certain prestige, which obviously is desirable for this position.'[18]

Sargent had distilled his unhappy experience at the BBC into a single letter: he was the victim of a vendetta because staff at Yalding House could not deal with a Chief Conductor whose standing and fame dwarfed them. True or not, Sargent had made a political error. He threatened to take matters higher up the chain of command and effectively issued to Howgill a declaration of hostilities. The Controller of Music, a BBC loyalist through and through, could not compete with Sargent as a musician, but he was a wily administrator. The day after receiving Sargent's letter, he started briefing against him at the highest level and succeeded in sacking him the following year. The clinching memorandum sent to Lindsay Wellington, Director of Home Broadcasting, in April 1956 was a model of apparent reasonableness. 'Sargent has enjoyed the title of Chief Conductor but has remained in essence a guest who conducts it more often than do other conductors,' claimed Howgill.[19] He advised that Sargent be given a year's notice during the 1956 Proms 'with no reason given other than that we shall wish to make a change after seven years'.[20] A thick file of internal minutes that claimed Sargent was too expensive, suspicious of unfamiliar music and had failed with the orchestra accompanied Howgill's memorandum.[21]

Arguments that Sargent was too expensive were clearly nonsense. The BBC paid him less than other conductors of his celebrity and box-office appeal enjoyed. Having sacked him, the Corporation neatly proved this point by immediately raising his fee.[22] The claim that Sargent was 'suspicious of unfamiliar, let alone new music' was based on his famous withdrawal in 1952 from a studio recording of Schoenberg's *Five Orchestral Pieces*. Sargent certainly could be scathing in his assaults on contemporary composers. In a 1957 address to the Society of Incorporated Musicians, of which he was president, he denounced much recent work as 'an awful lot of tripe' written by composers who sought only to hide their inadequacies behind intellectual obscurity.[23] To a Proms audience, he put it more simply: 'If I had a school for composers I would put up two mottoes: 1. If music be the food of love, play on. 2. If not, shut up, please.'[24]

This public posturing was the result of private unease at the direction in which modern music was heading and a feeling that too much composition was simply repugnant to audiences. His response in 1955 to the oratorio *Isaiah* by Polish composer Alexandre Tansman combined a typical bemusement and frustration in the face of contemporary techniques. 'These modern works of this type, of which I see so many, absolutely amaze me,' he wrote. 'I cannot understand how any composer could allow himself to write a work so completely lacking in melodic interest. If you glance through the whole work, the soprano line is absolutely terrifying in its lack of ideas and complete lack of any sense of melody. The part-writing too, of course, is absolutely square-cut and juvenile in its conception. There is no rhythmic variety or interest. It is just another succession of modern harmonies. I don't know what the modern composers are coming to but I really do feel they are a very uninspired lot!'[25]

'What a pity it is that his inexhaustible energy and his marvellous talents should almost always be wasted on such eternally repeated works . . .' complained Stravinsky of Toscanini, almost half of whose programmes between his sixtieth and seventieth birthdays comprised works just by Beethoven, Brahms and Wagner.[26] The BBC said much the same of Sargent, yet the spirit of the younger man, who had introduced so many important compositions from Europe to England through the Courtauld-Sargent Concerts and Liverpool Philharmonic performances, remained intact. He approached contemporary compositions with dedication. 'I am collecting a lot of scores, and going through them very seriously,' he wrote in 1955, and asked the BBC library to send anything new which they thought important.[27] While the sieve of history has proved him right about most of the composers he condemned, Sargent did help bring significant new works to English audiences for the first time. 'I have been working at it for a long time (on my holiday),' he wrote to the BBC from Bermuda of Shostakovich's Tenth Symphony. 'I assure you it is a very remarkable composition of definite musical import and impact.'[28]

Whatever Sargent's complaints about modern composers, he continued at least to give them a public hearing. Notable premieres included Howells's *Hymnus Paradisi* (composed in memory of his son, Mick), Martinu's Third Piano Concerto, Rachmaninov's *Symphonic Dances* and Vaughan Williams's Christmas cantata, *Hodie*. Less durable were works by Bax, Bliss, Sowerby, Jolivet, Malpiero, Castelnuvo-Dedesco, Fricker, Ibert, Bloch, Rubbra, Jongen and Burkhard. Howgill and the Music Division complained when dismissing Sargent that his interest lay only in 'established music', yet between 1950 and 1957 he conducted fifty premieres.[29] His predecessor, Adrian Boult, had conducted only fourteen more first performances in the previous seven years.[30] In his term as Chief Conductor, Sargent directed the equivalent of one new work every seven weeks.

The Music Division supplemented its false claims that Sargent was too expensive and too conservative with an opinion that the orchestra was not up to scratch. 'After nearly six years, none of us can say with conviction that the orchestra is the aesthetic body of the highest class that we feel it could and should be,' claimed Dick Howgill.[31] This did not match the orchestra's public reputation at home and abroad, which was at its highest point of the post-war period. Innovative reform and Sargent's own inspiring personality had wrenched it out of the doldrums. There had been triumphs at the Festival of Britain and the Edinburgh Festival.[32] The orchestra had played a leading role in national mourning after the death of George VI in 1952 and in celebrating the Coronation of Elizabeth II in 1953. Sargent's insistence that the orchestra perform outside London in ten regional towns and cities had increased its national profile.[33] The Proms thrived under his direction as he put new life into an ailing institution that many had thought beyond help.

Success at home was if anything exceeded by acclaim abroad. 'This English radio orchestra is of international standard and has developed a style of performance that lends it unmistakable individuality,' wrote a critic in Düsseldorf during a tour of Germany, Holland and Belgium in 1954. Sargent was praised as 'a master of the art, which might be called a British characteristic, that of remaining detached yet of giving what is actually in the score with fascinating definition and exactitude'.[34] When the orchestra moved to Hamburg, *Die Welt* praised 'the precision and effortless virtuosity of the ensemble, the clarity of sound even in the most powerful climax', and attributed it to 'the personal art of the youthfully slim, vital man on the rostrum with his energetic and vigorous gestures'.[35] In Holland and Belgium, critics again praised Sargent's vigour and the expressive playing he drew from the orchestra. Even his sharp instruction to latecomers – 'Sit down, please' – failed to dampen audience enthusiasm. The last concert of the tour took place in Brussels on 21 June in the presence of Queen Elisabeth of the Belgians. It was the kind of occasion that brought out the best in Sargent. Vaughan Williams's Sixth Symphony won an ovation, led from the royal box. The following morning, reported London papers, Sargent accompanied Queen Elisabeth on the piano while she played Mozart violin sonatas.[36]

Sargent's tour of Germany and the Low Countries won plaudits that left the orchestra's morale sky-high. 'The tour had proved that, in good conditions, the Orchestra could play excellently and was still responsive to the enlivening force of Sargent's direction,' writes Nicholas Kenyon, their official historian.[37] The tour of Scandinavia in June 1956 was possibly an even greater success. The opening concert was in Copenhagen at Tivoli Gardens. During rehearsals, the King of Denmark, a keen amateur conductor, sat in the hall following scores to *The Young Person's Guide* and Vaughan Williams's 'London' symphony. 'Would you like to conduct, sir?' Sargent asked. 'Better not, Malcolm,' replied the notoriously shy monarch, whose lack of physical presence had prompted Sargent to commit an appalling *faux pas* at Buckingham Palace the previous year. 'Malcolm was talking in a familiar way to a middle-aged man, when they were approached by an acquaintance,' remembers Kenneth Rose. 'Malcolm said "Do you know my friend the King of Norway?"; "Denmark," said the first man.'[38] Such slips were rare. Aside from attending all the rehearsals, the King summoned Sargent to his suite behind the royal box during the interval of the first concert. With the Third Programme broadcasting the concert, BBC officials began to fret as it became clear that royal gossiping would delay the transmission. 'Broadcasting ruins everything,' Sargent opined before taking his leave. After the concert, the King joined the orchestra and their Chief Conductor to celebrate late into the night.

From Denmark, the orchestra travelled to Norway and then Finland for an audience with musical royalty. Sargent had been a loyal advocate of Jean Sibelius since the 1920s and with members of the orchestra met the ninety-year-old composer at his home in Järvenpää. They took with them a book of signatures from the whole orchestra and were photographed with him. Sargent came away with a signed photograph that bore the inscription 'To Sir Malcolm Sargent, with gratitude and admiration from Jean Sibelius'. It later stood proudly on the piano at Albert Hall Mansions as an imprimatur of his Sibelius readings.[39]

Everywhere Sargent and the orchestra performed there were ovations, laurel wreaths and terrific reviews. The high point of the tour came in Sweden, where they performed in the presence of the British and Swedish royal families. It was amongst the most glamorous nights in the BBC orchestra's history. At the final rehearsal Sargent ran through the programme – *Young Person's Guide*, Sibelius's First Symphony and an overture by Swedish composer Hilding Rosenberg – and then turned to matters of etiquette. For more than an hour the orchestra practised standing for the national anthem and taking their calls. 'The orchestra had very mixed feelings about that sort of thing,' recalls Sidonie Goossens. 'He gave wonderful concerts but I often felt that he was distracted by royal families sitting up in the box.'[40] Whatever reservations the orchestra had about Sargent's attention to detail, the effect was stunning. Lord Mountbatten later remembered how 'the whole audience stood up' led from the royal box. The next day, King Gustav of Sweden made Sargent a Commander of the Order of the North Star. This was the zenith of the shining career of England's musical ambassador.[41]

'He thrives under festival conditions,' Howgill wrote of Sargent. Conducting the orchestra at prestigious concerts, he could make the musicians play out of their skins, but the kind of energy he expended to produce such fine results was impossible to sustain on a daily basis.

Both tours with the BBC Symphony Orchestra had seen his temperature rise to dangerous levels. George Willoughby, the orchestral manager, had been forced to call in a local doctor on more than one occasion. Sugar cubes and orange juice helped to keep up Sargent's vigour but were no substitute for proper rest. When he stood on the podium conducting for European royal families at major concerts, Sargent could fire performances of verve and intensity; that inspiration was more difficult to conjure at Maida Vale studios on a wet November morning recording a work that would soon sink without trace. Studio and Proms concerts brought out Sargent's talents, including his ability to draw a sufficiently competent performance on just a three-hour rehearsal. Without the intensive rehearsal and injection of adrenalin that an important concert provided, the BBC Symphony was just a routine orchestra.[42]

William Haley believed that the BBCSO was bedevilled by the fact that Toscanini had once called it the finest in the world. He might have appreciated the irony of Sargent scoring an international hit for the orchestra in Scandinavia in June 1956 only to be given a year's notice of dismissal almost as soon as he got off the plane. Sargent flew immediately to Bermuda for a holiday to mull events over. 'It's all rather unsettling,' he told Sir Ian Jacob before returning to meet him for lunch at Broadcasting House on 20 July to thrash out a new arrangement.[43] Sargent's own suggestion was that he should remain Chief Conductor of the orchestra during the Proms, with a new man appointed for the rest of the year. Jacob concurred and told Howgill that it was 'the kind of arrangement which might give us what we want while being fair to Sargent'.[44] The following day a formal offer was made to Sargent to ease the blow. He would become, like Sir Henry Wood before him, Conductor-in-Chief of the BBC Proms and continue as a guest conductor of the orchestra at other times in the year.[45] 'I am quite certain that the arrangement you suggest is the best for the BBC, of course providing that you really get the right man for the big job,' Sargent replied on 25 July in a letter that displayed both dignity and wounded pride. 'I take it you do not wish me to resign – I certainly hope you do not wish to sack me! We can easily fix a time when the press shall be notified of the new plans by mutual arrangement.'[46]

'I thinks this settles matters,' wrote Ian Jacob for the internal file. Sargent was invited to lunch at Jacob's house in Woodbridge, Suffolk, where they agreed a form of words for the official announcement. 'In order to give Sir Malcolm Sargent greater freedom for his many engagements,' the statement ran, 'it has been mutually agreed by him and the BBC that from the autumn of 1957 he will relinquish his post as Chief Conductor of the BBC Symphony Orchestra.' The formal announcement on 11 September coincided with the lavish Proms party that Sargent organised each year for the orchestra at London Zoo. He was in splendid form that night, performing his usual tricks with snakes and leopards whilst flitting from group to group with his customary rapid-fire conversation. Just before ten o'clock, he turned on the Home Service news. Amazingly the players did not know what was coming. When the newsreader announced that Sargent was leaving, the mood changed from end-of-term party to embarrassment. Members of the orchestra shuffled awkwardly towards the door, eager to make a hasty exit. There they found their Chief Conductor. His back was ramrod straight but as he shook hands with each in turn and wished them good luck, tears streamed down his face.[47]

15

Rolls-Royce, Whisky and Sir Malcolm Sargent

'I am a freelance and always have been,' Sargent bullishly told reporters after his separation from the BBC was announced. 'Anyone can employ me to conduct, any soloist can ask for me and any record company can issue me. I have never signed myself up exclusively anywhere or with anyone.' It was a wonder that 'this voluble and virile firecracker' had put up with 'the drearier chores of being a staff conductor' for so long, suggested the *Daily Mail*.[1] The BBC had hurt Sargent and even players in the Symphony Orchestra felt that he had been harshly treated. They presented him with an exquisite crystal decanter with seven engraved goblets of scenes from Holst's *The Planets* and images of his favourite animals at London Zoo. Sargent hid any humiliation under a veneer of unsquashable confidence. Peter Sargent recollects that 'he was very shaken when they pushed him out but he was absolutely damned if he was going to show it'.[2]

Sargent's fear that the split would cast a shadow over his career proved unfounded as the late 1950s turned out to be an unexpectedly golden period. He enjoyed continuing success in the happy relationship with his principal recording company, EMI.[3] While the BBC had tried to bend Sargent to its own obscure programming, EMI allowed him to conduct the great choral works in which he excelled. Sargent had been recording for the company since 1924 and the partnership had been unfailingly courteous. Where letters exchanged between Sargent and the BBC had been suffused with rancour, correspondence with EMI showed a genuine affection. 'He is a very old friend of ours and has been in the centre of our activities for the last thirty years or so,' wrote David Bicknell, Head of the Artistes Department, on Sargent in 1955. When EMI listed the principal conductors of their HMV label in 1956, Sargent was put in the illustrious company of Rudolf Kempe, Guido Cantelli and Beecham.

Sargent's greatest strength as a recording artist was his sheer professionalism, which maximised studio time by meticulous preparation. Unforeseen difficulties were overcome without fuss and with an absolute determination to finish on time. After an uncomfortable Mendelssohn recording in June 1956 during which Sargent was sick seven times, David Bicknell told him that 'it was very gallant of you to finish *Elijah* and Lawrance Collingwood [the producer] was full of admiration for the manner in which you did so when so many other artistes would have gone straight home to bed'.[4] Sargent went home immediately afterwards and telephoned a girlfriend: 'Darling, I'm in bed with flu.' 'Lucky flu,' came the sardonic reply.[5]

Sargent's dedication made him a reliable conductor for EMI; the popularity of his records also made him a commercial success. His recordings of choral works in particular enjoyed a wide audience and critical approval. New LPs by Sargent and the Huddersfield Choral Society of the central choral repertoire replaced 78s made in the 1940s. *Messiah*, *The Dream of Gerontius*, *Elijah*, *Israel in Egypt* and *Belshazzar's Feast* all sold well, particularly in America, where Angel Records brought them out. 'I agree that he does these things very well indeed,' Bicknell told Dorle Soria, founder of Angel, after she reported 'wonderful' reviews for *Israel in Egypt* and expressed hope that 'we can continue the Sargent-Angel tradition'.[6] These choral classics were EMI's biggest-selling Sargent records, especially when 'highlights' discs were released.

Sargent's orchestral LPs won critical praise even if sales figures did not match the extraordinary levels of his choral records. EMI considered his recordings of the Sibelius symphonies superb.[7] Through his concerto recordings, Sargent won yet more accolades. 'He was super to work with as a soloist,' says Jack Brymer, with whom Sargent performed the Mozart Clarinet Concerto. 'He had the ability to perceive what interpretation you wanted and convey it to the orchestra; you played as you wanted and he mirrored it.'[8]

Since recording Beethoven piano concertos with Artur Schnabel in the 1930s, Sargent had been much in demand. As Heifetz's favourite partner, he recorded works by Mozart, Bach, Vieuxtemps, Elgar and Bruch. 'When I lived in Los Angeles, Heifetz lived nearby and I used to see quite a lot of him,' remembers Sir Neville Marriner. 'He had a soft spot for Malcolm. Heifetz usually had not a good word to say for anybody and cut every conductor down to size, but I think he rather liked the meticulous way in which Malcolm prepared his scores and accompaniments.'[9] During the 1950s, EMI's leading international soloists including Paul Tortelier, David Oistrakh, Mstislav Rostropovich and Pierre Fournier queued up to record with him. These performers, like Schnabel and Kreisler before them, warmed to what the legendary sound engineer Frederick Gaisberg had called Sargent's 'modest and practical' way of working in front of the microphone.[10] Even the most eminent soloists could not always procure his services. When RCA told David Bicknell that Artur Rubinstein wanted to record concertos by Brahms and Beethoven 'and would like to get Malcolm Sargent to do them', they were turned down because the conductor's diary was full.[11]

These great soloists recognised depths of musicianship in Sargent that others missed. 'Malcolm was a much deeper man than his rather light-hearted, superficial aspect would convey and was much, much more of a musician than you would presume from his bearing,' suggested Yehudi Menuhin, who worked with him as a soloist for more than thirty years. 'From my experience with Russian or German conductors, they usually carry a certain portentous weight but Malcolm with his carnation never conveyed that over-seriousness. He was natural and elegant yet always master of his scores and no mean musician: a person of stature. I always enjoyed working with him.'[12]

Victor Hochhauser remembers that 'when it came to outstanding artists like Yehudi or David Oistrakh, he was very generous'.[13] Hochauser played an important role in bringing Russians to the west in the 1950s. Concerto recordings with Rostropovich and Oistrakh were part of Sargent's growing involvement with music of the Soviet Union. After the death of Stalin in 1953, restrictions on Soviet artists performing outside the state and foreigners performing in Moscow and Leningrad were relaxed. EMI, quick to snap up Russian talent, asked Sargent to help many brilliant but inexperienced recording artists. Complications often surrounded these sessions, not least because Soviet minders were reluctant to let charges out of their sight. When David Bicknell introduced Rostropovich in March 1955 as 'the best Russian cellist' and asked if it might be 'possible to fit him in', Sargent immediately invited him to Albert Hall Mansions. The Russian arrived with an interpreter and a bulky secret policeman who was introduced as a piano accompanist. 'It was obvious what kind of accompanist he was,' remembers Lady de Zulueta. 'You only had to look at his big boots.'[14]

Impressed by Rostropovich, Sargent agreed to an EMI recording of Prokofiev's *Sinfonia Concertante* with the Philharmonia. They booked Studio 1 at Abbey Road, but only days beforehand Rostropovich pulled out citing 'a hand injury'. Sargent recognised the political reality immediately and asked if David Bicknell 'realised that the Prokofiev concerto is on the banned list in Russia? He was not a member of the party when he wrote it.' It was obvious that 'pressure has been put upon Rostropovich not to record it'.[15] The following day, EMI asked Sargent if he was prepared instead to record a work he had never conducted, a concerto by Miaskovsky. 'Many thanks for your help over Rostropovich,' wrote a relieved Bicknell after it was successfully taped. 'It is always a pleasure to have you in the studio.'[16]

Rostropovich had been so delighted with Sargent that he encouraged the Soviet cultural ministry to invite him to conduct in Russia. Sargent was initially sceptical, not wanting to offer a propaganda advantage to a Cold War enemy. The decision to go was in part the result of encouragement from the highest levels of government. His former secretary, Marie-Louise Hennessy, was married to a high-flying diplomat, Philip de Zulueta, and Sargent often spent Christmases with them. De Zulueta worked as Private Secretary to the Prime Minister, Harold Macmillan, and was his most trusted adviser. Détente was central to Macmillan's foreign policy. Sargent asked de Zulueta's advice about the Soviet trip and was told that it could only help Macmillan's diplomatic efforts.[17] Sargent discussed the visit over dinner with the Prime Minister at the Beefsteak a few days before leaving.[18]

When Sargent arrived in the Soviet Union he conducted the USSR State Symphony Orchestra at four concerts in Moscow and the famous Leningrad Philharmonic for two, with Rostropovich and Igor Oistrakh as soloists. The programmes combined Sargent's usual repertoire with music from his host country, including Tchaikovsky and Prokofiev. In both cities, Sargent was greeted with curiosity by the public and courtesy by officials. At all his concerts, audiences responded with loud cheering and applause. In particular, Sargent's favourite showpiece, *The Young Person's Guide*, won enthusiastic ovations. His only deprivation was floral. By 1957, Sargent had become so identified with his carnation that, according to *Woman's Journal*, 'it is now a talisman and a symbol, a hallmark of fame and success, and an outward sign of that mysterious and priceless quality of glamour that sometimes – but not always – goes hand in hand with greatness'.[19] This Russian trip was a rare time when he could not acquire a carnation for his buttonhole (an aberration he was to avoid in 1962 by having one flown out from London for his first concert). Carnation or not, Sargent's Russian audiences loved him. Talking on Moscow radio after the first concert on 15 May, he told listeners that he had been 'rather overwhelmed' by the warmth of his reception.[20] So it seemed was Moscow. 'There are only three important British exports,' proclaimed a Russian journalist. 'Rolls-Royce, whisky and Sir Malcolm Sargent.'[21]

Sargent was thrilled by the genuinely affectionate welcome he received, but the highlight of the tour came in private not public. He had long been an advocate of the symphonies of Dimitri Shostakovich and took advantage of his first visit to Russia to call on the composer. Having recently conducted the first broadcast performance of Shostakovich's Tenth Symphony at the Edinburgh Festival, he was thrilled when the composer praised his interpretation. 'Shostakovich is in the line,' Sargent said afterwards.

'Like all the best composers, he is evolutionary.' The slow movements of his symphonies would secure his reputation as a great composer: 'the sadness of the slow movement is different from any other sadness in music. Sadness in Beethoven had beauty; here it is the sadness that comes to you as shock, as pain, the pain you feel when seeing starving children with the ribs breaking through their skin and hollow-eyed women in rags.'[22] Sargent's respect was reciprocated. During this first meeting in May 1957, the composer promised him the first performance outside the Soviet Union of his Eleventh Symphony and showed him the first two completed movements. Shostakovich was a man of his word. Sargent conducted the work at the Festival Hall the following January despite having received a photocopy of the score just eight days before the concert.

Sargent's informal diplomatic relations often encouraged goodwill towards his country but on occasion he was also an official British export. In July 1958, the British Council flew Sargent and the Huddersfield Choral Society to Brussels for an International Exhibition. They had been chosen to represent British music in the arts section with performances of *Belshazzar's Feast* and *The Dream of Gerontius*. Despite the appalling acoustics of the hall and a stage that left the choir standing behind the orchestra unable to see the conductor, they 'overcame this triumphantly'.[23] Only King Baudouin of Belgium seemed unimpressed. He sat stiffly in the royal box throughout *Belshazzar* and left almost immediately it had finished. The Duke of Edinburgh, who was in the box with him, shrugged his shoulders at Sargent before giving the surprised choir a morale-boosting thumbs-up. The King of Belgium was clearly less enamoured of Sargent than was the Queen. Sargent again found time for 'playing duets with Queen Elisabeth of the Belgians'.[24]

If Brussels was unexpectedly disappointing, Sargent and the choir carried all before them in visits to Vienna and Berlin on behalf of the British Council. On 1 June 1958, they performed *Messiah* at the Vienna Musikverein with the Vienna Symphony Orchestra in searing heat aggravated by the glare of television lights. The choir had travelled for two days by boat and train from an unseasonably cold Yorkshire to a glorious Austrian summer, but the magnificence of the golden hall and Sargent's inspiration ensured a sensational concert. For more than fifteen minutes afterwards, the Viennese audience stood and applauded. 'I almost cheered myself,' Sargent told journalists afterwards; it was 'a sight quite fantastic to behold'.[25] The astonished music critic of the *The Times* reported that 'It is plain from a score of press notices that the Viennese had not in living memory heard anything like the "English *Messiah*" – their own description – which, said the *Neues Kurier*, should lead us to ponder, stimulate and imitate.'[26] The visit, concluded the British Council representative, had been an 'outstanding success'.[27]

Reaction to the 'English *Messiah*' in West Berlin in September 1959 was, if anything, more ecstatic. Sargent and the choir gave two performances with the Berlin Philharmonic to commemorate the bicentenary of Handel's death. Three specially chartered aircraft took them from Manchester to West Berlin. After their first concert, they were given a tumultuous reception. Another 'Berlin Crisis' had been rumbling on for a year. Sargent's visit coincided with a major breakthrough for détente – Khrushchev's trip to the United States – and the power of their performance matched the optimism of the city. The ovation went on and on after the performance and included a traditional Berlin mark of respect: bringing the conductor back for another call after the orchestra leaves the stage. German music critics were overwhelmed by the sincerity of the performance. 'It almost gave the impression,' said *Die Welt*, 'that the state of creative trance in which Handel wrote this enormous work in just under three weeks has also descended upon its interpreters.'[28] Sargent received an immediate invitation to conduct the Berlin Philharmonic. The British Council judged the visit a 'great success'.[29] At the next Annual General Meeting of the Huddersfield Choral Society, the President, F.R. Armitage, suggested that 'historians might well record our visit to Berlin as the best work we had ever done'. It was 'our own effort at international relations'.[30]

Sargent had emerged from his unhappy BBC experience with his reputation secured. He enjoyed success at home and abroad both as conductor and celebrity. 'Britain's most elegant conductor, Sir Malcolm Sargent earns more than Tommy Steele and is better dressed than Douglas Fairbanks Jnr,' observed one admiring profile writer before the 1958 Proms season, his first after splitting with the BBC. 'He is a glutton for society, he works hard and plays harder and is probably the most brilliant conversationalist in London.'[31] Yet even the most gushing reporter could not fail to recognise one glaring truth: underneath the ebullient façade, Sargent was a troubled man. 'Of course, Sir Malcolm's appetite for society and his insistence on attending every first night that he can derives from loneliness which he conceals carefully and effectively,' wrote this astute observer.[32]

To most fans, and even enemies, Malcolm Sargent enjoyed an enviable lifestyle. He was recognised almost everywhere both as a musician and as a fashionable member of London society. When he wanted to go to the theatre, tickets were made available. Restaurants that were booked up found tables for him and full hotels offered their best rooms. Hostesses clamoured to have him to dinner or to stay at their country houses, and parties were organised in his honour. Photographers snapped him for society pages and journalists quoted him on virtually any topic. He had an image that was both instantly recognisable and unique. Chauffeur-driven cars whisked him from place to place so that he always arrived in the style of a matinée idol. His social success was based on one simple rule: never be dull. However tired he might be after a full day's work, Sargent's bright if brittle character would sparkle in company. Malcolm Sargent was more than a successful musician: he was a celebrity.

Whatever satisfaction Sargent gained from his glamorous life, it did not bring peace. By the late 1950s Malcolm Sargent's private life was in shreds. His ex-wife plagued him with constant alimony demands.[33] He enjoyed a love life that was physically active but emotionally stagnant. The 'social list' remained full and Sargent continued to take pretty, well-bred young women to opening nights and parties but without any sense of lasting commitment. Though never short of company, what Sargent lacked was companionship. His greatest fear was loneliness. This conductor always needed an audience even when the crowds had gone home. His friend Kenneth Rose recalls long evenings at Sargent's apartment after concerts. 'After supper, Malcolm would say "Please stay" because he was terrified to be left alone,' remembers Rose. 'Sometimes one would talk until four in the morning as he poured out his troubles. I would be absolutely dropping and he wanted to tell me about his wife. He had an absolutely horrible time.'[34]

Lady de Zulueta agrees that his demanding social life was an act of self-preservation. 'It was an anaesthetic for having no happy home of his own,' she says. 'If you have been doing something interesting and long to unwind and talk it over, it's rather glum to go home alone to an empty flat.' [35] Sargent's closest friends knew of his private angst and on occasion others glimpsed sadness behind the vivacious persona. Yehudi Menuhin recalled a train journey with Sargent when 'he told me about his children and I suddenly realised that here was a real human being who was going through agony'. This was a rare public sight of the inner man. 'He was so trained for the Salon that he never let that down. I mean an Englishman does not in company cry or wear his woes on the sleeve. You behave in a way that would not upset the Queen and that was Malcolm's style.'[36]

Sargent's despair immediately following Pamela's death in 1944 had been at first alleviated by time spent with his son. After Peter Sargent's marriage in 1951, that relationship gradually deteriorated. Even as a young boy Peter had felt the weight of paternal expectation, although his education at St George's Chapel, Windsor, Eton and Oxford provided him with an impeccable Establishment pedigree. That background, combined with the Sargent name and contacts, and the inheritance of his father's charm, meant that great things were expected. The problem for Peter Sargent was that he had little or no idea what or who he wanted to be. 'Looking back, I suppose I wanted – and he wanted me – to follow in his footsteps in music,' reflects Peter, 'but I knew that if I had been good they would have said everything I achieved was due to him and if not they would have said "not as good as his father". It was an impossible act to follow.'

Reluctant to pursue the career for which his early life had prepared him so well, Peter drifted from one job to another without settling. His workaholic father continued to set demanding standards. 'He thought I was lazy and in a way I was,' says Peter, 'but meeting his expectations was impossible.' After Oxford, he considered farming, and applied to study at Reading agricultural college. Sargent sent a secretary to Foyles to buy books on the subject to help Peter prepare. The night before the interview, Peter came home from a party at four in the morning and found his father sitting up in bed with only a book for company. 'Peter, boy! Come and talk about farming,' he instructed. For several minutes, Sargent grilled him about crop rotation and irrigation until it became obvious that his son knew nothing. Sargent was astounded. 'He had read the books himself, you see,' recalls Peter. 'In that split second I realised that whatever I chose I would never live up to his hopes. I never mentioned farming again.'[37]

The burden of being the son of a famous father proved too great for Peter Sargent. During the 1950s the two men became estranged. Peter married happily but to a woman who had no truck with Sargent's heavy-handed attitude. 'She stood up to him and he didn't like that,' Peter remembers. 'He wasn't used to someone saying "Don't be silly", because the Maestro was never silly. Really he had wanted me to marry someone with a title so that he could come and stay at my seat in the country.'[38] The relationship increasingly became financial rather than emotional. Sargent lent money to help his son buy a home and to educate his four grandchildren. Yet they saw each other rarely, particularly after a disagreement over a projected biography.[39] Sargent spent Christmas not with his son but with the de Zuluetas or the Stucleys at Hartland where his daughter was buried. 'Perhaps it is difficult having a famous father, although other people get by,' concludes Lady de Zulueta. 'He upset his father dreadfully.'[40]

Sargent's problems with his son cut him off completely from the family. His sister, Dorothy, lived in London but Sargent met her for tea only occasionally as a courtesy and otherwise avoided her. Her success, although less publicised, was as remarkable in its own way as her brother's. Dorothy not Malcolm had fulfilled their mother's aspirations by rising within the banking profession, becoming the first female head of personnel at Barclays. 'It was quite something back then for a girl to get into a bank,' observes Marjorie Gesior, who knew Dorothy in Stamford. 'You had done well even to get into the Post Office.'[41] With a toughness befitting her position, Dorothy refused to take any nonsense from her brother. They had been close as children but now she embarrassed him. When he moved to Albert Hall Mansions in 1947, Sargent had invited her to his housewarming party. 'I remember when we were in Stamford as children having to take letters from Malcolm to his girlfriends,' Dorothy announced to the assembled company. 'We don't need to hear about that,' Sargent snapped, unable to laugh it off. 'Am I really that bad?' she asked Peter on leaving. Dorothy was never invited to a party again. 'It was very sad,' suggests Peter Sargent. 'My father was always afraid that she would let him down in some way because she knew more about him than anyone.'[42]

Estranged from his family, and lonely, Sargent kept himself busy with work and his social list. Those who knew him best often felt that he was at his happiest when enjoying the company of children and animals. Children brought out an affectionate side to Sargent that few adults ever saw. He relaxed with them and could talk or play for hours. His gift was an ability to chat to children without any hint of condescension. He was interested in their opinions and revelled in their uncomplicated innocence. With young people, he was not the Maestro but simply 'Uncle Malcolm'. 'We had an elderly nanny whose heart would sink when she saw him coming because she knew there would be a riot,' remembers Lady de Zulueta. 'Children adored him and before you could blink he would be on the floor with them crawling all over him.'[43]

Sargent's love of children had been a consistent feature of his professional life. The Mayer children's concerts had influenced the musical tastes of a generation. Tours abroad, especially to Australia, often included special performances for children. He spoke with an uncomplicated truthfulness such as when, for example, telling a young audience in Liverpool at the end of the Second World War that music could help them: 'You will find it very difficult: there is no street today – not just here in Liverpool but in the average city – without loss and the sign of age and decay, and we have not been in a position to put it right. Our own homes are not as they were – our clothes are shabby – things are not too good. There are certain things which mankind has that always cheer him up under the most devastating circumstances. Religion is one, for those who can take it. We have something too that has always been an inspiration and help to man through any circumstances – the Arts.'[44]

During the 1950s, Sargent particularly enjoyed working with the National Youth Orchestra. While embroiled in bitter disputes as Chief Conductor of the BBC Symphony Orchestra, he found the enthusiasm of the young players was refreshing. NYO had been founded in 1948 with Boult as President, and Sargent, Barbirolli and Beecham as Vice-Presidents. Sargent's debut concert with the orchestra came in 1955 when he conducted its first live televised concert at the Royal Festival Hall with a nine year-old pianist as soloist. In 1958, he became the orchestra's President and to celebrate its tenth anniversary sent personally signed photographs to each of the players. 'There can be nothing more stimulating than to take a week with the best of the nation's musical youth and spend hours every day working with them,' Sargent said in 1959. 'They work hard under a discipline of practice hours, rest hours, feeding hours, rehearsal hours; a happy band of teenagers existing under St Cecilia for one purpose only – music-making.'[45]

Sargent's affection for children was matched by his love of animals. At home, like Churchill, he would often work in bed with the budgerigar, Hughie, perched on his head.[46] London Zoo provided a depth of solace that Sargent found almost nowhere else. 'He was a child at heart and the Zoo helped him keep going,' suggests Sylvia Darley.[47] Sargent was a member of the Garrick and the Beefsteak clubs, but the Fellows' dining room at London Zoo was his favourite for almost forty years.[48] As a boy in Stamford, Malcolm Sargent had waited with barely contained enthusiasm for the annual visit of the circus and each birthday asked his parents for a baby puma. He often said in later life that running a circus was the only job that might have tempted him away from music; and his stage manner as a conductor had something of the ringmaster's art.

Overseas tours were always punctuated by visits to local zoos. An old friend from Melton Mowbray, Harold Grenfell, owned a ranch in South Africa at which Sargent was a regular guest, spending days in the estate's game reserve. He was a familiar face at Melbourne Zoo, where he fed bananas to the tortoises and visited his favourite cockatoo, who always greeted him with 'Hello darling!'. 'Hello, indeed,' replied a well-practised Sargent.[49]

As much pleasure as Sargent took in the company of animals, he was even more active in guaranteeing their well-being. After the Second World War, he joined the sub-committee of the Zoological Society which oversaw animal welfare, and later joined its governing council. In 1950, the Royal Society for the Prevention of Cruelty to Animals, knowing his interest and in need of a celebrity, asked Sargent to appeal for funds. His broadcast on the Home Service recounted some of the appalling acts of cruelty inflicted on animals.

'The society needs funds and each one of you must help,' he urged. 'Unless you do so, you can never look your dog, or any dog, in the face again.'[50] The comeback was immediate and testament to this combined tug on the national heartstrings. Contributions addressed to him at the RSPCA totalled almost £6,000. 'The response exceeded all expectations,' recorded the Appeals Department.[51] Sargent personally signed thousands of letters of thanks to contributors. Such was his commitment and enthusiasm that the RSPCA immediately invited him to become a Vice-President of the society and President after Professor Gilbert Murray's death in 1957.[52] Sargent might have treated this as a nominal appointment but chose instead to devote to it considerable time. The new President asked to be sent agenda papers and minutes of council meetings and standing committees. He continued to issue appeals and significantly improved the financial resources of the society. His favourite duty was the annual animal service at St Martin-in-the-Fields for which he selected biblical passages about animals, arranged the music and even rehearsed the choir.[53]

Animals and their welfare provided a release from the pressures of celebrity for Sargent even if they reinforced his popular image. There was nothing contrived about his enthusiasm: colleagues noticed that he perceptibly relaxed at the Zoo. Hugh Maguire, who never warmed to Sargent, remembers regular lunches at the Zoological Society after BBC rehearsals that showed an easier side to the conductor. 'We always shared a bottle of Beaujolais and he laughed a lot, with sharp intakes of breath, his eyes bright,' Maguire remembers. 'Sargent was always happy at the Zoo.'[54]

16

Carnation Plucked

Wednesday 10 June 1959 was a rare day spent away from the podium for Malcolm Sargent. He used the morning for office work and the final preparations towards his first stereo recording of *Messiah* the following week. As Sylvia Darley passed him letters and forms for signature, one stood out: a proposed Zoological Society fellowship for the new Controller of Music at the BBC. Sargent examined it while casually wondering if he might fit in a visit to the Zoo that day. His holiday would begin two weeks later and he desperately needed to rest. It was essential to be on top form at that year's Proms in order to retain his pre-eminence. The BBC had that year appointed a Controller who was intent on revolution. Sargent signed William Glock's Zoological Society fellowship proposal without enthusiasm. He usually visited the Zoo to escape bureaucrats not to bump into them at lunch.[1]

The BBC's post-war policy of far-reaching reform in the Music Division had failed. Three heads in ten years had been unable to shake off the complacency and insularity of Yalding House. Dick Howgill, set to retire in 1959 and recognising the inadequacy of his own stewardship, had decided that only a complete overhaul would relieve the torpor. William Glock, in his own words, had been running a 'campaign of insurrection' against the British musical establishment throughout the 1950s.[2] The Dartington Summer School of Music, the International Music Association and the *Score* had provided vehicles to establish an agenda dominated by music of the European avant-garde. The BBC's appointment of this scholarly but waspish academic caused surprise and consternation. 'I feel rather as though I were a citizen of Wittenberg,' wrote Walter Legge, 'and Luther had just been elected Pope.'[3]

Glock's impact on the Music Division was immediate. Younger staff, sympathetic to his ideals, were recruited, including Alexander Goehr (later Professor of Music at Cambridge), David Drew and Leo Black. 'We [had] wanted to have nothing to do with the BBC,' says Goehr. 'It was the enemy and we were anti-Establishment.'[4] Now they were the new Establishment. Glock's most controversial appointment was Hans Keller, a musicologist who used pseudo-Freudian systems of analysis and was, according to taste, either a genius or a charlatan. Maurice Johnstone told Glock that Keller would join the department 'over my dead body'. Keller arrived in September 1959 and Johnstone left shortly afterwards, the first victim of Glock's coup.

Glock's revolution at the BBC was driven by the sense of restlessness and dissatisfaction that had swept through certain intellectual circles during the 1950s. Post-war Britain was a society uneasy with itself. While it continued to count the cost of war, Germany and France had risen phoenix-like to form a powerful trading area that further threatened Britain's economic interests. The dissolution of the British Empire had become a question of 'when' rather than 'if'. Even notions of what it meant to be 'British' were under challenge. Empire had lent Britain prestige on the world stage but also played a significant part in binding the nation together. Withdrawal from Empire initiated a slow move away from identification with notions of Britishness and encouraged the rise of nationalism in Wales and Scotland. Immigration from the West Indies and the Indian subcontinent also changed ideas of nationality, making Britain's collective identity both more cosmopolitan and complex.

The fragmentation of British post-war society was reflected in the manner by which it was entertained. A generation of writers, musicians and film-makers emerged who were deemed 'angry' with the Establishment. The 'angry young men' of the 1950s were not self-consciously a group but it is easy to see how themes consistent in their work gave them a single identity. In 1953 Stephen Spender wrote unflatteringly of 'a rebellion of the Lower Middlebrows . . . against the intellectual trends of Oxford, Cambridge and London, and the influence of Paris and Berlin'.[5] Kingsley Amis's best-selling novel, *Lucky Jim*, showed that attacks on those metropolitan values could be funny and popular. Amis was more amused than angry but his novel won similar iconic status to John Osborne's *Look Back in Anger*, the play that gave the cohort its tag. When 'Jimmy Porter' observed that his well-bred wife's family would 'kick you in the groin while you're handing your hat to the maid', he summed up the resentment and contempt that many felt towards an elite that dominated culture and society.[6]

Sargent came from a similar background to many of the 'angry young men' but by the 1950s any Wharf Road origins had been airbrushed from his life story. He was an Establishment figure in manner, dress and influence who epitomised the values of high culture. In 1961, he bumped into Malcolm Arnold, who had just completed the score to a film about the Eton and Oxford colonel of a battalion destroyed by his working-class second-in-command. 'It's called *Tunes of Glory*,' Arnold told him. 'John Mills plays a man just like you.'[7]

William Glock's 'angry' agenda for music at the BBC looked both forwards and backwards. At its heart was an advocacy of European new music and a rediscovery of Renaissance composers. His first invitation concert set a precedent by programming two Mozart string quintets with Pierre Boulez's *Le Marteau sans maître* (the flagship of the avant-garde, according to Alexander Goehr).[8] 'In general, the programmes set out to be both "fundamental" and venturesome,' wrote Glock. 'Just as they included not only Bach, Handel, Haydn, Mozart and Beethoven but also Machaut, Dunstable, Tallis, Gibbons, and Victoria, so in contemporary music there were basic works by Berg, Webern, Schoenberg, Stravinsky and Bartók, and then new pieces by Nono, Berio, Maderna, Stockhausen, Messiaen, Boulez, and Elliot Carter.'[9]

Glock's programme choices provoked controversy. British composers who rejected the ideas of the avant-garde found it increasingly difficult to get their work broadcast. Robert Simpson berated Glock for his 'unjustifiable exclusion of much valuable twentieth-century music that was either not fashionable or failed to meet with approval'.[10] John Manduell, a BBC producer in 1960, felt 'there were quite individual voices like Alan Rawsthorne, who became rather sad, simply because they were being cold-shouldered, or felt they were'.[11]

Glock's programming would have made little impact if confined to the lonely airwaves occupied by the Third Programme. *The Future of Sound Broadcasting*, published by the BBC in 1957, had confirmed earlier poor listening figures for the station: for every hundred people listening to a wireless, only one was tuned to the Third Programme.[12] The Proms, on the other hand, attracted widespread coverage at home and abroad. Where the average Third Programme audience was 5,000, broadcasts on radio and television of the Proms reached up to 100 million each season. Glock understood that if he wanted to achieve maximum exposure and court international controversy, this was the place to do it.

The new Controller's attitude to the Proms on taking up his post had been one of utter disdain. 'I never went to a Prom in the whole of the 1950s because they were so unattractive and there was nothing new,' he said, dismissing as irrelevant the fact that most concerts enjoyed full houses.[13] His first action as Controller was to disband the committee that chose programmes and to announce that in future Proms planning would rest with him. Older members of the department denounced Glock for behaving 'like Hitler', but he remained unmoved. When asked what he wanted to offer BBC listeners, his reply was emphatic: 'What they will like tomorrow.'[14] 'What we tried to do – and we all seemed to agree on this, I and the new members of staff – was to choose works that were really worth hearing, even if they might be a chamber of horrors from time to time.'[15] After Glock's first three seasons in charge, audiences at the Promenade concerts had dropped by ten per cent.[16]

The new Controller of Music and the Chief Conductor of the Proms could hardly have been less alike. Where Sargent was flamboyant and dapper, Glock was austere, yet these two very different characters quickly came to respect, even like each other. They had never met until Glock was appointed Controller. 'I'd

Above. Always dressed for the Club: Sir Malcolm, 1947, in a Baron photograph.

Above. Diana Bowes-Lyon.

Below left. When Harry met Larry: Sargent and Olivier both knighted at Buckingham Palace, 1947.

Below right. Another day at the office: Petronelle Reynolds (left) and Sylvia Darley (right) at IX Albert Hall Mansions, complete with view of the concert hall.

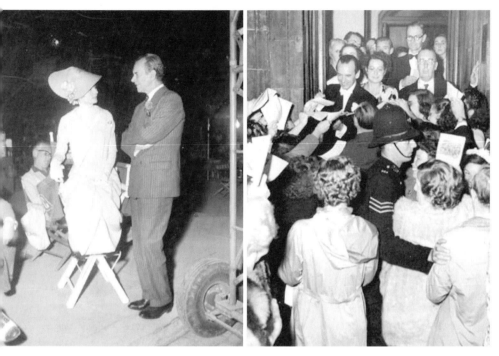

Above left. My Fair Lady: on the set with Audrey Hepburn, 1964.

Above right. 'One at a time, ladies please': post-prom, 1949.

Below. With Edwina Mountbatten, India 1948.

Above left. 'It's my opera and I'll cry if I want to': with William Walton at the Royal Opera House during rehearsals for *Troilus and Cressida*, 1954.

Above right. On Her Majesty's Service: Royal Festival Hall, 1962, with RFH manager, Mr Bean.

Below. With Ralph Vaughan Williams (and his OUP publisher) preparing for the premiere of the Ninth Symphony, Royal Festival Hall, April 1958.

Above. Royal rehearsal: King Paul of the Hellenes and his family on a private visit to the Royal Albert Hall, 1961. Princess Sophia (middle of picture) is now Queen of Spain.

Below. 'Hallelujah': stereo recording of *Messiah* in Huddersfield Town Hall, 1959.

Above left. The Python: London Zoo, 1955.

Above right. On safari in the Transvaal, 1964.

Below. With Hughie.

Above left. Sargent at 70.

Above right. Flash Harry.

Below. South Pacific: recuperating in Honolulu, 1966.

Above. The Last Night, 1967: with Colin Davis (left).

heard about him, knew about him to a certain extent and that the staff at Yalding House hated him,' said Glock of Sargent. At their first meeting they fell into talking about Artur Schnabel. Glock had studied in Berlin with the pianist in the 1930s and had watched Sargent conduct a 'masterly performance' with him of the Brahms B Flat Concerto at a Courtauld-Sargent concert at the Queen's Hall.[17]

What struck Glock at that first meeting and thereafter was Sargent's almost child-like enthusiasm. 'Each January I would show him the draft programme and he was always excited looking over it,' recalled Glock. 'He would look at everything not just to see who might have taken his favourites but to see what the whole season looked like. I liked his cheerfulness and that's mostly what I saw.'[18] Even small acts of courtesy were appreciated. When offered a drink by Sargent at their first meeting, the new Controller asked for kirsch. 'He didn't have any but the next time I went, it was there for me,' remembered Glock. 'He had that in him. I think I got on very well with him.'[19]

The charm offensive with Glock was consistent with Sargent's character. The Proms were a central feature of his life, emotionally and financially. After falling out with successive Controllers, he could hardly expect to emerge with credit from a broken relationship with a fourth. Yet what surprised many observers was not Sargent's tact in dealing with Glock but his enthusiasm for the new man's ideas. 'He always supported my enterprise, welcomed it, in fact,' reflected Glock.[20] Writing to Sir Henry Wood's widow, Jessie, shortly after the new Controller's appointment, Sargent displayed a barely contained excitement. 'He is very keen with regard to the musical situation at the BBC and will make changes as soon as possible,' he told her. 'This is itself a good thing. He has ideas about the Proms.'[21]

Sargent by 1960 had become a celebrity conductor famous for the Proms and inspirational performances of choral masterpieces. The pre-war Sargent who conducted for Diaghilev and forged his own revolutions had largely been forgotten. Sargent welcomed Glock's programmes as an extension of Courtauld-Sargent principles. Reservations about committing himself to conduct works before seeing the scores were easily overcome. 'I had the outrageous idea of asking him to give up part of his concerts to other, younger conductors,' remembered Glock. 'Others would not have done but he did.' Sargent willingly gave up serialist compositions to younger conductors such as John Carewe, Maurice Miles, Norman del Mar and John Pritchard. 'His view was pretty simple,' says Peter Sargent. 'He'd done his bit and it was time for the young men to have a go.'[22] 'I think he understood that audiences had been changed in the 1950s by the long-playing record and were receptive to new works,' concludes Glock. 'Sargent wanted to be in on that.'[23]

Throughout his career, Sargent had been prolific in the performance of contemporary music but faced the unpleasant fact that the composers he championed were burnt out, dead or no longer favoured. Jean Sibelius, 'the only real successor to Beethoven', had died in 1957.[24] Sargent had spoken to Sibelius the night before and was conducting the Fifth Symphony in Helsinki University at the exact moment of his death. The composer's son had hoped that the radio broadcast of the concert might help Sibelius gain consciousness (which prompted the unfortunate newspaper headline, 'Sibelius dies after hearing Sargent conduct Fifth Symphony').[25] Sargent had been in the process of recording all the composer's symphonies for EMI, but the cycle was instead cancelled. 'As so often happens when a great composer dies, there is now a slump, probably temporarily, in interest and not much business to be done,' explained David Bicknell.[26]

The death of Vaughan Williams, aged eighty-five, followed in August 1958. The previous April, Sargent had conducted the premiere of the composer's Ninth Symphony at the Royal Festival Hall. 'It was too long a journey from the box to the platform, so after the performance [Vaughan Williams] took his calls where he was,' wrote the composer's wife, Ursula, afterwards, 'and Malcolm, who appeared to have wings on his shoes, joined him to acknowledge the clapping and to share the flashing lights of the photographers.'[27] Sargent dedicated a Proms performance of *The Dream of Gerontius* to Vaughan Williams's memory and told the widowed Ursula how 'at the end of the concert there was no applause and the whole audience rose to their feet. The House was packed. They stood for an unbearably long time before any made a move to depart.'[28]

Sargent had supported Vaughan Williams's successor as England's leading composer, Benjamin Britten, early in his career, but latterly the relationship had cooled. Peter Pears, Britten's lover, detested

Sargent, and discouraged the composer from using him even when he was ideally suited. Sargent was not asked to conduct the premiere of Britten's monumental choral work, *War Requiem,* in Coventry Cathedral in 1962. Performed in the context of the Cuban missile crisis, it captured the public mood like no other serious English composition that century. The huge choral forces mobilised were Sargent's métier and he was distressed at not being asked to conduct. Having taken Britten's *The Young Person's Guide* around the world, he felt keenly this public humiliation.[29]

Sargent's popularity also suffered from the decline of other favourite composers, particularly Shostakovich and Walton. When Sargent premiered Shostakovich's Eleventh Symphony in January 1958, the critics had judged that the composer's symphonic genius had withered. Four more symphonies followed, but it was in his string quartets that Shostakovich found a more telling late voice. Shostakovich's best symphonic works lay behind him but at least his sound-world remained distinctive; William Walton, on the other hand, had allowed his talent to ebb away. He had always been lazy but his ability had flourished under the iron hand of his lover, Alice, Viscountess Wimborne. After her death in 1948, Walton had married Susana Gil Passo and moved to Italy. Life on the island of Ischia moved at a snail's pace and so did Walton's composing. He never recovered the verve of the pre-war years. New works when they finally emerged lacked the originality of earlier masterpieces. 'My own feeling is that unless somebody bullies you, you are not inclined to get on with it,' Sargent told him in 1958.[30] 'You are undoubtedly right about the bullying,' Walton replied tetchily. 'Perhaps an insulting note from you now and then would be a help!'[31]

Sargent tried to coerce Walton into writing a choral work to celebrate the 125th anniversary of the Huddersfield Choral Society in 1961. He had suggested an oratorio based on the story of Moses. 'Quite honestly, we could do with another *Belshazzar's Feast,*' he had told Walton.[32] 'The Moses script as I told you raises too much competition from *B's F* and would I fear be a hideous mistake to attempt it,' the composer responded. A work on the scale of *Belshazzar* was beyond Walton by now, but after much badgering by Sargent he proposed, 'while making no promises, a setting of *Gloria in excelsis*'.[33]

The first performance of *Gloria* should have been a celebration. The anniversary began well, with Sargent being granted the freedom of the town on 13 October 'in recognition and full appreciation of the illustrious service given to music in this country [and...] particularly the contribution he has made to music-making in this town as conductor of the Huddersfield Choral Society during the past twenty-nine years'. At a concert in the town hall that night, Sargent, conducting extracts from *Messiah*, told the audience that 'I am embarrassed as Sir Malcolm Sargent but proud if I can stand here in the name of music and of the choir which is second to none in the world.'[34]

Huddersfield had been through difficult times during Sargent's years. A thriving, prosperous town in the early 1930s, it had endured the Depression and a world war. It was now suffering from the industrial sclerosis that was eating away at urban communities in northern England. Sargent had given the people of Huddersfield a focal point for civic pride in the performances of a choir that was hailed as magnificent throughout the world.

Recognition, as so often with awards of this kind, also marked the end of an era. The choral society that had performed so spectacularly for three decades now struggled to recapture former glories. Choirs everywhere had been affected by the advent of television, which lessened the need for community activity, and were finding it increasingly difficult to attract young people. The era of mass choral societies was ending and even those with the reputation of Huddersfield were in decline. While in the midst of their 1959 triumph in Berlin, Sargent had been 'a little worried with regard to the pianissimo singing of the Huddersfield choir' and wondered 'if this is not because we are getting a surfeit of too-old people, particularly in the sopranos'.[35]

Many of the bright young things who had joined the choir when the charismatic Dr Sargent arrived in 1932 were still there, but now with grandmotherly looks and voices. Herbert Bardgett, their chorus master, was dying of cancer. This bad-tempered, abrasive man had bullied the choir for thirty years but trained them to an extraordinary standard. Most members disliked him yet tolerated his behaviour because he was among the finest choir trainers that England has ever produced. Illness kept him away from most rehearsals for *Gloria*, and those he did attend lacked the ruthless precision that had characterised his method. The result was that the night before the concert, Sargent had arrived in Yorkshire on a high after making his first recording with the Vienna Philharmonic Orchestra and found to his horror that the choir could not sing Walton's new work.

Gloria is a technically difficult piece for choir and orchestra with contralto, tenor and bass soloists in which, according to Walton's official biographer, 'invention simmers on a low light'. The composer was 'not sure that it is at all a good work, in fact not perhaps worth the hard labour necessary to make it really come off'.[36] Rehearsals for *Gloria* were shambolic. Complex rhythms in fast passages were beyond singers unsure of their parts. Walton listened in horror as his new work broke down time after time. 'Surely it would have been possible to rehearse them a few weeks previously so that you could give them the tempi etc. and the confidence in tackling a new work, which only you could give them,' he demanded of Sargent.[37] Sir Malcolm, as the master of the 'quick-fix' rehearsal, began teaching the choir bar by bar. Walton made testy interventions about speeds as Sargent attempted the more urgent task of getting the notes right.

The concert rehearsal was even worse. Walton was furious 'to discover that the soloists did not know their parts adequately and that they had not even had a piano rehearsal with you [Sargent] previously'.[38] Susana Walton urged her husband to humiliate the conductor by refusing to allow the performance to go ahead. 'I would and should have withdrawn the *Gloria* from the programme if I had not known the distress and disappointment this would have caused the organisation and yourself,' Walton told Sargent.[39] He would not speak to Sargent in the Mayor's Parlour before the concert but his wife launched a vicious attack. 'Willie's bad behaviour (and it *was* bad) may be excused by temperamental genius, nerves, etc. but this cannot apply to . . . Sue who was appallingly rude (I have told her so),' Sargent wrote to Lilias Sheepshanks.[40]

When Sargent left the parlour, choir members lining the corridors stood up as usual but looked edgy. The rumours of raised voices and flared tempers clouded what should have been a happy anniversary night. Sargent remained apparently unperturbed as he made his way through the singers, wishing them luck and exchanging pleasantries.

When he walked on to the stage of the Huddersfield Town Hall, the choir rose as one to applaud him. If Sargent felt any agitation, there were no visible signs. He launched into *Gloria* with his usual vigour and produced a performance that made up in excitement what it lacked in polish. Afterwards the conductor beckoned Walton to join him on the platform and held his arm aloft in a disingenuous sign of triumph.

The composer later admitted that 'You did indeed despite all these handicaps manage to "pull off" the performance.'[41] Yet immediately after the concert he told the press that Sargent had not given the work enough rehearsal time. Huddersfield officials, he charged, lacked commitment. At a dinner organised in his honour, Walton made these criticisms public with an appeal 'for this kind of thing not to happen again'. 'It was an unfortunate speech,' Sargent told him. 'It was not unfortunate enough,' Walton fired back.[42]

No one emerged unscathed from the first performance of *Gloria*. The work confirmed Walton as a composer in decline. 'An unkind critic – for such, I fear, exists – might have little to say about William Walton's *Gloria* except to suggest that the barrel labelled "Belshazzar's Feast" must be nearly empty now,' summed up the *Sunday Telegraph*.[43] Style and boldness remained but the imagination had long gone. *Gloria* was a mediocre work and its first performance confirmed that the Huddersfield Choral Society was in freefall. It was not the only choir tumbling from the heights.

If by 1961 the Huddersfield Choral Society was sounding frayed, the Royal Choral Society seemed in danger of unravelling altogether. Annual performances of *Messiah* and Christmas carols guaranteed full houses; at other concerts, audiences at the cavernous Albert Hall were embarrassingly small. 'If public response is the criterion,' wrote one critic after a performance of Honegger's *King David* in February 1962, 'the Royal Choral Society is having a bad time and has for some years past.'[44]

The decline in interest in choirs was more detrimental to the Royal Choral Society than most. Whereas the Huddersfield Choral Society was able to address recruitment problems with an appeal to civic pride, the Royal Choral had no such claims. Where before the war there had been a thousand voices, by the 1960s there was half that number. Of those who remained there was, like Huddersfield, 'a surfeit of too-old people'.[45] Sargent's performances of *Hiawatha* in the 1920s and 1930s had been stylish events that generated mass interest, but thirty years later the Royal Choral Society seemed out of touch. Even within classical music circles, the Society's performances of choral repertoire seemed old-fashioned. Audiences that once had thrilled to gigantic performances of *Messiah* now preferred, historically aware readings that stripped away tradition and returned to original scores.

Aware of changing demands but unwilling to adapt his own, Sargent began to lose interest in his mass choral societies in the 1960s. He had attended Royal Choral Society rehearsals on Monday nights for more than thirty years but now increasingly delegated to juniors. The style and charm remained, as did the devotion of the chorus. Graeme Tong, who joined the Royal Choral Society in 1960, remembers that 'everybody was blindly loyal and respected Sargent because he still made every individual believe that he was conducting them'. Yet the substance beneath the panache was increasingly fragile. 'Looking back on it, we sang very badly because nothing was ever adequately rehearsed,' Tong recalls. 'He would end the rehearsal by saying "You were wonderful; this is going to be the best performance ever!" and we believed him. But those concerts really were very poor. It was a big noise but it was not actually very controlled.'[46]

The decline of London's most prestigious choir was matched by a crisis in the capital's orchestral life, which by 1961 was characterised by dissent, betrayal and threats of extinction. The London Philharmonic Orchestra had come within hours of bankruptcy in 1957, not helped by the untimely resignation of Boult as Music Director to begin recording with the rival Philharmonia. The LPO re-formed as a self-governing organisation but operated on a hand-to-mouth basis, with players giving up salaries and pensions to keep afloat. Whatever problems the LPO faced, they were as nothing to those of the Royal Philharmonic Orchestra. Sir Thomas Beecham had founded the RPO in 1946 in yet another display of arrogant pique. During his long career, Beecham was intimately involved with Covent Garden, the BBC Symphony, London Philharmonic, London Symphony and Philharmonia orchestras. He came close to destroying all of them. The Royal Philharmonic Orchestra was last in the long line of Beecham orphans. He left it broke when he died in 1961, having not conducted it for a year and willing it no money. Imminent collapse seemed inevitable.

Beecham had formed the RPO after the breakdown of negotiations with Walter Legge about the Philharmonia, who instead appointed Herbert von Karajan ('a kind of musical Malcolm Sargent', quipped Beecham).[47] During the early 1950s, Karajan and the Philharmonia had set new standards of performance, much as Sargent and the LPO had done in the thirties.

By 1961, having already lost Karajan to Berlin, even this superstar orchestra was in trouble. Legge's influence at EMI was on the wane. During the 1960–1 season, the company did not even use the orchestra for its full allocation of recordings. 'What had started as a quest for perfection was turning into a battle for survival,' observed John Culshaw, Legge's rival at Decca.[48] Only the London Symphony Orchestra, under the benign influence of Pierre Monteux, continued to flourish. Of those struggling to survive, the Philharmonia had in its Principal Conductor, Otto Klemperer, a maestro of international renown who was prepared to fight on behalf of his players. Others were not so lucky. Boult had been first off the sinking ship at the London Philharmonic. His replacements, William Steinberg and John Pritchard, lacked any semblance of box-office pulling power. At the RPO, Rudolf Kempe, a magnificent conductor who inexplicably failed to excite English audiences, succeeded Beecham for two deeply unhappy years before resigning.

Sargent's relations with orchestral musicians in London remained strained. 'No one could criticise his musicianship,' remembers Sidonie Goossens. 'It was more a personal feeling.'[49] The 1936 'bread and butter' dispute had established a view of Sargent that remained to the end of his career. It became an unspoken rule among orchestral musicians that life should be made as difficult as possible for Sargent during rehearsal, although privately many admired him. 'When the orchestra were all together, they would say "Oh I *hate* Sargent" but if you met them on a train or for a cup of tea, they would be honest about his ability and his concentrated conception of a work because they knew he could hold an orchestra, a huge choir and soloists as if we were all mesmerised,' recalls Marjorie Thomas.[50] London players, having derided Sargent for decades, now found themselves in the disagreeable position of having to go to him cap in hand in order to secure a future.

Relations with the LPO, the original 'lifeblood' orchestra, had been so poor in the 1950s that Sargent was booked only in the last resort. This changed when the orchestra became self-governing and realities had to be faced, including, ironically, the abandonment of salaries and pensions. Sargent was a box-office draw at home and abroad, relatively cheap and the hardest-working conductor in England. The LPO booked him for twelve concerts in London and the English regions in 1962. Yet it was as a musical ambassador that Sargent was most valued. That same year he toured with the orchestra in Australia, India and the Far East. The box-office receipts gave a huge boost to the orchestra's finances.[51] It was a measure of Sargent's commercial value abroad that the LPO invited him to conduct twenty-four concerts on that tour while their Principal Conductor, John Pritchard, was on the podium for just eight.

Sargent and the orchestra left for India on 24 February on a journey that would see them travel more than 30,000 miles in just seven weeks. The last time Sargent had been in India, visiting the Mountbattens, he had suffered an unpleasant attack of dysentery that put him in bed for a week; the orchestra's management, keen to keep him well on this journey, spared no effort to surround him with luxury. Champagne was ordered on aeroplanes and Rolls-Royces stood by on airport runways. He was put up in grand houses and gubernatorial residences, at which he always politely requested the attic and instead was given palatial rooms. He attended parties held in his honour to network on behalf of his orchestra and country.

While he continued to glitter in public, he was slowing down in private. Where the younger Sargent had partied until four in the morning, he was now more interested in a good night's sleep. 'We have Sir Malcolm Sargent staying with us and what a strange man he is,' one teenage resident at the Embassy told her friends. 'I had a party last night and soon before midnight he came in wearing a silk dressing gown. He went over to the gramophone, switched it off and said "Never play music of that kind when I am a guest in this house." Then he stalked out.'[52] Ten years earlier, he would have been trying to coax her into bed.

In Delhi on 1 March, Sargent was reminded of another sadness.

He conducted the *Enigma Variations* at a concert attended by the Prime Minister, Jawaharlal Nehru. When Sargent had visited fourteen years earlier they had both been lovers of Edwina Mountbatten, who had died suddenly in North Borneo in 1960. Sargent, 'who was one of my wife's greatest friends', had organised music at her memorial service in Westminster Abbey that included 'Nimrod', Lord Mountbatten recalled.[53] While he conducted the same piece with Nehru looking on impassively, curious eyes watched for even a fleeting exchange between them.

From India, Sargent took the LPO to Hong Kong and the Philippines, neither of which had before received an English orchestra. All five concerts were sold out and tickets exchanged hands on the black market for five times their face value. To combat the searing heat in Manila, the orchestra played in shirtsleeves, although no one was surprised when Sargent walked on stage in full evening-dress complete with high stiff collar and carnation. While Harold Macmillan was blowing the 'winds of change' through the British Empire, here was one Englishman who did not see this as sufficient excuse to remove his coat in public.

Sargent and the orchestra flew next to Australia, where John Pritchard joined them. At Perth airport a trumpeter played them down the steps of their plane with 'When the Saints Come Marching In'. Audiences and critics in Perth, Adelaide, Melbourne and Sydney greeted the orchestra with rapturous applause and admiring reviews. Yet for Sargent this return to the country where he had triumphed in the 1930s was something of a disappointment. He was treated with familiar courtesy and enthusiasm but the state of frenzied excitement he had generated in 1936 had gone.

Where he had seemed dynamic and modern in the 1930s, introducing works never heard before in Australia, critics in 1962 observed that he seemed to be conducting the same repertoire. Eugene Goossens had been a post-war Director of the New South Wales Conservatorium and conductor of the Sydney Symphony Orchestra, and had injected an enthusiasm for the avant-garde into musical life. The ABC was about to appoint John Hopkins to be their own 'Glock' as Director of Music.[54] Times had changed but Sargent had not; as he looked at rows of empty seats in the Melbourne Town Hall, his mind turned back to happier days when cheering audiences stood on chairs to applaud and eager young women thronged around the artists' exit stretching out hands just to touch him. At his last Melbourne concert, more than a hundred people wandered in late. When Sargent pulled out his watch admonishingly, they seemed hardly to care. There would be other concerts and other conductors.

The final concert of the LPO's seven-week tour was much more to Sargent's liking. In Colombo he conducted the orchestra in an aircraft hangar at a concert billed as the social event of the year. Traffic on the roads to the airport beforehand was so jammed that coaches transporting the orchestra had to be escorted by police through fields and down the landing strip. They played Brahms's Second Symphony in shirtsleeves, with Sargent again in obligatory tailcoat. The audience treated them with enthusiasm that bordered on ecstasy. Time after time Sargent was brought back on to the stage as the audience thundered rapturous approval. 'Whoever wrote that East is East and West is West and never the twain shall meet was a donkey,' said Sargent. 'One of the bonds between us is Johannes Brahms.'[55]

The orchestra returned to London in ebullient mood. Sargent informed William Glock of 'a very successful and happy tour' and that 'the orchestra are playing magnificently'.[56] To David Bicknell at EMI, he was even more fulsome in his praise. 'I was very impressed by the playing of the London Philharmonic Orchestra,' he wrote. 'I can assure you they are excellent and are so keen to get recordings made that I know they would give every satisfaction. They play absolutely in tune. Their musical discipline is good, and what is more their orchestral discipline is magnificent.'[57] After years of unhappiness and recriminations, Sargent had finally made his peace with the orchestra that he founded in 1932.

While civilised relations resumed with the LPO, those with the Royal Philharmonic were less happy. By 1963, the RPO stood on the brink of collapse. The orchestra was 'sick at heart' said their manager, Robert Kendal-Frost.[58] Like the LPO, it turned to Sargent out of desperation. Two international tours were scheduled for 1963 on which it was hoped that his name would generate enough revenue to ensure survival. While the Royal Philharmonic Orchestra needed Malcolm Sargent, however, the players could not bring themselves to show respect. They were Beecham's orchestra, instilled with a collective arrogance that made them believe they were the best in London. They had fallen on hard times but could not lose the attitude. 'Flash Harry' was to their minds Beecham's nemesis.

In early 1963 Sargent took them on a tour of Eastern Europe. There were problems of orchestral discipline from the outset, not helped by Sargent's insistence that rehearsals on tour should be no different from those in London. After an arduous overnight journey by train from Germany, facing a concert that night, the orchestra needed sleep more than practice. 'Why must we rehearse this, Sir Malcolm, when we did it last night?' asked a principal. 'Not with me you didn't,' Sargent replied, and kept them rehearsing for the full three hours. This first rehearsal set the tone for the tour. There was dissent when he called 'seating rehearsals' but it was met only with a stiffening of Sargent's resolve and determination to exert his authority. 'We have a tradition of playing this solo in the RPO,' he was told after asking the Second Horn to slur the famous 'wrong' notes of Beethoven's 'Eroica' Symphony. 'You have no tradition in this orchestra, only my tradition,' Sargent snapped back. This was a bitter (not Beecham's) pill to swallow.

Tempers were not helped by the appalling conditions that the orchestra, and even Sargent, had to endure. Hotels in Czechoslovakia suffered constant electricity and water supply failures. Food was at best meagre and at worst nonexistent. Sleeping in unheated hotels with leaking roofs and no hot water combined with too much travelling to take its toll on the health of players. Sargent's sojourns at British embassies ensured that he did not share the orchestra's discomfort, but even he was not immune. At a concert in Bratislava on 29 January, Czech radio attempted to record the concert without having negotiated a broadcasting fee. An unpleasant row broke out between the orchestral management and the local authorities, which ended only when an RPO official marched into the sound booth and yanked out the lead. After the concert, the orchestra began another overnight train journey, this time from Bratislava to Krakow. When they arrived at the Polish border, Czech guards pretended not to know who they were. 'We stayed there all night and most of the next day with nothing to eat and no facilities,' remembers Jack Brymer. There were no first-class compartments and Sargent sat with the other musicians playing cards and drinking vodka. 'I can see Malcolm Sargent walking down that platform the next afternoon,' recalls Brymer. 'He had stubble on his face but he was erect and tall, striding along in an astrakhan hat, and by God they were not going to get him down. It was a real Englishman walking down that platform and I admired him more at that moment than at any other time.'[59]

After three concerts in Poland, Sargent and the RPO travelled to Russia to generate the kind of publicity the orchestra needed to secure its future. 'Sir Malcolm gets Moscow ovation,' headlined the *Daily Telegraph* after the opening concert.[60] They played *The Young Person's Guide* and the 'Eroica' Symphony to an audience that included the powerful Soviet Culture Minister, Yekaterina Furtseva, Shostakovich and a host of diplomats. After the performance, the minister went to Sargent's dressing room to congratulate him on a 'wonderful' performance. 'You are my favourite woman in Moscow,' Sargent replied flirtatiously.[61] The greatest triumph came in the final concert of the tour, on 16 February, held in the Kremlin in the presence of Soviet leader Nikita Khrushchev.[62] Furtseva had asked Sargent to conduct Tchaikovsky and brushed aside his objections about taking 'coals to Newcastle'. Six thousand of the Party faithful crammed into the Kremlin Hall to hear the orchestra play the Sixth Symphony. At the end they stood to applaud for more than five minutes. 'When he took us abroad, by God he carried the flag,' remembers Jack Brymer.[63]

The Royal Philharmonic Orchestra attracted a wonderful press for its European tour but was undermined by the civil war fought on returning home. In the summer of 1963 Lady Beecham announced that the orchestra, of which she remained Managing Director, would be wound up after the autumn tour of North America. 'We have had enough,' said her representative. 'We have offered them the chance to run the orchestra themselves.'[64] Prospects for a self-governing orchestra were appalling. The diary after the tour was empty. The Royal Philharmonic Society had given their concert series to a revitalised London Philharmonic. The *Evening Standard* reported that resignations were 'flooding in left, right and centre' while many players were not bothering to turn up for work. In an ultimate act of self-mutilation, the most disgruntled players began agitating for the cancellation of the forthcoming US tour. 'There was no prospect that we should survive into 1964,' remembered one player. 'It looked as if we were going to be taken to America by Sargent, brought back and scuttled.'[65]

Sargent returned to London on 12 July from a holiday in Honolulu to discover the RPO players objecting to a tour with him. He had always been sensitive to criticism from orchestral musicians but feigned indifference. While the RPO members bickered amongst themselves, he fired off a warning shot. 'I have not signed a contract and before going for my holiday in early June I wrote to the American agency arranging the tour and to Lady Beecham definitely stating that they were not to rely on me for the American tour,' he said in a press statement. 'I would be very happy to work again with the Royal Philharmonic Orchestra on this tour provided that I am satisfied with the personnel and rehearsal schedule.'[66] Only an appeal to Sargent's patriotism saved the day. Bob Boothby and Frederick Lloyd, an old friend from D'Oyly Carte Opera pleaded with him to resolve the situation. If he could make a small gesture towards the orchestra by promising that no seating rehearsals would be called, it would head off the rebellion and prevent the humiliation of an English orchestra cancelling a high-profile international tour. Sargent grasped the implications immediately. 'Things have gone too far to permit a cancellation of the tour,' he announced. 'With fifty-seven halls booked solid a cancellation would make this country's name stink.'[67]

At preliminary rehearsals in London before setting out for Canada, Sargent made a peace-offering to the orchestra by declaring himself willing to fight for its survival. 'I realise what difficulties the orchestra has been going through,' he said, and 'I know things were not always easy between us on the Russian tour. But here we have an opportunity of proving what a great orchestra this is, not only for the orchestra's sake but for the sake of Britain.'[68] They left for Ottawa on 28 September to begin an exhausting tour that saw the orchestra give fifty-seven concerts in sixty-four days. Sargent conducted thirty-seven performances, with Georges Prêtre conducting the remaining repeat programmes. From Ottawa the tour swept in an arc around the continent down the east coast, through the south, up the west coast and finally stopping in Alaska. Sargent conducted a run of eleven concerts in twelve days and another of twelve in thirteen. It was a punishing schedule but Sargent said later that the orchestra played as if 'fighting for its life'. There were moments of controversy, particularly in the Deep South where the orchestra found itself playing to a segregated audience in Jackson, Mississippi. An anonymous telephone caller made a death threat to Sargent and two white protesters were arrested before the concert. Afterwards Sargent went to the Sheriff's office to insist that they be released.[69]

The American tour was a triumph for Sargent and the Royal Philharmonic. Sell-out concerts, ovations and critical approval lifted spirits and consolidated their reputation. 'The American tour with the RPO was completely justified and an outstanding success,' Sargent later told the British Council. 'I have never known better playing or more fervent appreciation from an audience and the critics had not a word to say against the playing at any time. What the future of the orchestra will be I do not know.'[70] In fact, it had turned a corner. In 1964 an Arts Council committee recommended that each London orchestra receive a basic grant of £40,000. Sargent's willingness to take the RPO to America had bought time to stave off bankruptcy.

The tour had even established a semblance of good humour between Sargent and the players. He travelled with them and showed another side to his nature. 'I remember in one of those Bible-belt cities, we were invited to a reception by the League of American Daughters,' recalls Brian Smith. 'Sargent thrived at those kind of occasions but he could see that we were bored. He was talking to the woman in charge who had a huge chain of office. She said to him, "If I pluck your carnation will you blush?" to which he replied, "If I pull your chain will you flush?" We were back on the bus before our feet could touch the ground.'[71]

17

The Walk to the

Paradise Garden

Monday 20 January 1964 began typically for Malcolm Sargent. He woke up in a hotel room, this time the Mitre in Oxford, having conducted the BBC Symphony Orchestra at a live broadcast the night before. That morning, he was driven back to London, where he met Rab Butler, an acquaintance of many years through the Courtaulds, at the Travellers' Club in Pall Mall.[1] After lunch, Sargent was collected by Sylvia Darley and taken to the Maida Vale studios to rehearse Holst's Choral Symphony with the BBC Symphony Orchestra and chorus. He entered the studio, shook hands with the leader, Hugh Maguire, and exchanged pleasantries. Off came his pinstriped jacket, on went the black alpaca. The carnation was put into water. All in all, it was just another day at the office.

Holst's Choral Symphony is an uninspired work, rarely performed, and disliked by choirs and orchestras. As the rehearsal went on, players in the BBCSO became restless while Sargent in usual fashion went through the work in detail. 'Do we have to keep doing this?' Maguire asked. 'Yes,' replied Sargent, 'and don't tune while I'm talking to the choir.' Hugh Maguire was known throughout London for his temper and disregard for all but his favourite conductors. 'He disliked Sargent intensely,' believed William Glock.[2] Admonished in front of the players, Maguire retaliated. 'We are highly trained and skilled musicians and we don't need to be spoken to like that,' he fumed. 'You are treating us like a kindergarten.' Sargent never lost his temper even when seething. 'You had better leave,' he told the leader quietly. 'It's not your business to tell me to go; I am the host and you are the guest, but as it is, I am only too delighted,' Maguire replied. 'Anyone coming with me, boys?' Having held the initiative, Maguire had now surrendered it. No one went with him and he was left to march fifty yards to the back of the studio alone. Before he got halfway, Sargent had restarted.[3]

'Sargent tells orchestra leader to go,' proclaimed the *Daily Mail* the next day.[4] Reporters, immediately tipped off and lying in wait when he left Maida Vale, followed Maguire to the underground station, where a scuffle broke out. When he finally got home, BBC officials made frantic telephone calls begging him to make his peace with Sargent. Eventually it was made clear that if he did not, his contract would be terminated. The following morning, the two men met in a private office and exchanged apologies. They walked into the studio arm in arm to cheers from the orchestra. 'Everybody is absolutely happy,' Sargent told the press. 'Everything is all right between us. I do not want anything except that we should be perfectly happy and get on with making music together.'[5]

The tiff with Hugh Maguire was headline news in most newspapers. It confirmed Sargent's continuing celebrity status but added to a growing sense that he was losing his touch. Many critics who had previously been grudgingly respectful now sensed blood and moved in for the kill. Throughout his career, Sargent had been notoriously antagonistic towards critics and had on occasion even convinced proprietors to sack them. 'There was neither life nor emotions in Sir Malcolm's interpretation and the orchestra seemed to be disinterested in their playing,' wrote one after a Prom performance of Brahms's Third Symphony. He summed up critical opinion of Sargent's performances that season.[6] 'They are not Sir Malcolm's best friends,' observed David Bicknell at EMI.[7]

Even Sargent's friends were beginning to question whether his powers were fading. The Huddersfield Choral Society wrote in February 1964 complaining that 'we feel to be in danger of losing our spirit of adventure and are not seeking "fresh fields to conquer" through modern works. In short, life just now seems to be uneventful, there are no opportunities, musically speaking, involving incentive and a desire to achieve.'[8] These were harsh words from the executive committee of a choir to which Sargent had brought unprecedented fame. His rebuke was simple. 'With regard to Sir Malcolm's fee – you do realise, of course, he has always been extremely cheap for Huddersfield,' wrote Sylvia Darley, and demanded extra money.[9] Dissenting London voices echoed those in Yorkshire. The Royal Choral Society made a testy announcement in 1964 that for the first time in their history a chorus master had been engaged, 'this having become necessary because of Sir Malcolm's frequent journeyings abroad'.[10] Empty halls, flagging membership and poor musicianship demonstrated that the standing of the Royal Choral Society during Sargent's twenty-five-year conductorship had come full circle.

Dwindling audiences showed Sargent's popularity to be in sharp decline. Where in the immediate post-war years his name had been a box-office draw, now it guaranteed a disappointing house. At the Proms, the Controller brought in overseas conductors to spice up concerts. 'He didn't like me introducing foreign conductors and would never meet them,' Glock recalled. 'He objected because they were eminent rather than because they were not English.'[11] Sargent gave way because he had no choice but continued to fight any further 'trespassing on my preserves'.[12] Fading box-office appeal was matched by a dramatic fall in his commercial value to recording companies. Leonard Wood, managing director of British EMI, concluded in April 1964 that 'as it seems unlikely that Sargent at this stage in his career will sign an exclusive contract with another record company there really does not seem to be any need for us to negotiate a new contract with him [...] and as far as I am concerned the contract can be allowed to lapse'.[13] Only a rearguard action by Sargent loyalists saved him from loss of face. They drew up a list of popular works to record, including Christmas and highlights discs. 'He is quite happy at the moment and looking forward to recording the Handel choruses and therefore should be no problem for the immediate future,' the producer Peter Andry told a relieved David Bicknell, who had worked with Sargent for almost forty years.[14] Bicknell's constancy had touchingly masked the new reality at EMI: 'We do not want more Sargent records than necessary. He is not a seller.'[15]

As if to emphasise his failing powers, Sargent had become increasingly accident-prone and susceptible to illness. He fell in the snow while visiting the Stukelys in Devon and had to conduct for weeks afterwards on a velvet-covered bar stool. In Honolulu, he tripped on the stairs and reappeared at concerts with his arm in a sling. Illnesses occurred more frequently and lasted longer. In February 1964 his temperature went up to 101°F and he was sent to Hartland for complete rest. He returned to work three weeks later but was ill again within days and confined to bed for a week. The punishing diary schedule remained but the strain of fulfilling it was increasingly untenable.

Sargent was reluctant to slow down and his vanity stopped him from making life easier. Orchestral musicians noticed that he squinted at his music and with unfamiliar works even got lost. He tried wearing a monocle but recognised that he was slipping into caricature. Yet he would not wear glasses. 'The minute I go on stage in glasses, the illusion is broken,' he told his son.[16] Contact lenses eventually provided an answer but another weakness had been exposed. Poor eyesight was matched by creeping deafness, but he refused point-blank to wear a hearing aid even in private. Rumours spread that his black hair was dyed. Some whispered that he wore a corset to create a nipped waist. Proud of his figure, he took the opportunity during a trip to Hawaii in July 1964 to scotch this tittle-tattle by displaying his slim build to newspaper photographers whilst swimming with dolphins in the Sea Life Park at Makaputt. It was a valiant attempt to hide the march of time.

David Bicknell had been concerned for some time that Sargent's seventieth birthday would be a difficult, even embarrassing occasion, and worked hard to plan a thoughtful tribute. EMI presented Sargent with an album of his recordings spanning more than forty years, put his photograph on the front cover of *Gramophone*, and released new discs of Smetana's *Ma Vlast* and *Elijah* highlights. The question of a

birthday lunch, Bicknell explained to Sir Joseph Lockwood, head of
EMI, was more problematic. 'As [you] will recall ten years ago when
Sir Malcolm was 60 we had a conventional luncheon attended by the
leading music critics and journalists who, in fact, are never on very
good terms with Sir Malcolm and who these days provide very little
useful copy in their papers. It has therefore been thought advisable
for this luncheon to have a new theme – Sir Malcolm's wide personal
interests and activities and his long association with EMI.'[17]

Bicknell organised a private lunch at the Savoy Hotel for the day
preceding Sargent's birthday, at which Prince Philip was the guest of
honour. 'I suggest Sir Joseph does not mention him bringing a
companion!' observed Sargent when he heard the news.[18] Other
guests represented important influences and interests in his life: the
Marquess of Exeter; Lord Bruntisfield from the Royal Choral
Society; Lord Drogheda, chairman of the Royal Opera House; Sir
Robert Mayer; S.W. Garsed from Huddersfield; Lord Fisher, former
Archbishop of Canterbury; Sir Arthur Willet from the RSPCA; Sir
Solly Zuckerman from London Zoo; Sir Ian Jacob; Frederick Lloyd
from D'Oyly Carte; Keith Faulkner representing the Royal College
of Music; and Donald McCullough who had chaired the *Brains Trust*.
As he entered the Savoy on 28 April with the Prince at his side,
Sargent, observing his life story collected in the faces present, looked
fit to burst with pride.

Oliver woke the new septuagenarian early on his birthday. The
Royal Mail had sent a special postman to deliver two sackfuls of
birthday greetings that bizarrely included seventy brown eggs from
an admirer in Coventry. There was a telegram of greeting from the
Queen and Prince Philip. Perhaps the most touching letter was from
his boyhood contemporary, Sir Thomas Armstrong. 'God bless, my
dear friend,' he wrote. 'Count me always among the many people
who thank Him for having known you – and are devoted to you.'[19]
Downstairs in the lobby of Albert Hall Mansions, a security guard
had been hired to receive presents and stop fans attempting personal
visits.

A birthday concert had been organised at the Albert Hall. The
Huddersfield Choral Society and the Leeds Philharmonic Society
had both chartered trains to London, where they would join the
Royal Choral Society to sing settings of the *Te Deum* by Walton,

Verdi and Dvořák along with Elgar's *The Music Makers*. When Sargent walked on to the stage of the Albert Hall at half past nine that morning, the choirs rose to their feet and cheered. When he lifted his baton to rehearse Walton's *Te Deum*, 800 voices instead sang 'Happy Birthday', which was no less moving for being predictable. Princess Marina afterwards entertained Sargent to a birthday supper at Kensington Palace.

'Flash Harry is 70,' ran the headline in the *Daily Sketch*. Sargent might have worried that the magic was waning but his celebrity status ensured this birthday front-page coverage. 'Flash, they've called him down the years,' observed the *Sun*, 'and the mantle seems to settle aptly on the carefully tailored frame of today's most famous 70-year-old: Sir Malcolm Sargent.'[20] Reporters paid tribute to his energy, quick tongue and sharp Savile Row suits. He was the ambassador whose carnation had become a symbol of British values around the world. He hobnobbed with royalty and counted the stars of stage and screen among his friends. His charm with women was legendary. Sargent had presence, self-assurance and style. 'He stands out like a carnation in a nettlebed. Anywhere,' declared the *Daily Mirror*. 'Plant Sir Malcolm Sargent in a crowd of elegant stylish males and they suffer miserably from comparison.'[21]

'It just feels the same as being thirty-nine,' Sargent joked, echoing the wisecrack of American comedian Jack Benny. 'In fact I get less worried about my age. My doctor tells me I am fitter than I was forty years ago. I take active holidays and this year I hope to swim with a twelve-foot whale in Hawaii. I'm told it is a lady whale which should be fun.'[22] It was a bravura performance. Throughout the celebrations Sargent smiled and laughed, exchanging banter with public, press and musicians alike. Yet it was not a happy time for him. While newspapers covered his birthday on their front pages, articles in the arts sections read more like obituaries. His contribution to British musical life was acknowledged but Sargent, they implied, represented the past not the future. The birthday concert given by his three choral societies was a disaster. The Albert Hall was embarrassingly only half-full. Bitchiness between the three choirs ensured a poisonous atmosphere that translated into a wretched performance. Graeme Tong remembers it as The Night of the Three Tediums: 'It was such a dreary programme and did not draw an audience. We felt cheated because Sargent and the Albert Hall was us, so we thought why are these others here? The camaraderie was not what it should have been to say the least. It was sinking in that his magic was fading.'[23]

Rivalry between choirs for Sargent's affection could at least be counted as a compliment. The behaviour of orchestral players was altogether less whole-hearted. The London orchestras all made presentations to him but these were paid for out of management funds. The London Philharmonic's experience was typical. On 25 April, Sargent conducted the orchestra at a 'birthday' concert in the Royal Festival Hall. The board invited the players to have a whip-round beforehand. 'A few days later the management came back and said the response had been disappointing,' recollects Brian Smith, who had moved to the orchestra from the RPO. 'That was putting it mildly. It was such a paltry sum that it was too embarrassing to give to him.'[24]

The board made it clear to the players that work with Sargent was essential to the financial health of the orchestra and required some kind of gesture on their part. It was finally agreed that they would play Stravinsky's *Happy Birthday* at the concert and rehearse it in their own time. Sargent arrived at the Royal Festival Hall on the morning of the concert and a presentation was made on behalf of the orchestra to generous shuffling of feet. The orchestra behaved meticulously and the rehearsal finished at half past eleven when the conductor dismissed them. 'The plan was that we would all get a cup of coffee, wait for him to go home and then practise the Stravinsky,' recalls Smith. They had failed to take into account Sargent's controlling perfectionist nature. 'It must have been Sylvia who told him, because just as we went back he popped up and said, "Right, let's rehearse Happy Birthday to me." And he kept us all there until one o'clock.'[25] In one crass gesture Sargent had confirmed the prejudice of a generation of orchestral musicians.

The contrast between Sargent's public image and the view within musical circles that he was a spent force was perfectly drawn at his birthday Prom the following September. This time the Royal Albert Hall was packed and the programme inspired. Jacqueline du Pré had made her Proms debut with Sargent in 1962 and he now invited her to perform the Elgar concerto with the BBC Symphony Orchestra.

'This young artist also rose to the occasion as never before in her life alike in richness of tone and expressive intensity,' said *The Times*. 'The spontaneous accord between conductor and soloist made their recreation of this music akin to an act of creation.'[26] The audience roaring their approval for Sargent throughout the concert ignited memories of a time when such ecstatic applause greeted him night after night. 'It was a wonderful evening of very tense musical enjoyment and an enraptured house,' Sargent said afterwards.[27] Enraptured or not, it made no impact on the Controller of BBC Music, who had sponsored the concert. William Glock had not bothered to attend.

Sargent settled comfortably into a new role as the Grand Old Man of English music. The fires of radicalism, so bright in his early career, had subsided to embers and finally burnt out. Unsympathetic to the modern age, he lost no opportunity in expressing his disgust. As guest of honour at the 1965 British Musical Instruments Trade Fair in London, he gave a caustic assessment of pop music. 'They are going further into the jungle,' he said dismissively. 'This is called progress?'[28] The problem was 'loudness without emotion', he told astonished delegates in his keynote address. 'I fear that in this age we are getting louder and louder. In music, as in speech, loudness should be due to the emotion behind it. The moment you introduce a knob you can turn there is no emotional impact behind it. This is in itself a very grave danger.'[29] Given a demonstration of an electric guitar, Sargent exclaimed 'what a horrible sound' only to be rebuked by its maker. 'I think it is narrow-minded,' he told the conductor. 'After all, I go to the Proms as well as liking the Beatles.'[30]

Sargent was happy to appear old-fashioned, even bufferish, because he was content to carry on with his musical life exactly as it was and sought no new challenges. The Last Night of the Proms, 1965, was his 499th Promenade concert. World-famous conductors including Pierre Boulez, Rudolf Kempe, Istvan Kertesz and Georg Solti had appeared at the Royal Albert Hall during the season, but the faithful Promenaders still elected Sargent as their favourite conductor.[31]

It was a similar story when he conducted the New York Philharmonic Proms at the Lincoln Center and to audiences of more than 20,000 at the Myer Bowl in Melbourne. These tours, also in

1965 maintained his image with some aplomb. When a Commonwealth Arts Festival was organised at the Royal Festival Hall in September it came as no surprise that Sargent should have been presented to the press as its 'elder statesman'.[32] 'We are a mutual admiration society,' he purred of the Commonwealth before conducting a concert with the Sydney Symphony Orchestra in the presence of the Queen.

In October, he took the Huddersfield Choral Society to Boston to celebrate the 150th anniversary of the Handel and Haydn Society where he 'scored a triumph' according to local critics.[33] Later that month he flew to Helsinki, where it was announced that he was to become a Knight Commander of the White Rose of Finland for his services to the music of Jean Sibelius. In the midst of such headline-making activity was an ongoing commitment to choral societies in London, Huddersfield, Liverpool and Leeds, recordings for EMI and Decca, and orchestral performances throughout England. His diary remained punishingly full with barely a day's rest: this was business as usual.

By December 1965 Malcolm Sargent was exhausted. He had conducted the Proms throughout the summer but the Common-wealth Arts Festival afterwards had replaced his traditional holiday. As Christmas approached he began to look forward to a two-week holiday staying with friends in Northumberland. On Sunday 19 December, with three concerts still to conduct before Christmas, Sargent was driven to Broadstairs in Kent to make a charity appearance at a carol concert organised by Edward Heath, leader of the Conservative Party. 'Malcolm came down and made a very good appeal because his personality was so good,' says Heath.[34] At lunch, Sargent entertained assembled local worthies with his usual blend of flattery, anecdote and risqué jokes. After Heath conducted the concert, Sargent told the audience that 'the great thing about this member of parliament is that he starts everybody together and finishes everybody together and you cannot ask for more than that from a conductor'.[35] He made a witty speech and asked everyone to dig deep for charity. Afterwards, admirers thronged around him while he happily chatted and signed autographs for more than an hour. When Heath escorted him to the waiting car, a crowd waved him off. It had been a quintessential Sargent performance: bright, charismatic and energetic. No one that day could have guessed what it had cost him. 'The next thing we heard, he had collapsed in his car on the way home,' remembers Heath.[36]

Sargent was taken to a London clinic but after staying overnight ignored medical advice and returned to work. He was in agony conducting carols with the Royal Choral Society that night but showed nothing to the audience. He broke down in his dressing room afterwards and returned to the clinic. The next morning he was on the operating table for a prostatectomy and remained in hospital for a miserable Christmas and New Year. Convalescence was complicated by infection and a violent reaction to antibiotics.[37] 'I was very, very ill,' he told waiting journalists when he left hospital on 21 January after a month-long stay.[38]

The following week, he flew to Honolulu for an enforced holiday, accompanied by Sylvia Darley (because 'his doctors do not want him to travel alone').[39] He particularly regretted cancelling a concert in West Germany with the Berlin Philharmonic Orchestra, a surprising personal invitation from Herbert von Karajan.[40] Sargent returned to London on Sunday 19 February and three days later, on Ash Wednesday, was back at the Albert Hall to conduct his annual performance of *The Dream of Gerontius* with the Royal Choral Society. When he walked briskly on stage, he was given an affectionate ovation. He seemed fit, tanned and happy. Astonished critics reported how Sargent looked 'as brown as a nut and as energetic as ever' while conducting 'with undiminished vigour and alertness'.[41]

In reality, two months' recuperation had done very little to restore Sargent's long-term strength. Three weeks in the South Seas could usually be relied upon to restore his physical and spiritual well-being, but this period of rest had been less successful. He told a friend after the *Gerontius* performance of how 'the wretched wound refused to heal and I had a great deal of pain in my right leg'. Endless weeks in bed had left Sargent with pins and needles that 'advance into a really painful burning sensation and occasionally I get a sudden sharp pain which is exactly like being stung by a very big wasp'.[42]

Finding inactivity more frustrating than the pain itself, Sargent threw himself back into work with reckless abandon. Days after writing of his continuing illness, Sargent left for Canada, where he spent a week conducting in Montreal and Ottawa. Four weeks later, he undertook a nine-week tour of Australia during which he conducted twenty concerts. 'I am very well and thoroughly enjoying my work here,' he wrote from Melbourne to Peter Andry at EMI. 'The orchestra is excellent and sold-out houses in eleven cities think I am not bad!'[43] Sargent then spent a week in Honolulu before flying to the United States to conduct the New York Philharmonic Orchestra in five Promenade concerts. When he returned to London at the beginning of July, he was predictably exhausted. Sylvia Darley cleared his diary for a week that he spent recovering in bed at home. It was a short respite. On Monday 17 July he began rehearsals for the 1966 Proms during which he was scheduled to have just two days off until 18 September.

The opening night of the 72nd season was Malcolm Sargent's 500th Promenade concert. Backstage beforehand, the BBC Symphony Orchestra assembled and clapped politely when Sir Hugh Greene, Director-General, presented a print to Sargent of *Portrait in a Spandril* by Rembrandt to commemorate the occasion. As he emerged up the bull-run on to the stage of the Royal Albert Hall, a packed house greeted him with cheers of approval and thunderous applause. 'Carry on Sargent,' said a huge banner in the arena. 'Tonight I am five hundred!' he told Promenaders. The programme, to Glock's irritation chosen by the maestro himself, included works by Walton, Britten, Delius and Elgar. Audience and critics alike noticed his ebullience, particularly in Walton's *Façade*, which drew a massive ovation.

Sargent had grown adept at hiding not just physical discomfort but hurt pride. His 500th Prom should have been a night of celebration; instead it was a bitter commemoration of the passing of his influence. Back in January, William Glock had used Sargent's convalescence as an opportunity to loosen his stranglehold on the Proms. His concert appearances were reduced from twenty-three to eighteen. When he was told, Sargent was shocked, not least because he had been outmanoeuvred to accommodate Pierre Boulez, with whom Glock seemed half in love. 'I knew there would be a set-to,' remembered Glock. 'He was very, very upset – scowling – and there was a rather sharp skirmish. But eventually he agreed.'[44]

Glock had been unaware that the opening night would be

Sargent's 500th Prom until reminded by the conductor himself, and remained reluctant to amend the original programme. Eventually, with little grace, he wrote to Sargent agreeing to include a British work. 'It is difficult to change very much now,' Glock told the conductor cheekily, 'but would you agree to conduct Holst's *The Perfect Fool* instead of *L'Apres-midi*?'[45] Sargent's reaction to this insult was so fierce that Glock let him choose his own programme. 'People tell me that my readings of all music are getting better,' Sargent told a press conference before the concert. 'I hope I'll have the sense to come away when they're not. Mine is the most wonderful job in the world. I will continue until I conk out.'[46] Later in the season he broke down again at home but would not return to hospital or miss a single concert. 'We shall meet again on 22 July 1967, when we shall start our seventy-third season,' he told Promenaders at the Last Night. 'It's a date,' shouted back a pretty woman on the front row. It seemed inconceivable that he might not return.

With the Proms over, Sargent flew to the Italian Riviera for a week's convalescence and holiday. 'I was not well as you know this year and really did not want to spoil my holiday by thinking too much,' he told Peter Andry. 'I just lazed in the sun and got better.'[47] In fact, when he returned to London on 3 October, it was clear to his staff that Sargent was still a sick man. The pain in his leg remained and he was constantly nauseous. The autumn diary stretched interminably in front of him. Sylvia Darley pleaded with him to cancel commitments but he refused point-blank. He did eventually agree to her suggestion that fewer dates would be accepted in future if bigger fees were secured.[48] In desperation, she approached Sir Thomas Armstrong. On Friday 7 October, he went to Albert Hall Mansions for lunch and in his charming way gently suggested that Sargent might think about slowing down. It was not a happy occasion and Armstrong wrote poignantly of it to Sargent days later. 'We're now two of the senior boys, and among the last of those who know the older ways and the greater ones of the past. We are both made to feel more and more isolated, as the months go by, and the younger people will naturally want to make their way, and will push us aside. That's all right – natural enough, as long as they have something to offer that will be as good as the old or better. But it's quite an important thing to know how and when to get out and whether to do it gradually or to make a clean quick break.' The implication was clear enough.[49]

Sargent ignored him. 'That would be death,' he said of retirement.[50] He spent the rest of October recording Walton's First Symphony with the New Philharmonia for EMI, and conducted the usual round of orchestral and choral concerts in the north of England. On 8 November, he flew to the United States to conduct the New York Philharmonic and to Canada for concerts with the Montreal Symphony. He returned home on 25 November with a high fever, looking jaundiced and complaining of back pain. Two days later he collapsed and was rushed unconscious into hospital.

Tests revealed chronic pancreatitis, multiple liver abscesses and a blocked gall bladder. The pain worsened as doctors debated whether or not to operate. With Sargent's fever dangerously high, the strain of cutting him open risked death. As he deteriorated, doctors agreed on 7 December not to operate. That same day, Sargent began experiencing regular spasms and was in excruciating pain. Aware that this might precipitate a fatal seizure, doctors were forced to schedule operation for the next morning, after persistent badgering from Sylvia Darley. 'I gather Sir Malcolm has now been told that he could have had a heart attack during any one of these rigours, and only the fact that he has a strong heart saved him,' she wrote afterwards.[51] By 16 December, doctors declared Sargent out of danger but he faced another unhappy hospital Christmas. 'I am told I am making progress but confess I feel very ill,' he confided to Jessie Wood.[52]

Sargent was allowed home on 22 January 1967 after two months in hospital. 'I am much better, but still feel rather feeble and shan't be working for three or four weeks,' he wrote on his return. 'I am going to the south for a holiday as soon as I am allowed out of the doctor's clutches.'[53] The long flight to Honolulu was out of the question, so Sargent went to the Canary Islands for three weeks and returning on 19 February declared himself 'almost fully recovered'.[54] Six days later he was back on the podium conducting the Welsh Choral Union at the Philharmonic Hall, Liverpool, in Elgar's *The Kingdom*. When he walked on stage, an audience of 1,800 gave him a predictably tumultuous ovation that he acknowledged briskly. 'I am feeling completely fit whilst conducting, rather tired afterwards but will go on,' he wrote later.[55] It had been a low-key event but one greeted with characteristic gratitude by the audience and local critics.[56]

His return to the capital was less happy. On 9 March he conducted the Royal Choral Society in a performance of Beethoven's *Missa Solemnis*. The Royal Albert Hall was half-empty. 'It was a disappointment to see many empty seats on this auspicious occasion,' wrote the critic of *The Times*, 'but in all honesty one must say that the performance left much to be desired, and it is possible that Sir Malcolm will need a little while before he attains his former energy and ebullience.'[57] The following day, against doctors' orders, he caught a northbound train for a week of concerts in Liverpool, Leeds and Huddersfield.

Sargent was anxious to prove that he had the stamina to resume conducting regularly and could cope with travelling, for at the end of March he was due to leave for another Australian tour that involved twenty concerts in seven weeks. Stephen Blaikie, his doctor after the death of Lord Horder, begged Sargent not to go, predicting that the strain might be too much. 'So I will die in harness,' Sargent told him, and settled the matter. He left for Sydney on Easter Sunday and almost did not survive the journey, although not for the reasons that Dr Blaikie might have assumed. Flying at 30,000 feet, his Quantas aeroplane hit turbulence and plunged 4,000 feet. As the captain fought to regain control, Sargent, drink in hand, was thrown to the floor and only managed to scramble back into his seat and fasten his safety belt seconds before the plane made its emergency landing at Calcutta. 'It was a great shock to us all,' he wrote to Sylvia Darley. 'I was very fortunate.'[58] When he finally arrived in Sydney, worried officials clucked and fussed but Sargent retained his customary sangfroid. 'A monocle, a grey pin-stripe suit and a red carnation in the buttonhole,' said a Sydney newspaper. 'Sir Malcolm Sargent was back in town.'[59]

Sargent flew immediately to Melbourne to begin rehearsals. His first appointment, however, was not with the orchestra but a doctor. Dr Blaikie had provided a thick folder containing Sargent's medical history and prescriptions.[60] 'Well, theoretically you're dead,' observed the Australian doctor wryly after reading it. In fact, Sargent enjoyed a sustained period of reasonable health during his stay in Melbourne and felt well enough to play tennis most mornings.

Letters to the secretaries at Albert Hall Mansions exude the good humour and well-being of a man who thrived in sunshine. There were only occasional signs of frailty. 'I had a bad rigour the other night,' he reported in early May, having run out of pills, 'but woke up before dying, so all was well.'[61]

Reasonable physical fitness combined with a certain fragility born of the knowledge that he was still not a well man inspired in Sargent some of the finest performances of his life. Having always enjoyed working in Australia, he now conducted the Melbourne Symphony Orchestra in the country's first complete cycle of Beethoven symphonies. 'We are sold out everywhere and the press has been most flattering,' Sargent told William Glock.[62] Night after night, audiences stood in acclamation and reviewers rushed back to their typewriters to praise him.

Yet where on earlier visits critics had lauded his vivacity, now they noticed a more introspective interpretation. 'Last night there was a touch of nobility and often a great sadness in Sir Malcolm's direction,' observed one after a performance of the 'Eroica'.[63] On the podium for the Choral Symphony, Sargent's mind went back more than fifty years to Leicester where he had been so overwhelmed by the work that he had locked himself in the lavatory afterwards and would not take a curtain-call. In 1967 he brought to bear half a century's reflection on Beethoven and gave performances of the symphonies that, in his own words, were 'the best I have ever done'.[64]

Sargent left Australia for Honolulu on 25 May in high spirits and reasonable health. His diary for June was blank to give him time to prepare for another demanding Promenade season. 'I play tennis every day – also swim every day – but if I don't exercise, I don't sleep,' he wrote happily to Sylvia Darley mid-way through his holiday. 'I am *very well*. Sailing tomorrow and to polo on Sunday. I'm enjoying every day!'[65]

Refreshed and happy, he left for the United States at the beginning of July to conduct two concerts with the Chicago Symphony Orchestra. 'Am very well and exceedingly comfortable,' Sargent wrote on arrival.[66] His two concerts on 6 and 8 July 1967 were part of the summer festival in Ravinia Park, an hour and a half's drive from the city. Three thousand people packed into a small grandstand and thousands more sprawled on picnic rugs. 'With a white carnation in his lapel and suave manner to match, he sets a pattern for youthful elegance which many of his juniors cannot rival,' wrote the critic of the *Chicago Tribune* after the first concert. 'Without turning a hair or making an ungraceful gesture, he gets results.'[67]

Two days later he returned to the rostrum to conduct a programme including works by Delius and Sibelius. On a day of blazing sunshine, Sargent rehearsed the orchestra in the full heat of the afternoon. By evening, a hot wind had blown in from Lake Michigan, which kept temperatures high and the atmosphere sultry. The orchestra played in shirt-sleeves but there were no concessions to the weather from Sargent. Tailcoat, stiff wing-collar, slicked-back hair and white carnation were all in place as he conducted *The Walk to the Paradise Garden* by Delius. As always under such duress, Sargent changed shirt and tails during the interval to maintain an immaculate appearance for the second half.

Sargent believed that Jean Sibelius was the most important composer he had known personally, and the Second Symphony was his favourite. Those who had previously heard his interpretation noticed that on this occasion he gave a more sustained reading than usual, putting nobility before passion.[68] As the last movement came to its inexorable climax and the final sustained chords played by the magnificent Chicago orchestra washed over him, Sargent stood with baton aloft while the crowd erupted into a wild ovation. His arms came slowly down to his sides and he stood briefly motionless. Then he smiled to himself, brought the musicians to their feet and turned to face his audience. Malcolm Sargent had given everything on that hot July evening. He never conducted in public again.

The following day, Sargent caught the red-eye flight to London, where Sylvia Darley met him at the airport. When her Maestro walked through the gate she was appalled. Behind the bright smile and enthusiastic greeting, Sargent looked dreadful. His skin was stretched tight across hollow cheeks and his complexion a sickly yellow. He had lost almost a stone in weight. It did not take a doctor to recognise a very ill man. Within days of arriving home his temperature shot up to 101°F and his pulse rate was at over one hundred beats a minute.[69] Yet he would not cancel social engagements or even slow down. On 12 July, Sargent defied his doctors and went to the French Embassy in heavy morning-dress on a sultry afternoon to be invested as a Chevalier of the Legion of Honour. He collapsed at home immediately afterwards.

Dr Blaikie, initially diagnosing a 'sharp attack' of gastro-enteritis, insisted that Sargent take a week off work.[70] Norman del Mar replaced him on the podium at a concert with the BBC Symphony Orchestra at the Cheltenham Festival on Tuesday 18 July, while officials confronted the reality that Sargent might not be fit to conduct the first night of the Proms four days later. The discreet arrangements made by Glock with Colin Davis and Norman del Mar to cover the possibility of Sargent's ill health now took effect.[71] At the annual pre-Proms lunch at Broadcasting House the next day, the Controller quietly asked Davis to conduct the opening concert of the season while Sargent loudly told everyone that he would be 'all right on the night'.

The following morning, Sylvia Darley drove Sargent to Maida Vale for the rehearsal. When he walked into the studio, despite his straight back and forced smile, there was an audible gasp from the players. Having not seen Sargent for more than four months, they were astonished at how he had deteriorated. Deferential, embarrassed silence replaced the usual tricks. Sargent sat on a chair giving directions in a husky voice to rehearse Stravinsky's *Petrushka*. Away from the podium, edgy BBC staff huddled in corners discussing how to end the session before he collapsed, and implored Sylvia Darley to take him home. When the rehearsal finished, Sargent insisted on giving a press conference for waiting journalists. 'You know I had an operation last Christmas which should have killed me but it didn't,' he told them. 'Now I feel perfectly fit again.'[72]

Sargent woke early and in pain on Friday morning. His temperature again was 101°F. He was due to rehearse the BBC Symphony Orchestra at half past ten in preparation for the opening Prom, but when Dr Blaikie pronounced him too ill, Sargent uncharacteristically agreed to stay in bed. He instructed Sylvia Darley to tell Glock that he had a slight temperature but would be ready for action by the concert. In fact, Sargent grew worse, with a temperature running alarmingly close to a life-threatening 103°F.

One look at Sargent very early the following morning was enough for Dr Blaikie to declare him unfit to conduct. This bitter blow left Sargent with emotional distress to match his physical pain. Colin

Davis paid a courtesy call over breakfast to run through the scores. William Glock arranged for a television monitor to be installed at No. IX so that Sargent could watch the concert in bed. Young Promenaders in the arena of the Albert Hall held up 'Get well Flash!' banners. These acts of kindness did little to assuage Sargent's disappointment at missing the opening night of the Proms for the first time in twenty years.

During the following days, as Sargent's temperature remained dangerously high and his stomach pains intensified, a succession of eminent doctors visited Albert Hall Mansions. They diagnosed another acute biliary obstruction and admitted him to the nearby Sister Agnes Clinic to have his gall bladder removed. It was a common enough operation. Newspapers reported a successful procedure and predicted a quick return. 'A complete recovery will obviously take some weeks but it is hoped that Sir Malcolm will recover in time to conduct some final Promenade concerts,' reported the BBC.[73] Sylvia Darley issued a press release saying that 'his medical advisers are very pleased with his condition'.[74] This encouraging statement concealed a harsh truth. Doctors who opened up Malcolm Sargent on 26 July found him riddled with cancer. They predicted that he would not last until Christmas.

Sargent spent six weeks convalescing at the clinic unaware of his imminent demise. Having rallied after his operation, he began planning a month's tour of South Africa in late September. By the end of August he was allowed home and even wondered if he might get back on the podium to conduct the Last Night of the Proms on 16 September. The first week out of hospital he spent happy hours in a deckchair in Kensington Gardens. 'I am much better,' he wrote to Jessie Wood, 'and sit in the sun when I can so my yellow has gone and some brown is returning.'[75] Eating remained an effort, but Sargent seemed to be regaining his strength. Then on 6 September he collapsed unconscious after suffering violent stomach spasms. 'I thought he would die within hours,' recalls Sylvia Darley. 'He never went forward physically again.'[76]

Doctors refused to tell Sargent that he had cancer, fearing the shock would kill him, but the patient himself realised that his condition was serious when told to cancel all engagements until Christmas. He struggled around the apartment 'just to keep my legs going' but often fell to the floor. During interminable days in bed unable to eat or sleep, Sargent formed one remaining ambition: to stand in the Royal Albert Hall on Saturday 16 September for one last time at the Proms and say goodbye.

When Sargent asked Glock if this might be possible, the Controller of Music blithely agreed, believing him unfit to get out of bed let alone across the road to the hall. He had reckoned without Sargent's sheer bloody-mindedness. On 15 September, Sargent gathered doctors around his bed and discussed the detailed arrangements that would see him through the next day. He had not eaten for two weeks and even water was painful to swallow. Standing for just a few minutes caused unbearable abdominal pain. To get him to a physical condition at which he might realistically contemplate a visit to the Albert Hall, Sargent required an intravenous glucose drip for twelve hours and powerful painkillers.

Doctors arrived early at Albert Hall Mansions on the Saturday morning and began the process of medication that would bolster the conductor's failing body. Sargent himself seemed almost giddy at the prospect of what lay ahead. When a BBC official telephoned at half past eight to enquire after the conductor's health, he was astonished to be told that Sargent was determined to go on. Confronted suddenly with the reality of his appearance, an eight-man BBC delegation led by Colin Davis was rustled up to call on Sargent to change his mind. Sylvia Darley pulled Davis into her tiny office alone and told him the truth while he uneasily sipped a glass of sherry. 'Tonight will be Sir Malcolm's final appearance on any concert platform,' she said. 'He will never be seen in public again.'[77] Reluctantly, Davis conceded that Sargent must go on.

At seven o'clock, half an hour before the start of the concert, doctors removed the drip from Sargent's arm. His temperature was at an acceptable level; the pain had subsided. Tentatively, he stepped out of bed and with help reached his dressing room to begin the slow and painful process of changing. Almost an hour later, he had been transformed. The face remained drawn but he was recognisably Sir Malcolm Sargent, celebrity conductor. His charcoal chalk-stripe suit, having been re-tailored in Savile Row to fit a wasted figure, looked characteristically elegant. With Oxford shoes gleaming and hair immaculate, only one touch remained. He took the white carnation from a small crystal vase on his dressing table and carefully threaded it through his buttonhole. Sir Malcolm was ready for his final performance.

At nine o'clock Sargent, accompanied by secretaries and doctors, left for the Royal Albert Hall barely a hundred paces across the road. The Albert Hall Mansions lift had been out of action all day and ambulancemen stood by ready to stretcher Sargent down the stairs. With minutes to spare, technicians finally got the elevator working. With a heavy black overcoat draped across his shoulders and stick in hand, Sargent travelled down to the ground floor, where a car was waiting. Even the short journey across the road made him vomit and screw up his eyes in pain.[78] When he arrived at the artists' door of the Albert Hall, he breathed deeply, straightened his back and shot a broad smile to the astonished crowd milling around. Now he was in public, the showman's instinct rallied. He received the doorman's salute and then plunged down the long flight of stone steps into the bowels of the hall. In the green room, William Glock met him. 'I'll just sit down until Colin fetches me,' Sargent told the unhappy Controller. 'I just did not think he could go on and so he sat in the corridor with his back to me watching a TV monitor,' recalled Glock.[79]

When Colin Davis began the traditional Last Night speech, Sargent stood up and threw away his stick. For the first time in months, he walked unassisted. The orchestral intendant, Edgar Mays, remained one pace behind in case of emergency while Sargent stood at the bottom of the bull-run. 'Now I have a surprise for you,' Davis told the Promenaders. 'Sir Malcolm Sargent is in fact here, and I know you would like to pay to him your respects, and I will go and get him.'[80]

As Sargent emerged, the Albert Hall exploded with noise. The Promenaders shouted their approval. Those in seats stood to applaud. Sargent, upright and beaming, exuded the charisma that had made him a star. He moved apparently without effort towards the footlights and briskly leapt on to the podium. When he threw open his arms, the cheers grew louder. 'I was in the orchestra that night and was right next to the bull-run where he came up, hoping he would not collapse,' remembers Jack Brymer. 'It was very moving because he had come to the place where he had been loved best and gave himself over to the audience. It was tremendously theatrical but heartfelt.'[81] The ovation thundered on until Sargent suddenly held up his hands for quiet. 'Oh my God!' exclaimed Glock backstage. 'He is going to make a speech.'[82]

The hall that had been filled with sound just seconds earlier was now hushed in expectation. 'I am not going to make a long speech – Hear, hear! – I got that in first,' he told them drolly in clear, ringing tones, and set off cheers again.[83] He complimented the wonderful playing of 'my old friends and colleagues of the BBC Symphony Orchestra' and their 'new and very gifted conductor Colin Davis'. But the best he saved for last. 'I am going to say one more thing: next year the Promenade concerts begin on 20 July and I have been invited to be here that night.' Pandemonium broke out in the hall but was silenced again by a lift of the hand. 'I have accepted the invitation; God willing, we will all meet again then.' In the uproar that followed, Sargent stepped off the podium, shook hands with Davis and stood in silence to acknowledge his Promenaders. When Davis struck up the National Anthem, viewers watching the live television broadcast momentarily saw what those in the hall could not: a tear rolling down Sargent's face. This was farewell.

Back at Albert Hall Mansions, Sargent had a sip of champagne, took a handful of painkillers and slept for twelve hours, exhausted. The following afternoon, journalists arrived to interview him resplendent in a silk dressing gown while Hughie the budgerigar nibbled his ear. 'If anything conductors improve after illness,' he told them. 'It can deepen one's spirituality, one's understanding.' As to the future, 'I plan to go abroad a little later – somewhere warm – and in October leave for America to conduct the New York Phil-harmonic.'[84] This was not bravado or deceit on Sargent's part; he was genuinely planning his return. On Monday 18 September, he spent all day in bed studying scores and planning his 1968 diary. When the doctor arrived at six o'clock for his daily check-up, Sylvia Darley confronted him and a row ensued. 'You have got to tell him,' she shouted. 'He's up there now with his music and it's not fair. If you don't say something, I will.'[85]

The hapless doctor eventually agreed to deliver the gravest possible news. 'Is it cancer?' Sargent asked quietly. 'I am afraid it is, Sir Malcolm,' replied Blaikie. 'How long?' 'Christmas.' Sargent had suspected that his condition was serious, but faced now with the fatal reality, he wept openly. When the doctor had left, Sylvia Darley came up and stood beside him. 'The eyes were steady and we stared in silence,' she recorded in her diary. 'He had obviously shed a tear but was in command of himself now.'[86] 'Well, at least I can stop working now,' he told her.[87]

Sargent had two difficult weeks to live. Sylvia Darley moved into the apartment and slept on a camp-bed beside him. She gave the kind of practical medical care that eased his suffering; the loving attention of a wife and mother. Sargent could sleep for little more than an hour at a time; he ate and drank nothing, and was barely able to stand. The morphine that helped relieve pain was hallucinatory and gave him nightmares and delusions. After one exhausting day, Sylvia Darley awoke from dozing to find him staggering down the stairs wielding a Samurai sword and challenging imagined intruders to fight him. She tentatively coaxed him back to bed and the following morning Sargent could recall nothing of the incident.[88]

Days were spent making final arrangements. Donald Coggan, Archbishop of York, visited on several occasions to offer spiritual sustenance. 'He knew he was dying, so I prayed with him and we even talked of cricket,' recalled Coggan. 'And of course there were some tears.'[89] 'The Archbishop was very tactful,' Sargent told Sylvia Darley after one visit. 'If I weep, he goes round not looking at me while he talks and gazes at my pictures of Stamford.'[90] Coggan promised to bury Sargent when the time came and preach at his memorial service. Finding a final resting place was more problematic. Sargent decided that he wanted to be buried in Stamford next to his parents, only to discover that his sister, Dorothy, had purchased the plot years earlier. 'There is just room for one,' she told him bluntly. Only an imploring telephone call to the Canon of All Saints' church resolved the situation so that brother and sister would be closer in death than ever they had been in life.[91]

Sargent also received visits from old friends to say goodbye. His secretaries drew up a timetable and he saw around fifty people during ten days. 'I have always prayed for a foreknowledge of death so that I can see my friends,' he said.[92] Sylvia Darley told visitors, on Sargent's instruction, not to speak of his condition. 'I can't say goodbye as it is so tiring and wearing for me and them,' he had said. 'It is so much easier if I just say come again soon.'[93] Telephone calls from the Queen and Prince Charles, and visits by the likes of Lord Mountbatten and Princess Marina reflected Sargent's social and cultural eminence. Others callers, such as Sir Thomas Armstrong and Lilias Sheepshanks either pre-dated his fame or were family friends.

Sargent's most important visitors were his son and grandchildren. He had not spoken to Peter for more than a year after another quarrel and now had little time to effect reconciliation. When Peter nervously walked in to see his father on 30 September, he found him tearful and in pain. 'I haven't been too bad a father, have I?' Sargent asked his son, immediately dissolving any tension between them. They reminisced about happier days and talked of Pamela. Sargent's four grandchildren, aged between nine and fourteen, came in and knelt beside his bed. For twenty minutes, Sargent rallied and told jokes and stories to the children, all the time holding the hand of the youngest, Amanda. 'He laughed and joked right to the end,' Peter recalls. 'If there is a better way of dying than surrounded by your family and beautiful flowers, I cannot think of it,' Sargent told his son when the children had left.[94]

By Monday 2 October it was clear that Sargent was in agony. When Lord Mountbatten's secretary telephoned to ask when Dickie might visit he was told 'today or not at all'.[95] Early in the evening, Peter Sargent went alone to make his farewell. He found his father calm and apparently unfrightened by the prospect of death. 'You are lucky to have such strong faith,' Peter told him. 'I am much luckier than that,' Sargent replied. 'My faith has become knowledge.'[96] Only as Peter came to leave at ten o'clock did Sargent's tranquillity change to self-doubt. 'Am I forgiven?' he asked, clasping his son's hands tightly in his own. 'Of course, Papa,' Peter replied.[97] By eleven o'clock Sargent was in and out of consciousness. He managed a last telephone call to Anne Chapman, his wartime secretary. 'I am slipping away,' he told her. 'God bless you, goodnight and goodbye.'[98]

Shortly after midnight Sargent gently slipped into a coma.[99] For almost twelve hours the conductor quietly breathed away his life. When he started to falter, Sylvia Darley moved to the gramophone and put on his recording of *The Dream of Gerontius*. It was Tuesday 3 October, sixty-seven years to the day after the premiere of Elgar's meditation on death. As the 'Angel's Farewell' filled the room, Sir

Malcolm Sargent, England's maestro, fought momentarily for air and passed away. 'The voice of the Angel,' he had once written, 'was singing "Farewell, but not forever! Be brave and patient, swiftly shall pass this night of trial here, and I will come and wake thee on the morrow." Then the whole chorus breathed "Amen, Amen".'[100]

Notes

Prologue

1   *The Times*, 14 September 1970.
2   *Daily Telegraph*, 19 July 1968.
3   *Sun*, 10 October 1967.
4   *The Times*, 28 October 1967.
5   *The Times*, 16 September 1968.
6   'White heat of technology' was a phrase coined by Harold Wilson as Leader of the Opposition in 1963.
7   Sargent Papers: memorandum of agreement between Sargent, Reid and Hamish Hamilton Ltd, 16 July 1965. (All quotations from the Sargent papers appear by kind permission of Peter Sargent and Sylvia Darley.)
8   A full correspondence on the dispute is contained within the Sargent Papers.
9   Charles Reid, *Malcolm Sargent: a biography* (London, 1968). Sargent's ghosted memoir was to have been entitled *The White Carnation*.
10   *Guardian*, 4 October 1967.
11   *Observer*, 6 October 1968; review by John Lucas.

12 *Sunday Times*, 6 October 1968.

13 *Spectator*, 11 October 1968; review by Philip Hope-Wallace.

14 *Sunday Telegraph*, 29 August 1976; diary extract, 14 November 1963.

15 *The Times*, 30 December 1987.

16 Edward Heath, *The Course of my Life: the autobiography of Edward Heath* (London, 1998), p.68.

17 *BBC Music Magazine*, August 1998. Michael Kennedy is the author of biographies of William Walton, Ralph Vaughan Williams and Adrian Boult.

18 Maurice Miles gave Rattle his earliest opportunity to conduct and later taught him at the Royal Academy of Music. Kenyon, *Simon Rattle* (London, 1987), p.37.

1: One Day He'll Be a Knight

1 Author's interview with Ellis Miles, 23 February 2001.

2 Author's interview with Marjorie Gesior, 23 February 2001.

3 I am grateful to Judith Spelman and Derrick Fawcitt of the Stamford Civic Society, John Craddock, archivist of Stamford School, and Frieda Gosling, archivist of Stamford High School, for assisting my research.

4 Register Office (Ashford): certified copy of an entry of birth: Harold Malcolm Watts Sargent, 29 April 1895. Bath Villas is now 34 Beaver Road.

5 Register Office (Ashford): certified copy of an entry of birth: Harold Malcolm Watts Sargent, 29 April 1895.

6 Agnes Marion Hall, registration of birth (1864), marriage (1894) and birth of son, Malcolm (1895): International Genealogical Index (The Church of Jesus Christ of Latter-day Saints, 1997).

7 Judith Spelman, *Stamford Voices* (Stroud, 1999), p.73.

8 Author's interview with Marjorie Gesior, 23 February 2001; her husband sang in the choir under Harry Sargent.

9 Author's interview with Marjorie Gesior, 23 February 2001.

10 Martin Smith, *The Story of Stamford* (Stamford, 1994).

11 Christopher Hibbert, *The Virgin Queen* (London, 1992), p.244.

12 In the year of Sargent's birth, the 3rd Marquess of Salisbury won

a general election for the Conservatives/Unionists and became Prime Minister. He won another general election in 1900 and retired in 1902 to be replaced by his nephew, A. J. Balfour.

13 Author's interview with Marjorie Gesior, 23 February 2001.

14 Author's interview with Marjorie Gesior, 23 February 2001.

15 Author's interview with Marjorie Gesior, 23 February 2001.

16 H. G. Wells, *The History of Mr Polly* (1909); *The Shape of Things to Come* (1933); Peter Clarke, *Hope and Glory: Britain, 1900–1990* (London, 1996).

17 Sargent Papers: annotated copy of 'Sir Malcolm Sargent, interview with the BBC, 9 August, 1966'.

18 Phyllis Matthewson, *Sir Malcolm Sargent* (London, 1959), p.5. This book was written with help from Dorothy Sargent.

19 Sargent Papers: annotated copy of 'Sir Malcolm Sargent, interview with the BBC, 9 August, 1966'.

20 Spelman, *Stamford Voices*, pp.69–70.

21 Michael Tippett, *Those Twentieth Century Blues* (London, 1991), p.10.

22 Charles Reid, *Malcolm Sargent: a biography* (London, 1968), p.27.

23 Sargent Papers: annotated copy of 'Sir Malcolm Sargent, interview with the BBC, 9 August, 1966'.

24 B. L. Deed, *A History of Stamford School* (Stamford, 1982), p.67.

25 I am grateful to John Craddock for a guided tour of the school and inviting me to Evensong.

26 Reid, *Sargent*, p.43.

27 Reid, *Sargent*, p.36.

28 Walter Alcock enjoyed the distinction of playing in Westminster Abbey at the coronation of three kings: Edward VII, George V and George VI.

29 Reid, *Sargent*, p.49.

30 Sargent Papers: annotated copy of 'Sir Malcolm Sargent, interview with the BBC, 9 August, 1966'.

31 Peterborough Cathedral Archive: Dean and Chapter Minute Book, 1900–1913.

32 Author's interview with Dr Stanley Vann, 13 March 1999.

33 Author's interview with Dr Stanley Vann, 13 March 1999.

34 Sargent Papers: annotated copy of 'Sir Malcolm Sargent, interview with the BBC, 9 August, 1966'.

35 Sir Thomas Armstrong (1898–1994) was Choragus of Oxford University and Principal of the Royal Academy of Music. His son, Robert, was Cabinet Secretary between 1979 and 1987.

36 Rosemary Rapaport (ed.), *Thomas Armstrong: A Celebration by his Friends* (London, 1998), pp.25–6, 42.

37 Author's interview with Dr Stanley Vann, 13 March 1999.

38 Colin Matthews (ed.), *Brief Lives* (Oxford, 1997), p.479.

39 Author's interview with Dr Stanley Vann, 13 March 1999.

2: Malcolm in the Middle

1 James Fox, *The Langhorne Sisters* (London, 1998), p.74.

2 Anne de Courcy, *The Viceroy's Daughters: the lives of the Curzon sisters* (London, 2000), p.86.

3 Author's interview with Eva Dickings and Edith Hammond, 10 September 2000; I am grateful to Theo Mayfield, verger of the Church of St Mary the Virgin, Melton Mowbray, for arranging this interview and showing me round the church.

4 Greta Gastall, 'Memories of Sir Malcolm Sargent', archive of the Church of St Mary the Virgin, Melton Mowbray.

5 Author's interview with Eva Dickings and Edith Hammond, 10 September 2000.

6 Author's interview with Eva Dickings and Edith Hammond, 10 September 2000.

7 Author's interview with the Rector of the Church of St Mary the Virgin, Melton Mowbray, 10 September 2000.

8 Author's interview with Eva Dickings and Edith Hammond, 10 September 2000.

9 Greta Gastall, 'Memories of Sir Malcolm Sargent', archive of the Church of St Mary the Virgin, Melton Mowbray.

10 Tom Corfe et al (ed.), *The School on the Hill: An Informal History of King Edward VII Grammar School, Melton Mowbray* (Leicester; 2nd edition, 2000).

11 Author's interview with Eva Dickings and Edith Hammond, 10 September 2000.

12 Norman Davies, *Europe: A History* (London, 1996), p.1328.

13 Niall Ferguson, *The Pity of War* (London, 1998); Davies, *Europe: A History,* Chapter 11; Peter Clarke, *Hope and Glory: Britain, 1900–1990* (London, 1996), Chapter 3.

14 Ministry of Defence (Hayes), Defence Records 2b: 99935 Private Harold Malcolm SARGENT, Durham Light Infantry.

15 DLI Museum, 'The Story of the Durham Light Infantry'.

16 Cambridge University Library, E. J. Dent Papers, Add. Ms. 7972 (J. S. Wilson): Wilson to Dent, 2 September 1914, 7 August 1915.

17 Author's interview with Peter Sargent, 25 March 1998.

18 Gina Kolata, *Flu: the story of the Great Influenza Pandemic of 1918 and the Search for the Virus that Caused it* (London, 2000); Roy Porter, 'Atishoo! Atishoo! All fall down' in *Sunday Times*, 16 January 2000.

19 Cambridge University Library, E. J. Dent Papers, Add. Ms. 7972 (J. S. Wilson): Wilson to Dent, 9 January 1915.

20 Ministry of Defence (Hayes), Defence Records 2b: 99935 Private Harold Malcolm SARGENT, Durham Light Infantry.

21 *Melton Times*, 19 March 1920; I am grateful to Richard Snodin, whose family helped found the Melton Operatic Society, for access to his personal archive.

22 *Melton Times*, 4 March 1921.

23 See de Courcy, *The Viceroy's Daughters*, pp. 86–94.

24 Author's interview with Eva Dickings and Edith Hammond, 10 September 2000.

25 Fox, *The Langhorne Sisters*, p.75.

26 *Grantham Journal*, 20 February 1925.

27 De Courcy, *The Viceroy's Daughters*, pp. 86–9; Lady Irene Curzon was President of the Leicester Symphony Orchestra, which was set up as a vehicle for Sargent's conducting talents, and later appointed him conductor of the British Women's Symphony Orchestra.

28 Corfe, et al. (ed.) *The School on the Hill.*

29 Charles Reid, *Malcolm Sargent: a biography* (London, 1968), p.87.

30 See Arthur Jacobs, *Henry J. Wood: Maker of the Proms* (London, 1994); Stanley Sadie (ed.), *The New Grove Dictionary of Music and Musicians* (London, 1980), Vol. 20, pp.516–19.

31 Norman Lebrecht, *The Maestro Myth: Great Conductors in Pursuit of Power* (London, 1997, pbk.), p.155.

32 Leicestershire Record Office: Leicester Philharmonic Society (DE2969): Neil Crutchley, 'Sargent's early years in Leicestershire' in *Leicestershire and Rutland Heritage* (Winter 1989–90) pp.28–30; Leicester Symphony Orchestra, souvenir programme, Diamond Jubilee Concert, 4 November 1982.

33 Author's interview with Sir Malcolm Arnold, 22 February 2000. Sargent habitually referred to this work as *Impressions on a Windy Day*, *An Impression on a Windy Day* and *An Impression of a Windy Day*. I have used *Impressions on a Windy Day* throughout for consistency.

34 Leicestershire Record Office: Leicester Philharmonic Society (DE2969).

35 British Library, Music and Rare Books, Add. Ms. 56421, Wood Papers, Vol.3: Sargent to Wood, 25 October 1943.

36 Bernard Shore, *The Orchestra Speaks* (London, 1938), p.151.

37 *Daily Telegraph*, 12 October 1921.

38 Reid, *Sargent*, p.113.

3:   Une Spécialité Anglaise

1 Author's interview with Eva Dickings and Edith Hammond, 10 September 2000.

2 Author's interview with Eva Dickings and Edith Hammond, 10 September 2000.

3 Author's interview with Maisie King, 10 September 2000.

4 Author's interview with Eva Dickings and Edith Hammond, 10 September 2000.

5 Author's interview with Eva Dickings and Edith Hammond, 10 September 2000.

6 International Genealogical Index (The Church of Jesus Christ of Latter-day Saints, 1997): Eileen Laura Horne, registration of birth (1898) and marriage (1922); Pamela Stephanie Sargent, registration of birth (1923).

7 Greta Gastall, 'Memories of Sir Malcolm Sargent', archive of the Church of St Mary the Virgin, Melton Mowbray.

8 Leicestershire Record Office: Leicester Philharmonic Society (DE2969): Neil Crutchley, 'Sargent's early years in Leicestershire' in *Leicestershire and Rutland Heritage* (Winter 1989–90), pp.28–30.

9 Leicestershire Record Office: Leicester Symphony Orchestra, souvenir programme, Diamond Jubilee Concert, 4 November 1982.

10 Author's interview with Peter Sargent, 17 October 1999.

11 Sargent Papers: notes for Festival Hall tribute to Toscanini, undated (*c.* January, 1957).

12 Joseph Horowitz, *Understanding Toscanini* (London, 1987), p.112.

13 Michael Tippett, *Those Twentieth Century Blues* (London, 1991), p.14.

14 See J. A. Westrup, 'Sir Hugh Allen (1869–1946)' in *Music and Letters*, Vol.xxvii, No.2 (Oxford, 1946), p.46.

15 Tippett, *Those Twentieth Century Blues*, p.14.

16 Charles Reid, *Malcolm Sargent: a biography* (London, 1968), p.120.

17 Reid, *Sargent*, p.122.

18 Tippett, *Those Twentieth Century Blues*, p.15.

19 Stanley Sadie (ed.), *The New Grove Dictionary of Music and Musicians* (London, 1980), Vol.19, p.569.

20 Michael Kennedy, *The Works of Vaughan Williams* (Oxford, 1964), p.179.

21 Kennedy, *The Works of Vaughan Williams*, p.180.

22 Ursula Vaughan Williams, *RVW: a Biography of Ralph Vaughan Williams* (Oxford, 1964), p.155.

23 EMI Archive (Hayes), Sir Malcolm Sargent: J. K. R. Whittle to G. N. Bridge, 22 February 1965; Timothy Day, *A Century of Recorded Music: listening to musical history* (London, 2000), pp.6–12.

24 For a short history of the Mayer concerts see Charles Reid, *Fifty Years of Robert Mayer Concerts, 1923–1973* (Gerrards Cross, 1972).

25 Reid, *Sargent*, p.175

26 *Music Bulletin*, March 1926.

27 Reid, *Robert Mayer Concerts*, p.14.

28 Haberdashers' Aske's School for Girls, Yearbook, 1924–5. I am

grateful to Helen Dulley, the school's official historian, for providing this material.

29 Illness prevented Sargent conducting the 1933–4 season.

30 Reid, *Robert Mayer Concerts*, p.17.

31 Leslie Baily, *The Gilbert and Sullivan Book* (London, 1952), p.438.

32 Baily, *The Gilbert and Sullivan Book*, p.439. Sargent was music director at D'Oyly Carte Opera for the 1926, 1927 and 1929 seasons.

33 Theatre Museum Archive (Covent Garden): Princes Theatre File, 1926.

34 Anne Ziegler and Webster Booth, *Duet* (London, 1951), p.37.

35 Ziegler and Booth, *Duet*, p.37.

36 The Gilbert and Sullivan Archive: Memories of D'Oyly Carte, 'Bertha Lewis by Derek Oldham'.

37 The Gilbert and Sullivan Archive: Memories of D'Oyly Carte, 'Bertha Lewis by Derek Oldham'.

38 Ziegler and Booth, *Duet*, p.37.

39 Ziegler and Booth, *Duet*, p.37.

40 *Daily Telegraph*, 3 December 1929.

41 *The Times*, 5 November 1929. See also Tony Joseph, *The D'Oyly Carte Opera Company* (Bristol, 1994) pp. 194–8.

42 *Evening Standard*, 21 September 1926.

43 *Daily Telegraph*, 21 September 1926.

44 Theatre Museum Archive: Princes Theatre File, 1926.

45 *The Times*, 22 October 1929.

46 W.S. Gilbert, *Ruddigore* (1887), Act 1.

47 Ivor Novello studied with Sir Herbert Brewer, organist of Gloucester Cathedral.

48 Richard Rose, *Perchance to Dream: The World of Ivor Novello* (London, 1974), p.18.

49 Nicolas Slonimsky, *Music since 1900* (London, 1971, 4th edn.), p.1303.

50 Paul Arthur Schlipp, *Albert Einstein* (La Salle, Illinois, 1970), p.31.

51 Peter Conrad, *Modern Times, Modern Places* (London, 1998), p.16.

52 Although Berg in his violin concerto (1935) cleverly used a

twelve-tone row that identified itself with tonality, particularly J.S. Bach.

53 Stephen Walsh, *Stravinsky: a creative spring* (London, 2000), p.204

54 Michael Oliver, *Settling the Score: a journey through the music of the twentieth century* (London, 1999), p.274.

55 Walsh, *Stravinsky*, p.205.

56 Walsh, *Stravinsky*, p.207.

57 John Drummond, *Speaking of Diaghilev* (London, 1997), pp.36–9; Julie Kavanagh, *Secret Muses: The life of Frederick Ashton* (London, 1996), p.63.

58 Drummond, *Speaking of Diaghilev*, p.215.

59 Author's interview with Sidonie Goossens, 28 July 1999.

60 Theatre Museum (Covent Garden), Sargent Biographical File: Herbert Ashley, 'Vitality in Music' in *The Bystander* (1935).

61 Reid, *Sargent*, p.131.

4: *Make the Buggers Sing Like the Blazes*

1 Theatre Museum Archive (Covent Garden), Sargent Biographical File: Herbert Ashley, 'Vitality in Music' in *The Bystander* (1935).

2 Mrs J.F. Coleridge-Taylor, *Samuel Coleridge-Taylor: Genius and Musician* (London, undated); John MacKenzie, *Orientalism: history, theory and the arts* (Manchester, 1995), pp.30–1.

3 *The Times*, 11 June 1935.

4 Charles Reid, *Malcolm Sargent: a biography* (London, 1968), p.126.

5 Freddie Stockdale, *Three Great Impresarios* (London, 1998), p.166

6 Author's interview with Graeme Tong, Director of Administration, Royal Choral Society, 8 July 1998.

7 Stockdale, *Three Great Impresarios*, p.174.

8 Charles Reid, *Thomas Beecham: an Independent Biography* (London, 1961), p.186; Neville Cardus, *Sir Thomas Beecham*, (London, 1961).

9 West Yorkshire Archive (Sheepscar), Leeds Triennial Music Festival, Management Committee Minute Book 1926–39:

Notes of interview with Sir Thomas Beecham, 3 December 1930.

10   West Yorkshire Archive (Sheepscar), Leeds Triennial Music Festival, Management Committee Minute Book 1926–39: Minutes of Meeting, 17 December 1930.

11   Michael Kennedy, *Portrait of Walton* (Oxford, 1989), p.58.

12   John Brewer, *The Pleasures of the Imagination: English culture in the eighteenth century* (London, 1997).

13   Brewer, *The Pleasures of the Imagination*, p.404.

14   George J. Buelow (ed.), *The Late Baroque: from the 1680s to 1740*, (London, 1993); Neal Zaslaw (ed.), *The Classical Era: from the 1740s to the end of the 18th century* (London, 1989); Jim Samson (ed.), *The late Romantic Era: from the mid-19th century to world war one* (London, 1991); Nicholas Temperley (ed.), *Music in Britain: the Romantic age, 1800–1914* (London, 1981); Brewer, *The Pleasures of the Imagination*.

15   Owen Chadwick, *An Ecclesiastical History of England: The Victorian Church, part two* (London, 1970), p.10.

16   Jeremy Dibble, 'National developments in Britain and Ireland: a matter of style and morality' in *Welttheatre, Die Künste im 19 Jahrhundert*, Rombach Wissenschaften, Reihe Litterae Band 16 (1992), p.59; my thanks to Andrew Johnstone of Christchurch Cathedral, Dublin, for drawing this essay to my attention.

17   *Masterworks*, BBC2, 24 July 1999.

18   West Yorkshire Archive (Sheepscar), Leeds Triennial Music Festival, Press Cuttings 1928–34: *Yorkshire Evening News*, 7 October 1931.

19   West Yorkshire Archive (Sheepscar), Leeds Triennial Music Festival, Press Cuttings 1928–34: *Huddersfield Daily Examiner*, 31 August 1931.

20   Susana Walton, *William Walton: Behind the Façade* (Oxford, 1988) p.72.

21   *Masterworks*, BBC2, 24 July 1999.

22   West Yorkshire Archive (Sheepscar), Leeds Triennial Music Festival, Press Cuttings 1928–34: *Daily Mail*, 9 October 1931.

23   West Yorkshire Archive (Sheepscar), Leeds Triennial Music Festival, Press Cuttings 1928–34: *Daily Mail*, 9 October 1931; *Yorkshire Post*, 9 October 1931; *Yorkshire Observer*, 9 October

1931; *Leeds Mercury*, 9 October 1931; *The Times*, 10 October 1931; *Daily Telegraph,* 10 October 1931; *Masterworks*, BBC2, 24 July 1999. Newspapers (e.g. *Huddersfield Examiner*, 14 September 1931) before the performance reported that *Belshazzar's Feast* would take seventeen minutes when in fact it always takes more than half an hour. This led to erroneous stories that the first performance had been taken too slowly.

24 Isobel Baillie, *Never Sing Louder than Lovely* (London, 1982), p.117.

25 R.A. Edwards, *And the Glory: A History of the Huddersfield Choral Society* (Leeds, 1986), p.98.

26 West Yorkshire Archive (Kirklees), Huddersfield Choral Society, 1836–1986, KC200/1/1/9, Minute Book, 1929–35.

27 Author's interview with Dr Stanley Vann, 13 March 1999.

28 Sargent performed the B Minor Mass in his opening concerts as director of the Bradford (1925) and Huddersfield (1932) choral societies, and debuts at the Leeds Festival (1931) and with the Hallé Orchestra (1935).

29 West Yorkshire Archive (Kirklees), Huddersfield Choral Society, 1836–1986, KC200/8/2, Press Cutting: *Huddersfield Daily Examiner*, 5 November 1932; *Yorkshire Post*, 21 December 1932.

30 Author's interview with Marjorie Thomas, 30 April 1999.

31 Author's interview with Marjorie Thomas, 30 April 1999.

32 Author's interview with Marjorie Thomas, 30 April 1999.

33 Author's interview with Nancy Evans, 10 July 1999.

34 Baillie, *Never Sing Louder than Lovely*, p.48.

35 Anne Ziegler and Webster Booth, *Duet* (London, 1951), p.37.

36 Author's interview with Marjorie Thomas, 30 April 1999.

37 From a story told by Bob Boothby in *Sargent at Seventy*, BBC1, 22 April 1966.

5: *Dr Sargent is a Lucky Young Man*

1 Author's interview with Peter Sargent, 31 August 2000.

2 Author's interview with Peter Sargent, 31 August 2000.

3 Author's interview with Peter Sargent, 31 August 2000.

4   Author's interview with Peter Sargent, 31 August 2000.

5   Author's interview with Marjorie Gesior, 23 February 2001.

6   *Daily Telegraph*, 23 October 1929.

7   *Musical Times*, February 1932.

8   AKZO NOBEL (UK) Ltd (formerly Courtaulds PLC) Archives Department: *Notes on the Courtauld-Sargent Concerts* by Cicely Stanhope. These papers and others relating to the Courtauld-Sargent Concerts are also in the possession of Sir Adam Butler to whom I am grateful for allowing me to read them at his home.

9   Virginia Woolf, *The Common Reader* (London, 1929, 3rd edn.), p.11.

10 Robert P. Morgan (ed.), *Modern Times: from world war I to the present*, (London, 1993), p.67.

11 César Saerchinger, *Artur Schnabel: a Biography* (London, 1957), p.187.

12 AKZO NOBEL (UK) Ltd (formerly Courtaulds PLC) Archives Department: *Notes on the Courtauld-Sargent Concerts* by Cicely Stanhope.

13 Author's interview with Sidonie Goossens, 18 March 1998.

14 Bernard Shore, *The Orchestra Speaks* (London, 1938), p.158.

15 Shore, *The Orchestra Speaks*, p.152.

16 AKZO NOBEL (UK) Ltd (formerly Courtaulds PLC) Archives Department: *Notes on the Courtauld-Sargent Concerts* by Cicely Stanhope.

17 AKZO NOBEL (UK) Ltd (formerly Courtaulds PLC) Archives Department: *Notes on the Courtauld-Sargent Concerts* by Cicely Stanhope.

18 AKZO NOBEL (UK) Ltd (formerly Courtaulds PLC) Archives Department: *The Courtauld-Sargent Concerts* by Dorothy Middleton, published privately by Courtaulds PLC.

19 AKZO NOBEL (UK) Ltd (formerly Courtaulds PLC) Archives Department: *Notes on the Courtauld-Sargent Concerts* by Cicely Stanhope.

20 William Weber, *Music and the Middle Classes: the social structure of concert life in London, Paris and Vienna* (London, 1975), p.68.

21 John Brewer, *The Pleasures of the Imagination: English culture in the eighteenth century* (London, 1997), p.399.

22   *Daily News*, 23 October 1929.

23   *New Statesman*, 13 July 1929.

24   Nicholas Kenyon, *The BBC Symphony Orchestra, 1930–1980* (London, 1981), pp.49–50.

25   AKZO NOBEL (UK) Ltd (formerly Courtaulds PLC) Archives Department: *The Courtauld-Sargent Concerts* by Dorothy Middleton.

26   *Daily Telegraph*, 23 October 1929.

27   AKZO NOBEL (UK) Ltd (formerly Courtaulds PLC) Archives Department: *The Courtauld-Sargent Concerts* by Dorothy Middleton.

28   AKZO NOBEL (UK) Ltd (formerly Courtaulds PLC) Archives Department: *The Courtauld-Sargent Concerts* by Dorothy Middleton; *Evening Standard*, 30 January 1929; *Daily Telegraph*, 30 January 1929; *New Statesman*, 8 February 1930.

29   *Evening News*, 21 November 1929; *Evening Standard*, 3 February 1931; *Daily Mail*, 3 February 1931; Charles Reid, *Malcolm Sargent: a biography* (London, 1968), p.191.

30   *Musical Times*, 1 December 1931.

31   *Daily Telegraph*, 16 November 1931.

32   *Daily Telegraph*, 11 November 1931.

33   *Sunday Referee*, 24 January 1932.

34   AKZO NOBEL (UK) Ltd (formerly Courtaulds PLC) Archives Department: *Notes on the Courtauld-Sargent Concerts* by Cicely Stanhope.

35   Joseph Horowitz, *Understanding Toscanini* (London, 1987), pp.112–13.

36   Reid, *Sargent*, p.107.

37   Saerchinger, *Artur Schnabel*, p.206.

38   EMI Archives (Hayes), Sir Malcolm Sargent, Correspondence 1929–49: Harold Holt to Louis Sterling, 4 May 1932.

39   A. Susan Williams, *Ladies of Influence: women of the elite in interwar Britain* (London, 2000), p.18.

40   Lord Boothby, *Recollections of a Rebel* (London, 1978), p.189

41   I am grateful to Edmund Pirouet, the official historian of the LPO, for advice on this chapter. He explains the problems facing historians of this period: 'When, in September 1939, the existing company was put into voluntary liquidation, and the

members of the orchestra formed a new company, turning the London Philharmonic into a self-managed orchestra, their only inheritance was the orchestra's name. Our archive for this period is sketchy in the extreme, consisting of no more than a very few pre-war concert programmes. [...] In the absence of satisfactory evidence such as minutes, letters or other documentary evidence, it has been impossible to determine who bears the ultimate responsibility for the formation of the orchestra. There are many conflicting claims and attributions but a lack of hard evidence.' (Letter to the author, 23 September 1998.) See also Edmund Pirouet's history of the LPO: *Heard Melodies Are Sweet* (Lewes, 1998).

6: *It's a Wonderful Life*

1 Charles Reid, *Malcolm Sargent: a biography* (London, 1968), p.205.
2 Author's interview with Peter Sargent, 25 March 1998.
3 Author's interview with Peter Sargent, 31 August 2000.
4 Reid, *Sargent*, p.209.
5 *The Encyclopaedia Americana: International Edition*, Volume 27 (Danbury, Connecticut, 1988), 'Tuberculosis', pp.193–202.
6 Reid, *Sargent*, p.209.
7 Reid, *Sargent*, p.215.
8 London Metropolitan Archives, Royal Choral Society, ACC 2370/6, Sargent Concert Committee: Note by Robert Mayer, 24 January 1934.
9 Jim Ring, *How the English made the Alps* (London, 2000), pp.70–1.
10 London Metropolitan Archives, Royal Choral Society, ACC 2370/6, Sargent Concert Committee: Sir Hugh Allen to Commissioner of Customs and Excise, 8 January 1934.
11 César Saerchinger, *Artur Schnabel: a Biography* (London, 1957), p.237.
12 Author's interview with Peter Sargent, 25 March 1998.
13 Author's interview with Peter Sargent, 25 March 1998.
14 Author's interview with Peter Sargent, 25 March 1998.

15   Author's interview with Peter Sargent, 25 March 1998.
16   Author's interview with Peter Sargent, 25 March 1998.
17   Author's interview with Peter Sargent, 25 March 1998.
18   Author's interview with Peter Sargent, 25 March 1998.
19   West Yorkshire Archives (Kirklees), Huddersfield Choral
     Society, 1836–1986, KC200/1/9, Minute Book, 1929–1935:
     Minutes of Meetings, 10 March 1933, 7 April 1933, 5 May 1933
     and 17 November 1933.
20   West Yorkshire Archives (Sheepscar), Leeds Triennial Music
     Festival, Minute Book, Management Committee, 1926–39:
     Minutes of Meeting, 28 April 1933.
21   London Metropolitan Archives, Royal Choral Society, ACC
     2370/6, Sargent Concert Committee: Minutes of Meeting, 16
     October 1933.
22   London Metropolitan Archives, Royal Choral Society, ACC
     2370/6, Sargent Concert Committee: Minutes of Meeting, 14
     November 1933.
23   London Metropolitan Archives, Royal Choral Society, ACC
     2370/6, Sargent Concert Committee: Letters from Subscribers.
24   *Yorkshire Post*, 2 October 1934.
25   *Yorkshire Post*, 30 September 1934.

7:   *Bread and Butter*

1   Nicholas Kenyon, *The BBC Symphony Orchestra, 1930–1980*
     (London, 1981), p.245.
2   Author's interview with Jack Brymer, 18 March 1998.
3   Edmund Pirouet, *Heard Melodies are Sweet: A History of the
     London Philharmonic Orchestra* (Lewes, 1998), p.19.
4   Charles Reid, *Malcolm Sargent: a biography* (London, 1968),
     p.226.
5   Reid, *Sargent*, p.225.
6   Author's interview with Peter Sargent, 13 July 1998.
7   BBC Written Archives, RCONT1, Sir Malcolm Sargent,
     Artists File 2, 1940–1: Boult to Thatcher, 7 March 1940.
8   Author's interview with Sidonie Goossens, 18 March 1998.
9   Author's interview with Marjorie Thomas, 30 April 1999.

10   Author's interview with Sidonie Goossens, 18 March 1998.

11   BBC Written Archives Centre (Caversham), RCONT1, Sir Malcolm Sargent, Artists File 1, 1929–39: Programme Operator to Director of Talks, 23 November 1935.

12   West Yorkshire Archives (Kirklees), Huddersfield Choral Society, 1836–1986, KC200/1/1/10: Minute Book, 24 April 1936.

13   West Yorkshire Archives (Kirklees), Huddersfield Choral Society, 1836–1986, KC200/1/1/10: Minute Book, 29 November 1935.

14   Author's interview with Sidonie Goossens, 18 March 1998.

15   Norman Lebrecht, *The Maestro Myth: great conductors in the pursuit of power* (London, 1997), p.110.

16   Lebrecht, *The Maestro Myth*, p.91.

17   Lebrecht, *The Maestro Myth*, p.82.

18   Lebrecht, *The Maestro Myth*, p.137.

19   Lebrecht, *The Maestro Myth*, p.57.

20   Graeme Davison et al. (eds) *The Oxford Companion to Australian History (Oxford, 1998)*, p.46.

21   K.S. Inglis, *This is ABC: The Australian Broadcasting Commission, 1932–1983* (Melbourne, 1983), p.28.

22   Inglis, *This is ABC*, p.28.

23   Inglis, *This is ABC*, p.29.

24   Reid, *Sargent*, p.254.

25   Reid, *Sargent*, p.256.

26   *Teleradio*, 10 September 1938.

27   Rickard, *Australia*, pp.188–9.

28   *Advertiser* (Adelaide), 21 July 1938.

29   *Sydney Mail*, 3 August 1938; *Courier Mail*, 19 and 20 August 1938.

30   *Daily Sun*, 22 July 1938.

31   *Sydney Daily Sun*, 27 July 1938; *Sydney Morning Herald*, 27 July 1938; *Sydney Daily Telegraph*, 27 and 28 July 1938; *Sydney Sunday Sun*, 31 July 1938.

32   John Rickard, *Australia: a cultural history* (London, 1996), p.191.

33   *Mail*, 6 August 1938; *Sun*, 8 August 1938; *Argus,* 8 August 1938; *Age*, 8 August 1938; *Herald*, 8 August 1938; *Argus*, 15 August 1938; *Age*, 15 August 1938; *Herald*, 15 August 1938.

34 *Sun*, 9 August, 1938.

35 *Sydney Daily Telegraph*, 25 July 1938.

36 *Sydney Morning Herald*, 28 July 1938.

37 *Telegraph*, 6 September 1938.

38 *Daily Telegraph*, 6 September 1938; *Telegraph* (Brisbane) 6 September 1938.

39 *Woman*, September 1938.

40 *Sydney Morning Herald*, 12 September 1938.

41 *Sydney Morning Herald*, 12 September 1938.

42 *Sydney Morning Herald*, 19 September 1938.

43 *Telegraph* (Brisbane), 17 September 1938.

44 *Sydney Sunday Sun*, 18 September 1938.

45 Inglis, *This is ABC*, pp.28–9.

46 *West Australian*, 8 November 1938.

47 *West Australian*, 8 November 1938.

48 *West Australian*, 8 November 1938.

49 Author's interview with Peter Sargent, 17 October 1999.

50 EMI Archives (Hayes), Malcolm Sargent, Correspondence, 1929–49: Sargent to Gainsberg, 30 November 1938.

51 Author's interview with Peter Sargent, 25 March 1998.

52 Author's interview with Kenneth Rose, 13 July 1998.

53 Author's interview with Robin Sheepshanks, 14 August 1998.

54 Author's interview with Kenneth Rose, 13 July 1998. The Duke of Gloucester became Governor-General in 1945.

55 *Sydney Sunday Sun*, 18 September 1938.

56 Joseph Horowitz, *Understanding Toscanini* (London, 1987), pp.155.

57 EMI archives (Hayes): Malcolm Sargent, Correspondence, 1929–49: Sargent to Gaisberg, 30 November 1936; Gaisberg to Sargent, 1 December 1936; Gaisberg to Sargent, 11 February 1937.

58 BBC Written Archives Centre (Caversham), RCONT1, Sir Malcolm Sargent, Artists File 1, 1929–39: Sargent to Boult, 25 August 1937.

59 Sargent Papers: ABC to Sargent, 31 January 1939.

60 BBC Written Archives Centre (Caversham), RCONT1, Sir Malcolm Sargent, Artists File 1, 1929–39: Sargent to Boult, 25 August 1937.

61 Author's interview with Peter Sargent, 25 March 1998.

62   Author's interview with Peter Sargent, 25 March 1998.

8:   *The Baton and the Blitz*

1   Author's interview with Sir William Glock, 15 December 1997.
2   Charles Reid, *Malcolm Sargent: a biography* (London, 1968), p.264.
3   Reid, *Sargent*, p.264.
4   A precise figure, even to the nearest million, is impossible to ascertain; Norman Davis estimates the death toll at 41 million (Davis, *Europe: A History* (London, 1996), p.1328–9).
5   *Argus*, 5 September 1939.
6   Reid, *Sargent*, p.267.
7   Adrian Boult, quoted in Michael Kennedy, *Adrian Boult* (London, 1987), p.187; Andrew Sinclair, *War Like a Wasp: The Lost Decade of the Forties* (London, 1989), p.35.
8   Katharine Brisbane (ed.), *Entertaining Australia* (Sydney, 1991), p.245.
9   Historian Angus Calder, quoted in Robert Hewison, *Culture and Consensus: England, Art and Politics since 1940* (London, 1995), p.23.
10   Nick Hayes and Jeff Hill (eds.), *Millions Like Us: British culture in the Second World War* (Liverpool, 1999), p.211. I am grateful to Niamh McKeon for drawing my attention to this collection of essays. See in particular: Nick Hayes, 'More than music-while-you eat? Factory and hostel concerts, "good culture", and the workers', pp.209–235.
11   Hayes and Hill (eds.), *Millions Like Us*, p.218.
12   BBC Written Archives Centre (Caversham), RCONT1, Sir Malcolm Sargent, Artists File 2, 1940–1: Sargent to Weymouth, 9 June 1940.
13   Peter Martland, *Since Records Began: EMI the first 100 years* (London, 1997), p.85.
14   See Simon Frith's essay in Janes Curran, et al. (eds.), *Impacts and Influences: media power in the twentieth century* (London, 1987), pp.278–90.
15   Curran, et al. (eds.), *Impacts and Influences*, p.285.

16 Curran, et al. (eds.), *Impacts and Influences*, p.290.

17 Edmund Pirouet, *Heard Melodies Are Sweet: A History of the London Philharmonic Orchestra* (London, 1998), p.36; I am grateful to Edmund Pirouet for providing me with a complete listing of the London Philharmonic's wartime schedule.

18 Thomas Russell, *Philharmonic Decade* (London, 1944).

19 Author's interview with Sir Malcolm Arnold, 22 February 2000.

20 Clydebank was 'blitzed' on 19 March 1941 and almost every house damaged: Arthur Marwick, *The Home Front: The British and the Second World War* (London, 1976), p.58.

21 Russell, *Philharmonic Decade*.

22 Reid, *Sargent*, p.275.

23 Asa Briggs, *The Birth of Broadcasting:* the history of broadcasting in the United Kingdom, Vol. 1 (Oxford 1961), p.139.

24 Peter Clarke, *Hope and Glory: Britain, 1900–1990* (London, 1996), p.116–17.

25 Curran, et al. (eds.), *Impacts and Influences*, p.247.

26 BBC Written Archives Centre (Caversham), RCONT1, Sir Malcolm Sargent, Artists File 1, 1929–1939.

27 Nick Clarke, *Alistair Cooke: the biography* (London, 1999), p.138.

28 Author's interview with Sir Malcolm Arnold, 22 February 2000.

29 Victoria and Albert Museum Archives, EL3/83: *The Arts in Wartime in the Northwest of England*, Report by the Regional Officer of CEMA Region 10 to the General-Secretary, November 1944.

30 Pirouet, *Heard Melodies*, p.41.

31 Anne de Courcy, *The Viceroy's Daughters: the lives of the Curzon sisters* (London, 2000), p.333.

32 Author's interview with Peter Sargent, 31 August 2000.

33 BBC Written Archives Centre (Caversham), RCONT1, Sir Malcolm Sargent, Artists File 2, 1940–1: Secretary to Wyn, 15 November 1941.

34 Fees were cut across the board during wartime. At the Glasgow Empire, where Sargent began the Blitz Tour, average artists' fees were reduced from £672.10.0 per night before the war to £187.10.0. In July 1939, the Three Stooges had topped the bill

at £400 per night (University of Glasgow archives, Farmer Papers 4/2, Artists' Salaries 1939–40). I am grateful to Simon Ball for drawing this information to my attention.

35 Author's interview with Marjorie Thomas, 30 April 1999.

36 *NBC Trade News*, 15 February 1945.

37 Pirouet, *Heard Melodies*, p.38.

38 BBC Written Archives Centre (Caversham), RCONT1, Sir Malcolm Sargent, Artists File 2, 1940–1: *Frontline Family*, episode 79, transmitted 31 July 1941; Alan Melville to Empire Programmes, 22 June 1941; Peter Lewes, *A People's War* (London, 1986), p.189.

39 Anne Ziegler and Webster Booth, *Duet* (London, 1951), p.138.

40 Reid, *Sargent*, p.283.

41 Author's interview with Lord Menuhin, 13 October 1998.

42 Michael Kennedy and John R. Russell, *The Hallé Tradition: A Century of Music* (Manchester, 1960), p.282.

43 Susana Walton, *William Walton: Behind the Façade* (Oxford, 1988), p.150.

44 Norman Lebrecht, *When the Music Stops: Managers, Maestros and the Corporate Murder of Classical Music* (London, 1996), p.163.

45 Stanley Sadie (ed.), *The New Grove Dictionary of Music and Musicians*, Vol. 11 (London, 1980), p.94.

46 Asa Briggs, *The War of the Words* (London, 1970), p.111.

47 BBC Written Archives Centre (Caversham), RCONT1, Sir Malcolm Sargent, Chief Conductor File 1: Wilson to Howgill, undated (September 1950).

48 Sargent papers: Concert programme, Liverpool Philharmonic Orchestra, Thursday 10 August 1944.

49 Author's interview with Nancy Evans, 5 October 1999.

50 West Yorkshire Archives (Kirklees), Huddersfield Choral Society, 1836–1986, KC200/1/1/10, Minute Book: Minutes, 4 October 1940.

51 Reid, *Sargent*, p.280.

52 Robert Elkin (foreword by Dr Malcolm Sargent), *Queen's Hall, 1893–1941* (London, 1944), p.6.

53 Elkin, *Queen's Hall*, p.8.

54 Author's interview with Nancy Evans, 10 July 1998.

55 Elkin, *Queen's Hall*, p.128.

56   Lewes, *A People's War*, p.105.
57   Elkin, *Queen's Hall*, p.129.
58   AKZO NOBEL (UK) Ltd (formerly Courtaulds PLC) Archives Department: Notes on the Courtauld-Sargent Concerts by Cicely Stanhope.
59   Elkin, *Queen's Hall*, p.146.

9:   *Musical Ambassador*

1   Berta Geissmar, *The Baton and the Jackboot* (London, 1944), p.389.
2   BBC Written Archives Centre (Caversham), RCONT1, Sir Malcolm Sargent, Artists File 2, 1940–1: Appeal on behalf of London Philharmonic Orchestra.
3   Geissmar, *The Baton and the Jackboot*, p.390.
4   BBC Written Archives Centre (Caversham), RCONT1, Sir Malcolm Sargent, Artists File 2, 1940–1: Sargent to Murrill, undated (*c.*20 October 1940).
5   BBC Written Archives Centre (Caversham), RCONT1, Sir Malcolm Sargent, Artists File 2, 1940–1: Sargent to Murrill, undated (*c.*20 October 1940).
6   Author's interview with Peter Sargent, 13 July 1998.
7   Richard Aldous and Sabine Lee (eds.), *Harold Macmillan and Britain's World Role* (London, 1996), p.158.
8   Author's interview with Victor Hochauser, 20 March 1998.
9   David Greer (ed.), *Hamilton Harty: His Life and Music* (Belfast, 1979), p.60.
10   Andrew Motion, *The Lamberts: George, Constant and Kit* (London, 1986), p.217.
11   Michael Kennedy, *Adrian Boult* (London, 1987), p.189.
12   Humphrey Carpenter, *The Envy of the World: Fifty Years of the BBC Third Programme and Radio 3* (London, 1996), p.101.
13   Charles Reid, *John Barbirolli: a Biography* (London, 1971), p.220.
14   Joseph Horowitz, *Understanding Toscanini* (London, 1987), p.183.
15   Reid, *Barbirolli*, p.220.

16   *International Classical Record Collector,* Volume IV, no.16, p.34.

17   Author's interview with Sir Malcolm Arnold, 22 February 2000.

18   Kennedy, *Adrian Boult,* p.190; Edmund Pirouet, *Heard Melodies Are Sweet: A History of the London Philharmonic Orchestra* (London, 1998), p.42.

19   BBC Written Archives Centre (Caversham), RCONT1, Sir Malcolm Sargent, Artists File 2, 1940–1: Thomas to Sargent, 14 May 1941.

20   Robert Hewison, *Culture and Consensus: England, Art and Politics since 1940* (London, 1995), p.25; Nick Tiratsoo, *From Blitz to Blair: A New History of Britain since 1939* (London, 1997), pp.35–7.

21   Curran, et al. (eds.), *Impacts and Influences,* p.157.

22   Curran, et al. (eds.), *Impacts and Influences,* p.160.

23   Asa Briggs, *The War of the Words* (London, 1970), pp.318, 560–1.

24   Author's interview with Sylvia Darley, 9 October 1997.

25   Author's interview with Peter Sargent, 31 August 2000.

26   BBC Written Archives Centre (Caversham), RCONT1, Sir Malcolm Sargent, Artists File 2, 1940–1: Thomas to Sargent, 28 August 1941.

27   Sargent's answers from Charles Reid, *Malcolm Sargent: a biography* (London, 1968), pp.315–32.

28   Author's interview with Peter Sargent, 25 March 1998.

29   Reid, *Sargent,* pp.309–31.

30   Briggs, *The War of the Words,* p.562.

31   Howard Thomas, *Britain's Brains Trust* (London, 1944).

32   Author's interview with Peter Sargent, 31 August 2000.

33   Sargent/Darley Papers: letter from Sargent, 16 January 1950.

34   Author's interview with Peter Sargent, 31 August 2000.

35   Author's interview with Peter Sargent, 31 August 2000.

36   Sargent Papers: unidentified letter from Sargent, dated 23 October (possibly 1950).

37   Sargent Papers: unidentified letter from Sargent, dated 23 October (possibly 1950).

38   Author's interview with Peter Sargent, 25 March 1998.

39   Author's interview with Peter Sargent, 17 October 1999.

40 Author's interview with Peter Sargent, 25 March 1998.

41 Philip M. Taylor, *British Propaganda in the Twentieth Century: selling democracy* (London, 1999), p.71.

42 PRO (Kew): BW80/1, Music Advisory Committee, minutes 1939–45, 30th Meeting, 12 May 1942. In 1945, when it was clear that the Allies would win, musicians including Boult, Benjamin Britten, Peter Pears and John Barbirolli began appearing abroad on behalf of the Council.

43 Author's interview with Sylvia Darley, 9 October 1997.

44 PRO (Kew): BW2/137, Memorandum on Dr Sargent's concert tour in Sweden, 1942 (30 December 1942).

45 BBC Written Archives Centre (Caversham), RCONT1, Sir Malcolm Sargent, Artists File 3/1942–6: Mallet to Bliss, 8 January 1943.

46 *Yorkshire Post*, 8 December 1942.

47 Norman Lebrecht, *The Maestro Myth: Great Conductors and the Pursuit of Power* (London, 1997), p.92.

48 Ian Kershaw, *Hitler: nemesis, 1936–1945* (London, 2000), p.513.

49 Reid, *Sargent*, p.296.

50 Lebrecht, *The Maestro Myth*, p.91.

51 PRO (Kew): BW2/137, Memorandum on Dr Sargent's concert tour in Sweden, 1942 (30 December 1942).

52 *The Times*, 11 September 1943.

53 Karajan applied for membership of the Party in 1933. For a thoughtful discussion on Karajan and the Nazis, see Richard Osborne, *Herbert von Karajan: a Life in Music* (London, 1998), pp.742–50, which includes the text of Karajan's deposition to the Austrian Denazification Board in 1946.

54 Author's interview with Sylvia Darley, 9 October 1997.

55 *NBC Trade News*, 6 February 1945.

56 Author's interview with Sylvia Darley, 9 October 1997; Sargent kept the score, with Keeton's name inked in the top corner, until his death.

57 Reid, *Sargent*, p.106.

58 Theatre Museum (Covent Garden), Sargent Biographical File: Herbert Ashley, 'Vitality in Music' in *The Bystander* (1935).

59 'Sir Edward's Land of Hope and Glory' by Sir Malcolm Sargent. I am grateful to Maria Tippett for this reference.

60 Author's interview with Sylvia Darley, 9 October 1997.

61 Theatre Museum (Covent Garden), Sargent Biographical File: Herbert Ashley, 'Vitality in Music' in *The Bystander* (1935).

62 Author's interview with Peter Sargent, 25 March 1998.

63 Reid, *Sargent*, p.303; Howells wrote *Hymnus Paradisis* in memory of his son.

64 Author's interview with Lilias Sheepshanks, 14 August 1998.

65 Maurice Leonard, *Kathleen: The Life of Kathleen Ferrier, 1912–1953* (London, 1988), pp.42–3, 77.

66 Author's interview with Marjorie Thomas, 30 April 1998.

67 Author's interview with Nancy Evans, 10 July 1998.

68 Author's interview with Lilias Sheepshanks, 14 August 1998.

69 Author's interview with Peter Sargent, 25 March 1998.

70 Author's interview with Peter Sargent, 25 March 1998.

71 Author's interview with Peter Sargent, 25 March 1998.

72 2ER 834–57; C 3435–46, Edward Elgar, *The Dream of Gerontius*; Dr Malcolm Sargent, Huddersfield Choral Society, Liverpool Philharmonic Orchestra; Producer, Walter Legge; Engineer, Arthur Clarke.

73 PRO (Kew): BW2/178, Makower to Henn Collins, 24 May 1943.

74 Schwarzkopf, *On and Off the Record,* p.107; see also, Osborne, *Herbert von Karajan,* pp.207–13.

75 Legge to Beecham, undated (mid-January 1941): Alan Sanders (ed.), *Walter Legge: words and music, 1906–1979* (London, 1998), p.96.

76 PRO (Kew): BW2/178, Legge to Henn Collins, 22 September 1944.

77 PRO (Kew): BW2/178, Walton to Henn Collins, 17 July 1944.

78 PRO (Kew): BW2/178, Makower to Henn Collins, 7 September 1944; Henn Collins to Makower, 6 September 1944; Henn Collins to Legge, 18 September 1944.

79 PRO (Kew): BW2/178, Makower to Henn Collins, 7 September 1944.

80 PRO (Kew): BW2/178, Legge to Henn Collins, 22 September 1944.

81 Author's interview with Nancy Evans, 10 July 1998.

82 Testament CD SBT 2025, *The Dream of Gerontius* (1993),

accompanying booklet p.11.

83 Isobel Baillie, *Never Sing Louder than Lovely* (London, 1982), p.69.

84 R.A. Edwards, *And the Glory: The Huddersfield Choral Society, 1836–1986* (Leeds, 1986), p.108.

85 *Daily Telegraph*, 4 March 1946.

86 Author's interview with Hugh Maguire, 16 December 1997.

87 *Gramophone*, December 1999, p.41.

88 West Yorkshire Archives (Kirklees), Huddersfield Choral Society, 1836–1986, KC200/1/1/12: Minute Book, 28 June 1946.

89 DX 1283–1301; CAX 9572–9609; Producer, Lawrance Collingwood; Engineer, Arthur Clarke.

90 Baillie, *Never Sing Louder than Lovely*, p.119.

91 Edwards, *And the Glory*, p.111.

10: *Knight Errant*

1   Author's interview with Peter Sargent, 25 March 1998.

2   Author's interview with Peter Sargent, 25 March 1998.

3   Quoted in Andrew Roberts, *Eminent Churchillians* (London, 1994), p.58.

4   Charlotte Breese, *Hutch* (London, 1999).

5   Author's interview with Peter Sargent, 25 March 1998.

6   Sargent Papers: 'Inventory of items loaned to Sir Malcolm to help furnish No. 9 Albert Hall Mansions by Lady Mountbatten'; Janet Morgan, *Edwina Mountbatten: a life of her own* (London, 1992), pp.379–81.

7   Author's interview with Sylvia Darley, 9 October 1997. The description of Albert Hall Mansions is drawn from Chris Partridge, 'The British House: apartments designed to be in a different class' in *Sunday Times*, 17 September 2000.

8   Author's interview with Sylvia Darley, 17 July 1998.

9   Author's interview with Peter Sargent, 25 March 1998.

10 Author's interview with Peter Sargent, 25 March 1998.

11 Author's interview with Peter Sargent, 25 March 1998.

12   Author's interview with Lady de Zulueta, 13 July 1998.

13   Author's interview with Sylvia Darley, 17 July 1998.

14   Author's interview with Lilias Sheepshanks, 13 August 1998.

15   Author's interview with Peter Sargent, 25 March 1998.

16   Author's interview with Lilias Sheepshanks, 13 August 1998.

17   Author's interview with Sylvia Darley, 9 October 1997.

18   Charles Reid, *Malcolm Sargent: a biography* (London, 1968), p.372.

19   Author's interview with Sylvia Darley, 9 October 1997.

20   Author's interview with Lady de Zulueta, 13 July 1998.

21   Author's interview with Kenneth Rose, 13 July 1998.

22   Author's interview with Peter Sargent, 31 August 2000.

23   Author's interview with Robin Sheepshanks, 13 August 1998.

24   Private information.

25   Susana Walton, *William Walton: Behind the Façade* (Oxford, 1988), p.147.

26   Author's interview with Sylvia Darley, 9 October 1997.

27   Author's interview with Kenneth Rose, 13 July 1998.

28   Author's interview with Kenneth Rose, 13 July 1998.

29   Author's interview with Peter Sargent, 31 August 2000.

30   Author's interview with Peter Sargent, 31 August 2000.

31   Author's interview with Neville Marriner, 3 August 1998.

32   Author's interview with Peter Sargent, 17 October 1999.

33   Author's interview with Peter Sargent, 25 March 1998.

34   Jonathan Croall, *Gielgud: a theatrical life* (London, 2000), p.385.

35   Private information.

36   Sargent Papers: 'Sylvia's Diary' (1947–67).

11: Olympian

1   Sargent received this most prestigious degree at Oxford on the same day as William Walton.

2   Author's interview with Peter Sargent, 25 March 1998; Charles Reid, *Malcolm Sargent: a biography* (London, 1968), pp.346–7.

3   *Stamfordian*, Vol. 14, No.VI, p.5.

4   At the June 1947 Haringey Festival, Sargent secured full houses

of 10,000 while Sir Thomas Beecham conducted on successive nights to between 1,000 and 2,000 people.

5 British Library, Music & Rare Books, Add. Ms. 56421, Wood Papers, Volume 3: Lady Jessie Wood to Sargent, 15 April 1945 and 16 May 1945.

6 BBC Written Archives Centre (Caversham), RCONT1, Sir Malcolm Sargent, Artists File 4, 1947–9: Wright to Howgill, 13 August 1947.

7 BBC Written Archives Centre (Caversham), RCONT1, Sir Malcolm Sargent, Artists File 4, 1947–9: Sargent to Thompson, 26 August 1947.

8 Author's interview with Sir Edward Heath, 27 April 1999.

9 Michael Kennedy, *Adrian Boult* (London, 1987), p.198.

10 Kennedy, *Adrian Boult*, p.211.

11 BBC Written Archives Centre (Caversham), RCONT1, Sir Malcolm Sargent, Artists File 2, 1940–1: Boult to Thatcher, 7 March 1940.

12 Author's interview with Sir Neville Marriner, 3 August 1998.

13 Colin Seymour-Ure, *The British Press and Broadcasting since 1945* (Oxford, 1991), pp.86, 147.

14 Joseph Horowitz, *Understanding Toscanini* (London, 1987), p.272.

15 Collin Brooks, journal, 3 September 1953. I am grateful to N.J. Crowson, editor of these journals, for this unpublished quotation.

16 The Queen made her first televised Christmas broadcast in 1957. Asa Briggs, *The History of Broadcasting in Britain, Vol.V: Competition, 1955–1974* (London, 1995), p.144.

17 Author's interview with Sir Edward Heath, 27 April 1999.

18 Author's interview with Sir Neville Marriner, 3 August 1998.

19 BBC Written Archives Centre (Caversham), RCONT1, Sir Malcolm Sargent, Artists File 4, 1947–9: Nicolls to Sargent, 27 September 1948.

20 EMI Archives, Sir Malcolm Sargent, Correspondence, 1929–49: Mittell to Sargent, 21 September 1948.

21 BBC Written Archives Centre (Caversham), RCONT1, Sir Malcolm Sargent, Artists File 4, 1947–9: Sargent to Streeton, 24 November 1948.

22 BBC Written Archives Centre (Caversham), RCONT1, Sir Malcolm Sargent, Artists File 4, 1947–9: Sargent to Streeton, 2 December 1948.

23 BBC Written Archives Centre (Caversham), RCONT1, Sir Malcolm Sargent, Artists File 4, 1947–9: Streeton to Sargent, 9 December 1948.

24 BBC Written Archives Centre (Caversham), RCONT1, Sir Malcolm Sargent, Artists File 4, 1947–9: Sargent to Nicolls, 16 December 1948.

25 BBC Written Archives Centre (Caversham), RCONT1, Sir Malcolm Sargent, Artists File 4, 1947–9: Nicolls to Sargent, 17 December 1948; Sargent to Nicolls, 20 December 1948.

26 BBC Written Archives Centre (Caversham), RCONT1, Sir Malcolm Sargent, Artists File 4, 1947–9: Howgill to Streeton, 20 December 1948.

27 BBC Written Archives Centre (Caversham), RCONT1, Sir Malcolm Sargent, Artists File 4, 1947–9: Howgill to Streeton, 31 December 1948.

28 Sargent Papers: ABC to Sargent, 31 January 1939; Fees Book, 1949–1967.

29 BBC Written Archives Centre (Caversham), RCONT1, Sir Malcolm Sargent, Artists File 4, 1947–9: Streeton to Howgill, 30 December 1948.

30 Horowitz, *Understanding Toscanini*, p.153. 1 guinea = £1.05. In 1949 £1 = $2.80.

31 Author's interview with Victor Hochauser, 20 March 1998.

32 Author's interview with Peter Sargent, 31 August 2000.

33 London Metropolitan Archives, Acc 2370/74, Royal Choral Society: Sargent's fees.

34 EMI Archives, Sir Malcolm Sargent, Correspondence, 1929–49: Skandinavisk Colombia Gramophone Company to Artistes' Department, 21 October 1948.

35 PRO (Kew): BW80/1, Minutes, 44th Meeting of Music Advisory Committee, 11 January 1944.

36 PRO (Kew): BW2/137, Donald to McNab, 18 March 1946.

37 *Daily Telegraph*, 3 March 1947.

38 *Manchester Guardian*, 10 March 1947; *The Times*, 4 March 1947; *The Times*, 11 March 1947.

39 The defaced passport remains in the Sargent Papers.

40 PRO (Kew): BW2/137, press cutting from papers re. Graz Festival, Das *Steirblatt*, June 1946.

41 PRO (Kew): BW80/2, Minutes, 69th Meeting of Music Advisory Committee, 8 March 1949.

42 *The Times*, 11 October 1949; Reid, *Sargent,* p.354.

43 Reid, *Sargent,* p.351.

44 Reid, *Sargent,* p.352.

45 Sargent Papers, Darley to Annie, City Hall, 27 May 1948.

46 Reid, *Sargent,* p.352.

47 Reid, *Sargent,* p.353.

48 Sargent Papers: South American Diary, 1950,'Argentina'.

49 Sargent Papers: South American Diary, 1950,'Argentina'.

50 Jock Balfour's time in Argentina is described in his memoir, *Not Too Correct an Aureole: the recollections of a diplomat* (Wilton, 1983). Sargent is not mentioned.

51 Reid, *Sargent*, p.357.

52 Sargent Papers: South American Diary, 1950, 'Argentina'.

53 Sargent Papers: South American Diary, 1950, 'Argentina'.

54 Sargent Papers: South American Diary, 1950, 'Argentina'.

55 Reid, *Sargent*, p.358.

56 Reid, *Sargent*, p.360.

57 Reid, *Sargent*, p.356.

58 Sargent Papers: South American Diary, 1950, 'Brazil'.

59 Sargent Papers: South American Diary, 1950, 'Brazil'.

60 Sargent Papers: South American Diary, 1950, 'Brazil'.

61 Sargent Papers: South American Diary, 1950, 'Brazil'.

62 Sargent Papers: South American Diary, 1950, 'Chile'.

63 Sargent Papers: South American Diary, 1950, 'Chile'.

64 Sargent Papers: South American Diary, 1950, Homeward Journey.

65 Sargent Papers: South American Diary, 1950, Homeward Journey.

66 Sargent Papers: South American Diary, 1950, Homeward Journey.

67 Humphey Carpenter, *The Envy of the World: Fifty Years of the BBC Third Programme and Radio 3, 1946–96* (London, 1996), p.101.

12: *God's Gift to BBC Music*

1   *Evening Standard*, 20 December 1951.
2   BBC Written Archives Centre (Caversham), RCONT1, Sir Malcolm Sargent, BBC Chief Conductor File 1, 1950–4: Note of meeting of DG, et al., with Sargent, 28 April 1950.
3   *Daily Telegraph*, 5 May 1950.
4   Humphrey Carpenter, *The Envy of the World: Fifty Years of the BBC Third Programme and Radio 3, 1946–96* (London, 1996) p.101.
5   Author's interview with Hugh Maguire, 16 December 1997.
6   Author's interview with Hugh Maguire, 16 December 1997.
7   Author's interview with Jack Brymer, 18 March 1998.
8   Author's interview with Sir Neville Marriner, 3 August 1998.
9   Author's interview with Sir Neville Marriner, 3 August 1998.
10 Author's interview with Sir Neville Marriner, 3 August 1998.
11 Cambridge University Library, E.J. Dent papers, ADD, W, J.S. Wilson: Wilson to Dent, 2 September 1914.
12 Michael Kennedy, *Adrian Boult* (London, 1987), pp.81, 111,161–3.
13 Kennedy, *Adrian Boult*, p.215.
14 Churchill College Archive: Haley Papers, 13/6, 13 July 1950.
15 Kennedy, *Adrian Boult*, p.214.
16 BBC Written Archives Centre (Caversham), RCONT1, Sir Malcolm Sargent, Artists File 4, 1947–9: Wilson to Sargent, 6 January 1948; Sargent Papers: Sargent's diary, 12 and 19 January 1948; Nicholas Kenyon, *The BBC Symphony Orchestra, 1930–1980* (London, 1981), p.217.
17 Kenyon, *The BBC Symphony Orchestra*, p.218.
18 Carpenter, *The Envy of the World*, p.101.
19 BBC Written Archives Centre (Caversham), RCONT1, Sir Malcolm Sargent, Artists File 4, 1947–9: Wilson to Nicolls, 30 December 1948.
20 Carpenter, *The Envy of the World*, pp.101–2.
21 Kenyon, *The BBC Symphony Orchestra*, p.218.
22 BBC Written Archives Centre (Caversham), RCONT1, Sir Malcolm Sargent, Chief Conductor File 1, 1950–4: Wilson to

Sargent, 11 January 1950; Sargent Papers: Sargent's diary, 6 January 1950.

23 Labour had won a slim majority at the polls in 1950 but would be defeated the following year.

24 Robert Hewison, *Culture and Consensus: England, Art and Politics since 1940* (London, 1995), p.61.

25 Hewison, *Culture and Consensus*, p.61.

26 Kenyon, *The BBC Symphony Orchestra*, p.227.

27 BBC Written Archives Centre (Caversham), RCONT1, Sir Malcolm Sargent, Chief Conductor File 1, 1950–4: Nicolls to Board of Governors, 26 January 1950; Sargent Papers: Sargent's diary, 18 and 21 January 1950.

28 BBC Written Archives Centre (Caversham), RCONT1, Sir Malcolm Sargent, Chief Conductor File 1, 1950–4: Sargent to Nicolls, 21 February 1950.

29 BBC Written Archives Centre (Caversham), RCONT1, Sir Malcolm Sargent, Chief Conductor File 1, 1950-4: Sargent to Nicolls, 22 February 1950.

30 BBC Written Archives Centre (Caversham), RCONT1, Sir Malcolm Sargent, Chief Conductor File 1, 1950–4: Sargent to Nicolls, 23 February 1950.

31 Sargent Papers: Fees Book, 1950.

32 BBC Written Archives Centre (Caversham), RCONT1, Sir Malcolm Sargent, Chief Conductor File 1, 1950–4: Howgill to Nicolls, 25 April 1950.

33 Kenyon, *The BBC Symphony Orchestra*, p.230.

34 For a list of Yalding House staff, see Kenyon, *The BBC Symphony Orchestra*, p.440.

35 Carpenter, *The Envy of the World*, p.125.

36 BBC Written Archives Centre (Caversham), RCONT1, Sir Malcolm Sargent, Chief Conductor File 1, 1950–4: Sargent to Howgill, undated (April 1951).

37 BBC Written Archives Centre (Caversham), RCONT1, Sir Malcolm Sargent, Chief Conductor File 1, 1950–4: Note of Meeting between Haley and Sargent, 2 July 1951.

38 BBC Written Archives Centre (Caversham), RCONT1, Sir Malcolm Sargent, Chief Conductor File 1, 1950–4: Sargent to Nicolls, 26 April 1951.

39   Kennedy, *Adrian Boult*, p.221.

40   Kennedy, *Adrian Boult*, p.221.

41   BBC Written Archives Centre (Caversham), RCONT1, Sir Malcolm Sargent, Chief Conductor File 1, 1950–4: Sargent to Nicolls, 5 July 1951.

42   BBC Written Archives Centre (Caversham), RCONT1, Sir Malcolm Sargent, Chief Conductor File 1, 1950–4: Sargent to Nicolls, 23 February 1950.

43   BBC Written Archives Centre (Caversham), RCONT1, Sir Malcolm Sargent, Chief Conductor File 1, 1950–4: Sargent to Nicolls, 9 November 1951.

44   BBC Written Archives Centre (Caversham), RCONT1, Sir Malcolm Sargent, Chief Conductor File 1, 1950–4: Sargent to Nicolls, 9 November 1951.

45   BBC Written Archives Centre (Caversham), RCONT1, Sir Malcolm Sargent, Chief Conductor File 1, 1950–4: Murrill to Nicolls, undated (9 November 1951).

46   Herbert Murrill died in July 1952.

47   BBC Written Archives Centre (Caversham), RCONT1, Sir Malcolm Sargent, Chief Conductor File 1, 1950–4: Murrill to Nicolls, 15 November 1951.

48   BBC Written Archives Centre (Caversham), RCONT1, Sir Malcolm Sargent, Chief Conductor File 1, 1950–4: Murrill to Nicolls, 10 December 1951.

49   Author's interview with Sidonie Goossens, 18 March 1998.

50   BBC Written Archives Centre (Caversham), RCONT1, Sir Malcolm Sargent, Chief Conductor File 1, 1950–4: Sargent to Haley, 18 September 1950.

51   Author's interview with Brian Smith, 12 November 1999.

52   Kenyon, *The BBC Symphony Orchestra*, p.245.

53   *Daily Telegraph*, 2 May 1952.

54   Author's interview with Sidonie Goossens, 18 March 1998.

55   Kenyon, *The BBC Symphony Orchestra*, p.247.

56   Charles Reid, *Malcolm Sargent: a biography* (London, 1968), p.372.

57   BBC Written Archives Centre (Caversham), RCONT1, Sir Malcolm Sargent, Chief Conductor File 1, 1950–4: Sargent to Nicolls, 26 April 1951.

58 Reid, *Sargent*, pp.8–9; Victoria and Albert Museum Archives, EL6–94, Festival of Britain, arrangements for opening ceremony: Weldon to Arts Council, 8 February 1951.

13: *Malta Dog*

1 Joseph Horowitz, *Understanding Toscanini* (London, 1987), pp.153–4; in September 1949, £1 = $2.80. Concert fees converted into sterling saw Toscanini earning at least £1,500, Koussevitzky £357 and Ormandy £178 each time they stood on the rostrum.

2 EMI Archives, Sir Malcolm Sargent, Correspondence, 1929–49: Darley to Bicknell, 22 September 1948.

3 Sargent Papers: Sargent's diary, October 1951.

4 Sargent Papers: Sargent's diary, October 1951.

5 Sargent Papers: Sylvia Darley's diary, October–December 1951; Fees Book.

6 Author's interview with Lady de Zulueta, 13 July 1998.

7 Author's interview with Peter Sargent, 25 March 1998.

8 Sargent had paid an unhappy visit to India in early 1948. Lady Mountbatten's biographer points out that the day Sargent returned to London also coincided with the first reference to Nehru in Edwina's diary using his first name. Janet Morgan, *Edwina Mountbatten: a life of her own* (London, 1992), pp.462–7.

9 Sargent Papers: Commander-in-Chief, Portsmouth, to Sargent, 7 December 1949.

10 Andrew Roberts, *Eminent Churchillians* (London, 1994), p.106.

11 Sargent Papers: Diary: 'Mediterranean Cruises, September and October 1952'.

12 Sargent Papers: Diary: 'Mediterranean Cruises, September and October 1952'.

13 Sargent Papers: Diary: 'Mediterranean Cruises, September and October 1952'.

14 Sargent Papers: Diary: 'Mediterranean Cruises, September and October 1952'.

15 Sargent Papers: Mountbatten to Sargent, 8 April 1953; Sargent to Lady Mountbatten, 12 May 1953.

16 Charles Reid, *Malcolm Sargent: a biography* (London, 1968), p.378–9.

17 A. Susan Williams, *Ladies of Influence: women of the elite in interwar Britain* (London, 2000), p.133; Helena Matheopoulos, *Maestro: encounters with conductors of today* (London, 1982), p.144.

18 Michael Kennedy, *Portrait of Walton* (Oxford, 1989), p.190.

19 Susana Walton, *William Walton: behind the Façade* (Oxford, 1988), p.144.

20 Walton, *William Walton*, p.144. Such was the mediocrity of Walton's podium skill that when EMI recorded *Belshazzar's Feast*, Walter Legge suggested engaging a young German to conduct while putting Walton's name on the album cover as conductor (Walton, *William Walton*, pp.145–6). Walton did not enjoy conducting in public. When Dick Howgill invited him to conduct the First Symphony at the Proms, the composer asked Sargent to 'persuade them that you've got more glamour than I have (which shouldn't be too difficult) [and] I shall be only too happy to hand the baton to you' (BBC Written Archives Centre (Caversham), RCONT1, Sir Malcolm Sargent, Artists File 7, 1956–7: Walton to Sargent, 3 March 1956).

21 Kennedy, *Portrait of Walton*, p.180.

22 Nigel Nicolson (ed.), *Harold Nicolson: diaries and letters, 1945–62* (London, 1968), p.239.

23 Walton, *William Walton*, p.148.

24 Reid, *Sargent*, p.383.

25 John Tooley, *In House: Covent Garden, 50 years of opera and ballet* (London, 1999), p.76.

26 BBC Written Archives Centre (Caversham), RCONT1, Sir Malcolm Sargent, Artists File 7, 1956–7: Walton to Sargent, 3 March 1956.

14: *The Gospel According to St Malcolm*

1 BBC Written Archives Centre (Caversham), RCONT1, Sir Malcolm Sargent, BBC Chief Conductor File 1, 1950–4: Howgill to Jacob, 3 September 1953. Sir Ian Jacob was Director-General between 1952 and 1959.

2   BBC Written Archives Centre (Caversham), RCONT1, Sir Malcolm Sargent, BBC Chief Conductor File 1, 1950–4: Howgill to Jacob, 3 September 1953.

3   William Glock, *Notes in Advance: An Autobiography in Music* (London, 1991), p.101.

4   BBC Written Archives Centre (Caversham), RCONT1, Sir Malcolm Sargent, BBC Chief Conductor File 1, 1950–4: Sargent to Bruno Walter, 24 November 1953.

5   BBC Written Archives Centre (Caversham), RCONT1, Sir Malcolm Sargent, BBC Chief Conductor File 1, 1950–4: Sargent to Bruno Walter, 24 November 1953.

6   BBC Written Archives Centre (Caversham), RCONT1, Sir Malcolm Sargent, BBC Chief Conductor File 1, 1950–4: Howgill to Sargent, 3 December 1953.

7   BBC Written Archives Centre (Caversham), RCONT1, Sir Malcolm Sargent, BBC Chief Conductor File 1, 1950–4: Sargent to Howgill, 4 December 1953.

8   BBC Written Archives Centre (Caversham), RCONT1, Sir Malcolm Sargent, BBC Chief Conductor File 1, 1950–4: Sargent to Howgill, 7 December 1953.

9   BBC Written Archives Centre (Caversham), RCONT1, Sir Malcolm Sargent, BBC Chief Conductor File 1, 1950–4: Johnstone to Howgill, 22 January 1954.

10   BBC Written Archives Centre (Caversham), RCONT1, Sir Malcolm Sargent, BBC Chief Conductor File 1, 1950–4: Johnstone to Howgill, 22 January 1954.

11   BBC Written Archives Centre (Caversham), RCONT1, Sir Malcolm Sargent, BBC Chief Conductor File 1, 1950–4: Johnstone to Howgill, 13 July 1954.

12   BBC Written Archives Centre (Caversham), RCONT1, Sir Malcolm Sargent, BBC Chief Conductor File 2, 1955–6: Sargent to Whewell, 19 February 1955.

13   BBC Written Archives Centre (Caversham), RCONT1, Sir Malcolm Sargent, BBC Chief Conductor File 2, 1955–6: Johnstone to Sargent, 28 February 1955.

14   BBC Written Archives Centre (Caversham), RCONT1, Sir Malcolm Sargent, BBC Chief Conductor File 2, 1955–6: Sargent to Howgill, 1 March 1955.

15 BBC Written Archives Centre (Caversham), RCONT1, Sir Malcolm Sargent, BBC Chief Conductor File 2, 1955–6: Howgill to Sargent, 2 March 1955.

16 BBC Written Archives Centre (Caversham), RCONT1, Sir Malcolm Sargent, BBC Chief Conductor File 2, 1955–6: Johnstone to Sargent, 18 March 1955; Sargent to Johnstone, 22 March 1955.

17 BBC Written Archives Centre (Caversham), RCONT1, Sir Malcolm Sargent, BBC Chief Conductor File 2, 1955–6: Sargent to Howgill, 23 March 1955.

18 BBC Written Archives Centre (Caversham), RCONT1, Sir Malcolm Sargent, BBC Chief Conductor File 2, 1955–6: Sargent to Howgill, 24 March 1955.

19 BBC Written Archives Centre (Caversham), RCONT1, Sir Malcolm Sargent, BBC Chief Conductor File 2, 1955–6: Howgill to Wellington, 12 April 1956.

20 BBC Written Archives Centre (Caversham), RCONT1, Sir Malcolm Sargent, BBC Chief Conductor File 2, 1955–6: Howgill to Wellington, 12 April 1956.

21 BBC Written Archives Centre (Caversham), RCONT1, Sir Malcolm Sargent, BBC Chief Conductor File 2, 1955–6: Howgill to Wellington with documents, 12 April 1956.

22 Sargent's fee was raised to 100 guineas for promenade concerts and 125 guineas for studio concerts; BBC Written Archives Centre (Caversham), RCONT1, Sir Malcolm Sargent, Artists File 7, 1956–7: Head of Programme Contracts to Music Bookings Manager, 27 March 1957.

23 *The Times*, 2 January 1957.

24 Charles Reid, *Malcolm Sargent: a biography* (London, 1968), p.444.

25 BBC Written Archives Centre (Caversham), RCONT1, Sir Malcolm Sargent, Artists File 6, 1954–5: Sargent to Isaacs, 18 June 1955.

26 Joseph Horowitz, *Understanding Toscanini* (London, 1987), p.133.

27 BBC Written Archives Centre (Caversham), RCONT1, Sir Malcolm Sargent, Artists File 6, 1954–5: Sargent to Howgill, 18 April 1955.

28   BBC Written Archives Centre (Caversham), RCONT1, Sir Malcolm Sargent, Artists File 6, 1954–5: Sargent to Howgill, 21 July 1955.

29   Nicholas Kenyon, *The BBC Symphony Orchestra, 1930–1980* (London, 1981), appendix b.

30   Kenyon, *The BBC Symphony Orchestra*, appendix b.

31   BBC Written Archives Centre (Caversham), RCONT1, Sir Malcolm Sargent, BBC Chief Conductor File 2, 1955–6: Howgill to Wellington, 12 April 1956.

32   BBC Written Archives Centre (Caversham), RCONT1, Sir Malcolm Sargent, BBC Chief Conductor File 1, 1950–4: Howgill to Jacob, 3 September 1953.

33   In the 1953–4 season, for example, the orchestra visited Newcastle, Manchester, Hanley, Birmingham, Bristol, Belfast, Liverpool and Chester (*The Times*, 5 October 1953).

34   Kenyon, *BBC Symphony Orchestra*, p.259.

35   Kenyon, *BBC Symphony Orchestra*, pp.259–60.

36   *Daily Telegraph*, 25 June 1954.

37   Kenyon, *BBC Symphony Orchestra*, p.261.

38   Author's interview with Kenneth Rose, 13 July 1998.

39   Sargent Papers: signed photograph of Sibelius.

40   Author's interview with Sidonie Goossens, 18 March 1998.

41   *Daily Telegraph*, 14 June 1956; Reid, *Sargent*, p.10; Kenyon, *BBC Symphony Orchestra*, pp.268–9.

42   BBC Written Archives Centre (Caversham), RCONT1, Sir Malcolm Sargent, BBC Chief Conductor File 2, 1955–6: Simpson to Johnstone (copied to Howgill), 29 March 1955.

43   BBC Written Archives Centre (Caversham), RCONT1, Sir Malcolm Sargent, BBC Chief Conductor File 2, 1955–6: Sargent to Jacob, undated (July 1956).

44   BBC Written Archives Centre (Caversham), RCONT1, Sir Malcolm Sargent, BBC Chief Conductor File 2, 1955–6: Jacob to Howgill, 23 July 1956.

45   BBC Written Archives Centre (Caversham), RCONT1, Sir Malcolm Sargent, BBC Chief Conductor File 2, 1955–6: Jacob to Howgill, 24 July 1956.

46   BBC Written Archives Centre (Caversham), RCONT1, Sir

Malcolm Sargent, BBC Chief Conductor File 2, 1955–6: Sargent to Jacob, 25 July 1956.

47 Kenyon, *BBC Symphony Orchestra*, p.273.

15: *Rolls-Royce, Whisky and Sir Malcolm Sargent*

1   *Daily Mail*, 12 September 1957.
2   Author's interview with Peter Sargent, 17 October 1999.
3   Sargent also recorded for Decca.
4   EMI Archives (Hayes): Sir Malcolm Sargent, Correspondence, 1956–7: Bicknell to Sargent, 26 June 1956.
5   Author's interview with Lilias Sheepshanks, 13 August 1998.
6   EMI Archives (Hayes): Sir Malcolm Sargent, Correspondence, 1956–7: Bicknell to Soria; Soria to Bicknell, undated.
7   EMI Archives (Hayes): Sir Malcolm Sargent, Correspondence, 1958–60: Scott to Andry, 8 April 1958.
8   Author's interview with Jack Brymer, 18 March 1998.
9   Author's interview with Sir Neville Marriner, 3 August 1998.
10 Timothy Day, *A Century of Recorded Music: listening to musical history* (London, 2000), p.49.
11 EMI Archives (Hayes): Sir Malcolm Sargent, Correspondence, 1950–5: Marek to Bicknell, 15 April 1952.
12 Author's interview with Lord Menuhin, 13 October 1998.
13 Author's interview with Victor Hochauser, 20 March 1998.
14 Author's interview with Lady de Zulueta, 13 July 1998.
15 EMI Archives (Hayes): Sir Malcolm Sargent, Correspondence, 1956–7: Sargent to Bicknell, 1 March 1956.
16 EMI Archives (Hayes): Sir Malcolm Sargent, Correspondence, 1956–7: Bicknell to Sargent, 15 March 1956.
17 Author's interview with Lady de Zulueta, 13 July 1998; on Macmillan's détente policy see Richard Aldous and Sabine Lee (eds.), *Harold Macmillan and Britain's World Role* (London, 1996), pp.9–35.
18 Sargent Papers: Diary, 6 May 1957.
19 *Woman's Journal*, January 1956.
20 Charles Reid, *Malcolm Sargent: a biography* (London, 1968), p.420.

21 Theatre Museum, Sargent Biographical File: quoted in 'Pin Up of the Proms' by Ronald Duncan, 26 July 1958.

22 Reid, *Sargent*, p.421.

23 Sargent Papers: Huddersfield Choral Society, Annual Report and Balance Sheet, 1959–60.

24 Sargent Papers: Sargent to Kenneth Rose, 22 July 1958.

25 R.A. Edwards, *And the Glory: The Huddersfield Choral Society, 1836–1986* (Leeds, 1986), p.118.

26 *The Times*, 27 June 1958.

27 PRO (Kew): BW80/2, 92nd meeting of the Music Advisory Committee, 14 July 1958.

28 Edwards, *And the Glory*, p.119.

29 PRO (Kew): BW80/2, Mus (1959) 3rd meeting of the Music Advisory Committee, 3 December 1959.

30 Sargent Papers: Huddersfield Choral Society, Annual Report and Balance Sheet, 1959–60.

31 Theatre Museum, Sargent Biographical File: quoted in 'Pin Up of the Proms' by Ronald Duncan, 26 July 1958.

32 Theatre Museum, Sargent Biographical File: quoted in 'Pin Up of the Proms' by Ronald Duncan, 26 July 1958.

33 Sargent Papers: Gordon Dadds & Co. (Mrs Sargent's solicitor) to Charles Russell & Co. (Sargent's solicitor), 29 October 1958.

34 Author's interview with Kenneth Rose, 13 July 1998.

35 Author's interview with Lady de Zulueta, 13 July 1998.

36 Author's interview with Lord Menuhin, 13 October 1998.

37 Author's interview with Peter Sargent, 25 March 1998.

38 Author's interview with Peter Sargent, 25 March 1998.

39 *The Times*, 17 September 1956; *The Times*, 14 January 1957.

40 Author's interview with Lady de Zulueta, 13 July 1998.

41 Author's interview with Marjorie Gesior, 23 February 2001.

42 Author's interview with Peter Sargent, 25 March 1998.

43 Author's interview with Lady de Zulueta, 13 July 1998.

44 Sargent Papers: Remarks by Dr Sargent at the First *Daily Herald* Concert for Youth, 8 December 1945.

45 Ruth Railton, *Daring to Excel* (London, 1992), p.263.

46 *Evening News*, 29 March 1965.

47 Author's interview with Sylvia Darley, 9 October 1997.

48 Library of the Zoological Society of London: Recommendation for a Fellow, Malcolm Sargent, 19 November 1930.

49 Reid, *Sargent*, p.452.

50 RSPCA Archives (Horsham): *Animal World*, March 1950. I am grateful to the Archivist of the RSPCA, Chris Reed, for his advice on Sargent's work for the society.

51 RSPCA Archives (Horsham): Annual Report, 1950.

52 RSPCA Archives (Horsham): Minutes of Council Meeting, 17 July 1958.

53 RSPCA Archives (Horsham): *Animal World*, February 1964.

54 Author's interview with Hugh Maguire, 16 December 1997.

16: *Carnation Plucked*

1 Zoological Society of London Library, Membership Correspondence, 1958–64: Darley to Harrison Matthew, 16 June 1959.

2 William Glock, *Notes in Advance: an Autobiography in Music* (Oxford, 1991), p.87.

3 Glock, *Notes in Advance*, p.99.

4 Humphrey Carpenter, *The Envy of the World: Fifty Years of the BBC Third Programme and Radio 3, 1946–96* (London, 1996), p.196.

5 Robert Hewison, *Culture and Consensus: England, Art and Politics since 1940* (London, 1995), p.89.

6 John Osborne, *Look Back in Anger: a play in three acts* (London, 1960), p.21; Peter Clarke, *Hope and Glory: Britain, 1900–1990* (London, 1996); Ross McKibban, *Classes and Cultures: England 1918–51* (Oxford, 1998).

7 Author's interview with Sir Malcolm Arnold, 22 February 2000. *Tunes of Glory* (1960) starring John Mills as Colonel Basil Barrow and Alec Guinness as Major Jock Sinclair; directed by Ronald Neame; based on the novel by James Kennaway. John Mills won Best Actor at the Venice Film Festival for his performance.

8 Carpenter, *The Envy of the World*, p.202.

9 Glock, *Notes in Advance*, p.113.

10   Carpenter, *The Envy of the World*, p.204.

11   Carpenter, *The Envy of the World*, p.203–4.

12   Asa Briggs, *Competition, 1955–1974: The History of Broadcasting in the United Kingdom, Volume 5* (Oxford, 1995), p.39.

13   Author's interview with Sir William Glock, 15 January 1998.

14   Glock, *Notes in Advance*, p.115.

15   Carpenter, *The Envy of the World*, p.195.

16   Glock, *Notes in Advance*, p.117.

17   Glock, *Notes in Advance*, p.17.

18   Author's interview with Sir William Glock, 15 January 1998.

19   Author's interview with Sir William Glock, 15 January 1998.

20   Author's interview with Sir William Glock, 15 January 1998.

21   British Library, Music and Rare Books, Add. Mss 56421, Wood Papers, Volume 3: Sargent to Lady Jessie Wood, 23 November 1959.

22   Author's interview with Peter Sargent, 17 October 1999.

23   Author's interview with Sir William Glock, 15 January 1998.

24   Charles Reid, *Malcolm Sargent: a biography* (London, 1968), p.403.

25   Erik Tawaststjerna (trans. Robert Layton), *Sibelius, Volume 3, 1914–57* (London, 1997), pp.330–1; *Musical Times*, April 1965.

26   EMI Archives (Hayes), Sir Malcolm Sargent, Correspondence, 1959–60: Bicknell to Wood, 20 May 1959.

27   Ursula Vaughan Williams, *RVW: a Biography of Ralph Vaughan Williams* (Oxford, 1964), p.391.

28   Sargent Papers: Sargent to Ursula Vaughan Williams, undated.

29   The relationship is illustrated by the sparse nature of the correspondence between the two men in the Sargent Papers and that held in the Britten archive at The Red House, Aldeburgh.

30   Sargent Papers: Sargent to Walton, 27 May 1958.

31   Sargent Papers: Walton to Sargent, 11 June 1958.

32   Sargent Papers: Sargent to Walton, 27 May 1958.

33   Sargent Papers: Walton to Sargent, 11 June 1958.

34   R.A. Edwards, *And the Glory: The Huddersfield Choral Society, 1836–1986* (Leeds, 1986), p.120.

35   Sargent Papers: Sargent to Bardgett, undated (29 November 1959).

36 Michael Kennedy, *Portrait of Walton* (Oxford, 1989), p.216.

37 Sargent Papers: Walton to Sargent, 2 December 1961.

38 Sargent Papers: Walton to Sargent, 2 December 1961. The soloists were Marjorie Thomas, Richard Lewis and John Cameron.

39 Sargent Papers: Walton to Sargent, 2 December 1961.

40 Sargent Papers: Sargent to Lilias Sheepshanks, undated (November 1961).

41 Sargent Papers: Walton to Sargent, 2 December 1961.

42 Sargent Papers: Walton to Sargent, 2 December 1961.

43 *Sunday Telegraph*, 26 November 1961.

44 London Metropolitan Archives, Royal Choral Society, ACC 2370/173: *The Choir*, February 1962.

45 Sargent Papers: Sargent to Bardgett, undated (29 November 1959).

46 Author's interview with Graeme Tong, 8 July 1998.

47 Harold Atkins and Archie Newman (eds.), *Beecham Stories* (London, 1978), p.61.

48 Peter Heyworth, *Otto Klemperer, Volume 2, 1933–1973* (Cambridge, 1996), p.308.

49 Author's interview with Sidonie Goossens, 18 March 1998.

50 Author's interview with Marjorie Thomas, 30 April 1999.

51 *Daily Telegraph*, 12 April 1962.

52 Reid, *Sargent*, p.415.

53 Sargent Papers: Mountbatten to the Dean of Westminster, 28 February 1960.

54 K.S. Inglis, *This is ABC: The Australian Broadcasting Commission, 1932–1983* (Melbourne, 1983), p.231.

55 Reid, *Sargent*, p.419.

56 BBC Written Archives Centre (Caversham), Sir Malcolm Sargent, Artists File 11a, 1962: Sargent to Glock, 27 March 1962.

57 EMI Archives, Sir Malcolm Sargent, Correspondence, 1962–5: Sargent to Bicknell.

58 *Evening Standard*, 18 June 1963.

59 Author's interview with Jack Brymer, 18 March 1998.

60 *Daily Telegraph*, 5 February 1963.

61 *Daily Telegraph*, 5 February 1963.

62   Boothby, *Recollections of a Rebel* (London, 1978), pp.104–6.
63   Author's interview with Jack Brymer, 18 March 1998.
64   *Evening Standard*, 18 June 1963.
65   Reid, *Sargent*, p.429.
66   *Guardian*, 15 July 1963.
67   Reid, *Sargent*, p.430.
68   Reid, *Sargent*, p.429.
69   *Guardian*, 6 December 1963.
70   Sargent Papers: Sargent to Cruft, 10 December 1963.
71   Author's interview with Brian Smith, 12 November 1999.

17:   *The Walk to the Paradise Garden*

1   Butler was still in a state of shock at having been passed over as
     Prime Minister for the second time in six years. He was
     favourite to become Prime Minister in 1957 and 1963 but was
     outmanoeuvred on both occasions by Harold Macmillan.
2   Author's interview with Sir William Glock, 15 January 1998.
3   Author's interview with Hugh Maguire, 16 December 1997.
4   *Daily Mail*, 21 January 1964.
5   *Daily Mail, The Times*, 22 January 1964.
6   *New Daily*, 2 September 1964.
7   EMI Archive (Hayes), Sir Malcolm Sargent, Correspondence,
     1962–5: Bicknell to Wood, 10 November 1964.
8   Sargent Papers: Cranshaw to Sargent, 1 February 1964.
9   Sargent Papers: Darley to Cranshaw, 15 May 1964.
10   London Metropolitan Archives, Royal Choral Society Papers,
     Acc 2370/175: *Musical Events*, November 1964.
11   Author's interview with Sir William Glock, 15 January 1998.
     Until Glock's Controllership, no foreign conductors had
     performed at the Proms.
12   BBC Written Archives Centre (Caversham), Sir Malcolm
     Sargent, Artists File 12, 1965–6: Sargent to Glock, 21 January
     1965.
13   EMI Archive (Hayes), Sir Malcolm Sargent, Correspondence,
     1962–5: Wood to Matthis, 22 April 1964.

14   EMI Archive (Hayes), Sir Malcolm Sargent, Correspondence, 1962–5: Andry to Bicknell, 24 April 1964.

15   EMI Archive (Hayes), Sir Malcolm Sargent, Correspondence, 1962–5: Whittle to Andry, 20 October 1964.

16   Author's interview with Peter Sargent, 17 October 1999.

17   EMI Archive (Hayes), Sir Malcolm Sargent, Correspondence, 1962–5: Bicknell to Lockwood, 13 April 1965.

18   EMI Archive (Hayes), Sir Malcolm Sargent, Correspondence, 1962–5: Sargent to Bicknell, 5 April 1965.

19   Sargent Papers: Armstrong to Sargent, 28 April 1965.

20   *Sun*, 29 April 1965.

21   *Daily Mirror*, 24 August 1965.

22   *Sunday Times*, 25 April 1965.

23   Author's interview with Graeme Tong, 8 July 1998.

24   Author's interview with Brian Smith, 12 November 1999.

25   Author's interview with Brian Smith, 12 November 1999.

26   *The Times*, 2 September 1965.

27   BBC Written Archives Centre (Caversham), Sir Malcolm Sargent, Artists File 12, 1965–6: Sargent to Glock, 2 September 1965.

28   *Evening News*, 23 August 1965.

29   *Daily Telegraph, Daily Mirror*, 24 August 1965.

30   *Evening News*, 23 August 1965.

31   *Spectator*, 8 October 1965.

32   *Daily Telegraph*, 16 September 1965.

33   *Daily Telegraph*, 1 November 1965.

34   Author's interview with Sir Edward Heath, 27 April 1999.

35   Author's interview with Sir Edward Heath, 27 April 1999.

36   Author's interview with Sir Edward Heath, 27 April 1999.

37   Sargent Papers: Note by Dr Blaikie, 25 January 1966.

38   *Evening Standard*, 24 January 1966.

39   Sargent Papers: Darley to Crawshaw, 27 January 1966.

40   Author's interview with Peter Sargent, 25 March 1998.

41   *Financial Times, The Times*, 24 February 1966.

42   Sargent Papers: Sargent to Cohen, 24 February 1966.

43   EMI Archive (Hayes), Sir Malcolm Sargent, Correspondence, 1966: Sargent to Andry, 6 May 1966.

44   Author's interview with Sir William Glock, 15 January 1998.

45 BBC Written Archives Centre (Caversham), RCONT 1, Sir Malcolm Sargent, Artists File 12, 1965–6: Glock to Sargent, 22 March 1966.

46 *Newsweek*, 15 August 1966.

47 EMI Archive (Hayes), Sir Malcolm Sargent, Correspondence, 1966: Sargent to Andry, 20 October 1966.

48 Sargent Papers: Darley to the Secretary, Leeds Philharmonic Society, 5 October 1966.

49 Sargent Papers: Armstrong to Sargent, 10 October 1966.

50 Sargent Papers: Unidentified press cutting (1967).

51 Sargent Papers: Darley to unidentified correspondent, 30 December 1966.

52 British Library, Music and Rare Books, Add. Mss. 56421, Wood Papers, Volume 3: Sargent to Lady Jessie Wood, 16 December 1966.

53 Sargent Papers: Sargent to Eric Chadwick, 24 January 1967.

54 BBC Written Archives Centre (Caversham), RCONT 1, Sir Malcolm Sargent, Artists File 13, 1967: Sargent to Samuelson, 21 February 1967.

55 BBC Written Archives Centre (Caversham), RCONT 1, Sir Malcolm Sargent, Artists File 13, 1967: Sargent to Gillard, 2 March 1967.

56 *Liverpool Daily Post and Echo*, 27 February 1967.

57 *The Times*, 10 March 1967.

58 Sargent Papers: Sargent to Darley, 30 March 1967.

59 Sargent Papers: Unidentified press cutting (April/May 1967).

60 Sargent Papers: Dr Stephen Blaikie, re. Sir Malcolm Sargent, 23 March 1967.

61 Sargent Papers: Sargent to Darley, undated (May 1967).

62 BBC Written Archives Centre (Caversham), RCONT 1, Sir Malcolm Sargent, Artists File 13, 1967: Sargent to Glock, 22 April 1967.

63 Sargent Papers: Unidentified press cutting (April 1967).

64 Sargent Papers: Sargent to Darley, 6 April 1967.

65 Sargent Papers: Sargent to Darley, 16 June 1967.

66 Sargent Papers: Sargent to Darley, 4 July 1967 (misdated as 4 June 1967).

67 Charles Reid, *Malcolm Sargent: a biography* (London, 1968), p.455.

68   Reid, *Sargent*, pp.455–6. Sargent later asked for *The Walk to the Paradise Garden* to be played at his memorial service. It was the favourite work of his son, who as a child had thought it a work about death instead of the reality: a walk to the pub.

69   Sargent Papers: Clinical chart, July 1967.

70   BBC Written Archives Centre (Caversham), Sir Malcolm Sargent, Artists File 13, 1967: Blaikie to Glock, 16 July 1967.

71   BBC Written Archives Centre (Caversham), Sir Malcolm Sargent, Artists File 13, 1967: Glock to Gillard, 22 March 1967.

72   *Daily Mail*, 22 July 1967.

73   *Daily Telegraph*, 25 July 1967.

74   *Daily Telegraph*, 27 July 1967.

75   British Library, Music and Rare Books, Add. Mss. 56421, Wood Papers, Volume 3: Sargent to Jessie Wood, 28 August 1967.

76   Sargent Papers: '28 August–3 October' by Sylvia Darley.

77   Sargent Papers: '28 August–3 October'.

78   Sargent Papers: '28 August–3 October'.

79   Author's interview with Sir William Glock, 15 January 1998; Sargent Papers: '28 August–3 October'.

80   Sargent Papers: '28 August–3 October'.

81   Author's interview with Jack Brymer, 18 March 1998.

82   Sargent Papers: '28 August–3 October'.

83   Reid, *Sargent*, p.462.

84   *The Times*, 18 September 1967.

85   Author's interview with Sylvia Darley, 9 October 1997.

86   Sargent Papers: '28 August–3 October'.

87   Sargent Papers: '28 August–3 October'.

88   Sargent Papers: '28 August–3 October'.

89   Author's interview with Lord Coggan, 16 July 1998.

90   Sargent Papers: '28 August–3 October'.

91   Sargent Papers: '28 August–3 October'.

92   Sargent Papers: '28 August–3 October'.

93   Sargent Papers: '28 August–3 October'.

94   Author's interview with Peter Sargent, 25 March 1998; *Daily Sketch*, 5 October 1967.

95   Reid, *Sargent*, p.6.

96   Author's interview with Peter Sargent, 25 March 1998.

97 Author's interview with Peter Sargent, 25 March 1998.
98 Reid, *Sargent*, p.6; author's interview with Peter Sargent, 25 March 1998.
99 Author's interview with Sylvia Darley, 29 August 2000.
100 Robert Elkin, *Queen's Hall, 1893–1941* (London, 1944), p.129.

Index